Mohammed Chris Alli's
The Federal Republic of Nigerian Army
Symposium on Sage Philosophy

Mohammed Chris Alli's
The Federal Republic of Nigerian Army
Symposium on Sage Philosophy

Edited by

Maduabuchi Dukor
Professor of Philosophy, Nnamdi Azikiwe University, Awka
Nigeria

Malthouse Press Limited
Lagos, Benin, Ibadan, Jos, Port-Harcourt, Zaria

© Maduabuchi Dukor 2018
First Published 2018
ISBN: 978-978-55798-2-6

Malthouse Press Limited
43 Onitana Street, Off Stadium Hotel Road,
Surulere, Lagos, Lagos State
E-mail: malthouselagos@gmail.com
Tel: +234 (0)802 600 3203

All rights reserved. No part of this publication may be reproduced, transmitted, transcribed, stored in a retrieval system or translated into any language or computer language, in any form or by any means, electronic, mechanical, magnetic, chemical, thermal, manual or otherwise, without the prior consent in writing of Malthouse Press Limited, Lagos, Nigeria.

This book is sold subject to the condition that it shall not by way of trade, or otherwise, be lent, re-sold, hired out, or otherwise circulated without the publisher's prior consent in writing, in any form of binding or cover other than in which it is published and without a similar condition, including this condition, being imposed on the subsequent purchaser.

Distributors:

African Books Collective Ltd
Email: abc@africanbookscollective.com
Website: http://www.africanbookscollective.com

Dedication

This work is dedicated to General Chris Mohammed Alli (rtd.), GCON, former Chief of Staff, Army and all Nigerians who, by their actions and writings, consistently defend and defended the cause of true federalism.

Acknowledgements

First, I should express my gratitude to General M. Chris Alli (rtd.) for rendering the permission to do an anthological symposium on such an invaluable work of his. Then, the responses, corporations and commitments from distinguished Professors of Philosophy in this country who x-rayed this important work in the light of ancient, modern and contemporary imperatives of philosophy is very unalloyed. I am referring to erudite scholars Professors Jim Unah, Egbeke Aja, Ben Eboh, Dorothy Oluwagbemi-Jacob, Andrew Uduiguemen, Chris Ukhun, Oladele Bologun, Philip Ujomu and Dr Christopher Udofia.

My gratitude also goes to my son Kenechi Dukor (B.Sc. Mechanical Engineering) for his technical and editorial assistance. Obiozor Ekeze R. N. did the indexing and should be thankfully acknowledged. Ultimately, we are grateful to our distinguished Professor-Emeritus of philosophy at the University of Ibadan, Professor Godwin Sogolo, for accepting to write the foreword to this anthology.

Foreword

The Federal Republic of Nigerian Army: The Siege of a Nation, by Mohammed Christopher Alli, deserves the kind of critical attention given to it by the eminent scholars in Philosophy and the Humanities, assembled at this Symposium. Much has been left to be desired in the role the Nigerian military has played in governance and the protection of the nation's territorial boundaries and sovereignty. This book captures, masterfully, the essentials of military misrule in Nigeria and its undue influence on the body polity.

Here, the dominant and damaging role of the military is being subject to the rigours of philosophical analysis. The African scholar-philosophers in this Symposium are on a historical assignment of interrogation and conversation, which George Hegel, the German philosopher, rightly said, in his *Logic of Philosophy of History*, would produce thesis, anti- thesis and synthesis of a just, fair, equitable and free Republic such as Nigeria, with a disciplined military institution under a civil Constitution.

Major General M. Chris Alli has set the ball rolling in this critical master-piece on the role played by the Nigerian military in decapitating the country's federalism. Indeed, an intellectual and critical conversation on the book has actually begun with Professor Maduabuchi Dukor and his team. This is the logic of civilized discourse which must be revisited now and again in different relevant forums to pre-empt the morbidity or neglect of progressive thoughts, like those of Alli, especially in a materialistic society like ours. The failure of the military in governance, in Nigeria, must be subjected to the rigorous horn of reason. Thus, this auspiciously timed conversation, through a Symposium, deserves high commendation.

While the traditional role of the military is easy to sum up as the defence, protection and preservation of a country's territorial integrity against attacks and wars of aggression, we must always bear in mind that every contemporary democracy has a duty to uphold and critically reinforce the subordination of the military to civil authority. Nigeria's military institutions cannot afford to derail from this cherished tradition and constitutional obligation. The era of military coups and military regimes in Africa is now history such that the rank and file of the Nigerian military and its command structure and architecture are today firmly subordinated to civil and democratic rule. Not only does power belong to the people, the institutions of the state and civil society are under their overall authority and control. This is the message of Chris Alli's book. As a critical survey of past military misadventures, and a satire against false federalism, it is a firm warning against future corruption and impunity in the military.

Professor Dukor and his co-African philosophers have added a second order philosophical voice, not only to Alli's Magnum Opus, but also to the reform of the military and its institutions in Nigeria. This is being done in line with the admonition of Karl Jaspers, the German existentialist philosopher, that "theory without practice is blind and practice without theory is empty." Our African philosophers are trying to bridge the yawning gap between theory and practice in understanding military and civilian democratic practice in Africa. They deserve great commendation.

I confidently say that this current Anthology as well as the original work that preceded it, The Federal Republic of Nigerian Army : The Siege of a Nation, are a must read for students and researchers in Higher Institutions, Universities, Research and Diplomatic Institutes, Defence Colleges, Military Schools and Establishments. It should be a companion to officers in the Army, Navy, Air Force and, indeed, the Nigerian readership in general.

Emeritus Professor Godwin Sogolo

Editor

Dukor, Maduabuchi PhD (UNN), M.Phil (Unilag), B.A. (Ibadan) PGD (Journalism), Professor of Philosophy, Nnamdi Azikiwe University, Chairman of Board and Director, Prescience Programme Nnamdi Azikiwe University (2012-2014). President/Editor-in-Chief, ESSENCE LIBRARY (www.essencelibrary.org). Visiting Scholar at the Department of Philosophy, University of Ghana, Legon, Accra, Ghana (1999-2002), Adjunct Professor of Philosophy; Joseph Ayo Babalola University (2010-2015), Delta State University (2015), Odumegwu Ojukwu University (2015), and Niger Delta University (2015). Founding Head of the Department of Philosophy, Lagos State University. He has to his credit 7 books, 42 chapters in Anthology and 69 journal articles including 36 international publications. He is a Visiting member of the Editorial Board of Guardian newspapers

Contributors

Aja, Egbeke hails from Amangwu Ohafia in Ohafia Local Government Area of Abia State and holds PhD (Nig.) 1992 M. A. (Nig.) – 1986, B.Sc (Hons. Nig.) – 1981, N.C.E. (A.I.C.E. Owerri) – 1975. He has served University of Nigeria, Nsukka as Acting Head of Department (2005-2008), Associate Dean, Faculty of Social Sciences (2008), and rose to the rank of Professor of African Philosophy in October 01, 2002. Professor Aja Served as the Deputy Vice Chancellor (Administration), UNN 2010-2012. He has published in many professional journals of Philosophy and also to his credit are over ten texts in core areas of Philosophy. Professor Egbeke Aja is married with children and grandchildren.

Balogun, Oladele Abiodun, received his PhD in Philosophy from the University of Ibadan. He is a Professor of Philosophy at Olabisi Onabanjo University Ago Iwoye Ogun state. His papers have appeared in several international journals and he has attended several international philosophical conferences across the globe. His research interests are in African Philosophy, Philosophy of Education and Philosophy of Law. Balogun is a recipient of the Thabo Mabeki award of leadership at the University of Texas at Austin in 2017.When not engaged in deep thought and writing he enjoys hanging out with his marvellous children and lovely wife, Temitope.

Eboh, Rev. Fr. Ben Okwu is a priest of the Catholic Diocese of Nsukka. He is a native of Umerum in Ayamelum LGA of Anambra State. He is a Professor of Philosophy of the Department of Philosophy, University of Nigeria, Nsukka. And he retired from the services of University of Nigeria, Nsukka in December 2008. Currently, he is on a contract appointment and the Head of Department of Philosophy, Anambra State University, Igbariam Campus, now renamed Chukwuemeka Odumuegwu Ojukwu University (COOU).

Okoro, Chidozie, Professor of Philosophy at the University of Lagos, Akoka, Lagos, Nigeria. He specializes in Applied Ontology, Metaphysics of the Kantian, Hermeneutic Phenomenology ad African traditions. He also specializes in the Philosophy of Development. He has published widely and has attended conferences both home and abroad.

Oluwagbemi-Jacob, Dorothy is Professor of Philosophy at University of Calabar and Former Head of Department and Dean of Faculty of Arts.

Udofia, A Christopher, PhD is a Senior Lecturer, in the Department of Philosophy, University of Calabar.

Uduigwomen, Andrew F. is a Professor of Philosophy and Former Head of Department of Philosophy, and Dean, Faculty of Arts, University of Calabar.

Ujomu, Philip Ogochukwu, Associate Professor, Department of Philosophy, Faculty of Humanities, Management and Social Sciences [FHMSS], Federal University Wukari (FUW), Taraba State, Nigeria.

Ukhun, Chris, PhD. Professor of Philosophy. Former Head of Department of Philosophy and Dean of Faculty of Arts, Ambrose Ali University. Ekpoma, Edo State, Nigeria.

Unah, Jim Ijenwa, PhD, FNPA, Distinguished Professor of Philosophy at the University of Lagos October 2017. Former Head of Department of philosophy and currently President, Philosophical Association of Nigeria (PAN)

Contents

Dedication
Acknowledgements
Foreword
Chapters

The Military and National Security

1. Reading Mohammed Chris Alli - *Maduabuchi Dukor* - **1**

2. M. Chris Alli, Nigerian statist – Militarist Realism and National Security - ***Philip Ugochukwu Ujomu*** - **23**

3. M. Chris Alli and the Politics in the Nigerian Army: A Philosophical Approach - ***Oladele Abiodun Balogun*** - **57**

4. On M. Chris Alli's Morality of War - *Egbeke Aja* – **69**

5. M.C. Alli On Security And Media Within The Context Of Jeremy Bentham's Ethics - ***Chris Ukhun*** - **83**

Morality and National Question

6. Moral Character and Holistic Development in M. Chris Alli - ***Jim Ijenwa Unah*** - **97**

7. M. Chris Alli and Moral Perspectives of National Question – ***Ben Okwu Eboh*** - **111**

8. M. Chris Alli and The Peril of Religious Exclusivism: Religious Pluralism As a Panacea - ***Andrew F. Uduigwomen & Christopher A. Udofia*** - **131**

Federalism and Philosophy of Development

9. M. Chris Alli, Militocracy and the Crisis of Leadership in a Plural State - *Chidozie Okoro-* **149**

10. The Matter of Justice and Equity in Nigeria: A reflection on M. Chris Alli - *Dorothy Oluwagbemi-Jacob* - **183**

11 Neo-liberalism and M. Chris Alli's Hermeneutics of Federalism - *Maduabuchi Dukor* - **207**

Index - 235

Chapter 1

Introduction

-Maduabuchi Dukor

Reading Mohammed Chris Alli's *The Federal Republic of Nigeria Army: the Siege of a Nation*

When the debate on the existence of African philosophy erupted like a ripple in water, it spread like wild fire in the Anglophone and Francophone philosophical organizations, departments and faculties of universities, yet even radiated from the unaffiliated intellectuals in town and religious organizations. The interlocutions were like a symposium on the philosophy mainstream as well as in the side-lines and margins of modern and contemporary issues in the social sciences, sciences and medicine seeking to enact the classical relevance of philosophy to all. In the classical philosophical tradition, the methodology was in the form of raising questions and attempting to answer them in the most rational and critical attitude as much as possible. For instance, the leading questions are: what is African philosophy and who is an African philosopher? Re-inventing this canon in this anthology, a group of ten philosophers/teachers of philosophy have affirmed the existence of African philosophy in the debate which was concluded in the early 1990s and wish to propagate ideas in Africa as African philosophy and identify notable thinkers, institutions and groups in Africa as rational and critical enough to be categorized in the mould of philosophical entrepreneurs.

In this anthology, organized as a symposium on Mohammed Christopher Alli's great work, *The Federal Republic of Nigerian Army: The Siege of a Nation*, we hereby identify M Chris Alli as one of those critical and rational thinkers, philosophers, albeit, a General in the Nigerian Army, whose work finds a befitting logical space in the contemporary African philosophical tapestry. His work is fittingly and squarely thunderous in the genre of philosophy and canonically within the ambit of African philosophy. Philosophy is however, "a universal and impersonal discipline and African philosophy is part of this world heritage because it is pursued and accepted in the positive progressive sense of the second order mode of scientific and critical inquiry..." (Dukor, 2005:5). There had been disputations in the 1990s whether a genre of philosophy like mathematics and physics can be described as African philosophy or not just because the philosopher is African or the philosophy is non-African.

Perspectively, African tradition, culture and values can pass as philosophy even though, as Henry Odera Oruka would argue, "one cannot rationally combine a belief in the universality of philosophy with a belief in African philosophy" (Oruka, 1989:132), The question of M. Chris Alli's philosophy implicit in his aforementioned work is tumultuously universal in critical and logical sense, save it is a philosophical praxis in Africa and by an African which qualifies it to be called an African philosophy. Pauline Hountondji would tacitly accept our stance with semantic and utilitarian modulation on it thus: "the problem is whether the word 'philosophy' when qualified by the word 'African' must retain its habitual meaning, or whether the simple addition of an adjective necessarily changes the meaning of the substantive. My own view is that its universality must be preserved..." (Hountondji, 1989:108).

In this anthology, we are to ex-ray this work of M. Chris Alli not only because of its universality, logic and appeal in extricating sufficient and logical arguments from moral, military and political questions of contemporary times but also because the philosophy in his work abides by the notion of "a conscious creation" (Bodunrin, 1989: 32) as one cannot be said to have a philosophy in the strict sense of the word until one has consciously reflected on one's belief" (Ibid). M. Chris Alli's *The Federal Republic of Nigerian Army: The Siege of a Nation* is therefore not only a metaphor for military misrule of Nigeria for three decades in the name of a federal republic but also a critical reflection on the core values of life, which straddles through idealism, existentialism to utilitarianism in periscoping critical questions of nationhood, democracy, military, security, good governance and human right. Beyond ethnographic and personal matters of a biographic interest the book is a chronicle of socio-political ideas based on his life and military career.

Background

As the saying goes; some are born great, some achieve greatness and some have greatness entrusted on them. Also, some are born philosophers, some achieve the philosophic and some have the philosophic entrusted on them. Similarly, some are born sagacious, some achieve sagacity and some have sagacity encrypted in them. Wherewithal does M. Chris Alli fit in on these supra-natural and existential schemes? His distinguished career in the Nigerian Army and occasional postings to diplomatic and political assignments fortuitously was neither for seeking knowledge for knowledge sake enterprise like the ancient African and Greek tradition nor the rational and critical inquiry of contemporary teachers and thinkers in the Universities. But he had what it takes to engage in philosophic enterprise; he is well educated along his military career, has the eloquent use of English, has the philosophic and sagacity entrusted in him and has the critical and rational wherewithal to reflect on his beliefs and that of others as they affect the actions and inactions of moral and rational agents in his society. This is the turf with which great philosophers in the world were born with. Some had an equally distinguished career in the Army before settling down to write and philosophize on a variety of human problems. Some were ascetics and withdrawn. Most world renowned philosophers belong to these groups in addition to those of us that teach in the universities to help generations of thinkers and students imbibe the rigour of critical reflections and reasoning on humanities challenges.

This artist and philosopher in space and time was born to Mohammed Baba Alli and Mrs Manaswe Rebecca Alli on 25 December, 1944 at Lokoja in the present Kogi State in Nigeria. What could appear to be a seeming or apparent difficult thing today was that his father was a Muslim and his mother a Christians and all his siblings without exception happened to be Christians without any untoward rancour and acrimony between father and mother. It was a family hinged on the pedestal of religious tolerance, a virtue which is variously and intermittently advertised and exhibited as a moral virtue in his philosophy.

He was brought up at Onitsha Town in the Old Eastern region and present Anambra state of Nigeria where he attended the famous metropolitan college of Onitsha. He joined the Nigerian Air Force from where he was enlisted into the Nigerian Army, after completing the six months officer cadet training on 22 October, 1967, the heat of the Nigerian civil war. A gentle man and committed soldier on the Nigerian side against the secessionist, Biafra, he served as Adjutants and Commanding Officer of various infantry brigades and battalions during the war.

Having remained unbroken in persecuting the war, his career in the military was unchequered rising to the exalted position of Chief of Army staff before retiring.

Major General Chris Alli received Grand Commander of the Order of Niger (GCON), Republic Medal (RM), Service Medal (NSM), General Service Medal (GSM), Forces Service Star (FSS), National Silver Jubilee Medal (SIM) and Commander of the National Order of the Republic of Gambia.

He has professional trainings in Nigeria, UK, Pakistan and the National Defence College India. He also received Masters Degree in Strategic Studies, University Allahabad, Distinguished Scholar and Student of the National Defence College, New Delhi, India, Commandant's Honour and Graduate of Nigeria Army, Command and Staff College, Jaji, Grand Commander of the Republic of Gambia.

Major General M. C. Alli (RTD) is former; Nigerian Defence Attachй to Zimbabwe, Military Governor of Plateau state of Nigeria, Director of Military Intelligence and General Officer Commanding Mechanized Division.

He was an intelligent officer whose academic and literary inclination was sustained in his appointments and services in military intelligence circles. To sum it up he has continued to sustain this not only in his writings but also in the Guardian Newspaper Editorial Board as erudite lead speaker on literary, economic, security, political, social, national and international issues. However, his penchant, and propensity, for anything literary in a second order and critical engagement with political, economic and social order of his society was not maverick but reminiscent of the tradition of great philosophers before him such as Martin Heidegger (1889-1926) who, like him, worked as a soldier but in the final year of World War I.

Activism for justice is more often endowed in particular individual human nature. M. Chris Alli's writings, erudition, interlocutions and activism for social justice speak to this fact of quintessential gadfly. His predecessors in this philosophical heritage were Jean Paul Sartre (1905-1980), Anton William Ammo (1703-1759) a philosopher in Europe from Ghanaian African ancestry and the German Philosopher Friedrich Nietzsche (1844-1990) who also influenced the intellectual culture of his own country, Germany and so on.

Conceptual schemes

A philosophical symposium on M. Chris Alli's moral and political philosophy is an exposition of critical development questions and answers in his book, *The Federal Republic of Nigerian Army: the Siege of a Nation*. It is an interrogation and extrapolation of the political and moral values extant in his book with the objective of pushing further their epistemological boundaries and widening the frontier of knowledge. In the main, reading *The Federal Republic of Nigerian Army: The Siege of a Nation* reveals a consistent and coherent body of political and moral knowledge as a substratum undergirding the empirical vistas and postulations of the key words; namely, Federalism, Republic, Nigeria, Army, Siege and Nation. It is easy, perhaps, to capture in M. Chris Alli the character of a spasmodic and original thinker whose thoughts are of eclectic tradition re-inventing the echoes of broad schools of philosophy namely; theism, theistic humanism, idealism, existentialism, consciencism, historicism, liberalism, neo-liberalism, federalism, republic, post-humanism, and his own deductive monological logic about Nigerian society like Nigeria Factor and the Big Three in the quest for a proper articulation of moral values and political realities of Nigerian Republic and federalism.

Theism

This is a philosophical and theological doctrine maintaining the existence of one personal God, creator of the universe. This is M. Chris Alli's heritage. He was born of dual theological heritage (Alli, 2001:7); his father was a Muslim while his mother was a Christian. He became inclined to Christianity because of the mother's influence. But all the same theistic consciousness never departed him as subsequent confessions and associations consolidated his faith in one God. He and his siblings celebrated both "Charismas and Eidel Kabir days, in addition to other holy but less boisterous festivities like Easter day had Eidel Fitr' (p.7). His names are conceptually syncretism amalgams of the two religions thus: Mohammed, Baba, Christopher and Emmanuel Alli, however, but popularly known as M. Chris Alli. Theism undergirds his entire philosophy. When he veered off from his houseboyship under a teacher contracted by his disciplinarian father at Onitsha to live a vagabond life, he later reflected thus:

> Those three nights of vagabond living taught me by and large, that a man must be able to stand alone even in a crowd. It taught me that there is a spiritual difference between external influences and internal power. I realized that some internal and inexplicable force existed in me from which reservoir I can often, draw spiritual faith and strength. (p.10)

Reflecting on his teacher, Mr. Okafor, his master as a houseboy, he said: "he might just be with our Lord. From my heart and in my mind, he was a good man who set me on a path of hard work and self realization." (p.11). On his military career he said it had been "a profound and complex experience, but the driving force was my abiding faith in God, hard work and self-confidence, rather than lobby or patronage" (p.23). One thing discernable in his philosophical dispositions and thoughts is that barring any foreseen or unforeseen psychological trauma, his moral and political philosophy had been guided not by fate but by free-will, hard work and self-confidence under the surveillance and supervenience of an anthropomorphic ultimate reality who is the governor of the universe. This, directly and indirectly, has informed his philosophical appurtenances and eclectic views bordering on idealism, historicism, existentialism, liberalism, neo-liberalism, consciencism and utilitarianism.

Theistic Humanism

One of the common features of M. Chris Alli's work is theism even as all applications of theories and concepts in his work are undergirded by humanist philosophy. He can be said to be first and foremost a humanist notwithstanding that Humanism notoriously understood as secular humanism without belief in God or gods is not the kind of Humanism captured in his thought-provoking neo-liberal political and economic philosophy for Nigeria. He is rather a theistic Humanist in thinking by his rational disposition and by the fact that he is an African. This is what I call "Theistic Humanism" of African philosophy which is "a philosophical principle or doctrine of African ideas of man, universe and god...the ideas of Theism and Humanism are jointly and inseparably applicable to African culture" (Dukor, 2001:65). M. Chris Alli's theistic humanistic principles are extant in his thinking and writings as he would reflect more often than not that "you can hardly go wrong if you are guided by the consideration of and rationalization with your maker, the nation, humanity. For him the contradictions in the Nigerian society are off the mark or bench mark of Theistic Humanism qua Theistic Humanism of African philosophy such that:

> the dividing line between honesty and 'Kleptocracy' in Nigeria lies in the realm of opportunity. Those who had a chance and access to public treasury, do not grumble, those who did not have the opportunity to exercise quick fingers blame everyone else for corruption. This is the depth and culture of corruption in Nigeria. It is also more than the factor of money and thievery (Alli, p.53)

And in one of his critiques of the military incursions in Nigerian politics he argues that the Armed Forces "are neither the custodians of the nation, nor the defenders of the Constitution. They are a miniscule part of the whole..." (p. 317). Alli's humanism is predicated on theism and so naturally adheres to the theory of theistic Humanism of African philosophy.

Idealism

This conceptual scheme is a philosophy prone to many definitions. But whether it refers to ideas or ideals as etymologists would suggest, it can be reduced to a concept within which metaphysical impulse is strong, hence can be defined as a metaphysical vision which seeks to present a coherent, inclusive view of the universe and of man's plan within it for which mind is the fundamental principle of explanation and understanding (Beck, 1979:87). M. Chris Alli seems to be an objective idealist who in the tradition of Plato and St. Augustine would argue that values are in some sense objective and part of the nature of reality. From this metaphysical fulcrum he is always penchant to establish a nexus among purpose in life, ideal self-hood, self-realization, reason, consciousness, human personality, community, man, ideal and society. Reflecting on the essence or ideal of life and in a word, 'idealism' M. Chris Alli enunciates as follows:

a) The future belongs to those who prepare for it and a mission without knowledge is like a boat on dry land;
b) Ali manner of factors bear on character formation and response to the needs of existence; the part played by "a parental moralizing, the Christian doctrine, cultural values and ethics;
c) You have to use what you have to get what you need – good name, connections and patronage, wise counsel and more importantly, pragmatism;
d) One needs not degrade one's conscience in responding to the pressure of goods, inordinate ambition and unprincipled life style or be over awed by the trappings of power and the powerful;
e) The dividing line between honesty and 'Kleptocracy' in Nigeria lies in the realm of opportunity. Those who had a choice and access to public treasury, do not grumble, those who did not have the opportunity to exercise quick fingers blame everyone else for corruption. This is the depth and culture of corruption in Nigeria. It is also more than the factor of money and thievery. (pp 52-53)

These are some of M. Chris Alli's idealist romances and excretions which form and perforates his stakes and pontifications, on federalism liberalism and neo-consciencism, existentialism and most importantly state, power and authority.

Existentialism

As a disciplined, patriotic officer and gentleman of modern military formation who rose to the highest rank in Nigerian Army, the Chief of

Army Staff, M. Chris Alli is paradoxically an existentialist in thought and prose. At some subtle subliminal level his discipline and firmness in the military professional exercises commits him to existentialism which in principles is a reaction against various forms of dehumanization resulting from technology, nationalism, militarism and scientific objectivism. Also, Alli shares Existentialism's revolt against alienation and forms of dehumanization and their effects, hence, his philosophy like other existentialists is man centred and based on the truth of subjectivity and freedom. Like wise, he agrees with Protagoras, an ancient Greek philosopher that "man is the measure of all things" (Warner, 1958:57). Existentialism, however, may not be incorrect in many relevant forts. There are theistic existentialists like Koren Kierkegaard and Karl Jaspers and atheistic ones like Martin Heidegger, Fredrick Nietzche and Jean Paul Sartre. What qualified Alli as theistic existentialist is the same onto-theological tendency of Kierkegaard and Jaspers configured in a transcendental conception of ultimate reality, a deity to which man is looking up to in his existential experience. As an idealist qua existentialist he says that three elements combine to design and affect one's fortune or misfortunate on earth namely: the guidance of the Supreme Being (2) natural intelligence, and (3) environment which has a moderating impact on the first two (Alli, p.22). But on the flip side is the subjective truth for an officer and gallant soldier like Ali who when confronted by the enemy in the war front would not hesitate to decimate him. He argues: "A solder is expected to apply all the factors of combat geography and terrain, equipment, ecology and the art and means of defeating and ruling his enemy..." (p. 31). His moral and political philosophy is gauged intermittently, served and weaving around Existentialism in concomitance with Theism, Idealism and Historicism

Consciencism

Conscience is an attribute of mind and quality of human spirit. Metaphysically, it is the divine spark of God in man from where Kwame Nkrumah's consciencism as an ideology and philosophy is etymologically derived. M. Chris Alli's inclination towards Nkrumah's philosophical consciencism as a conceptual scheme is a synchronic and inadvertent approval of the role of conscience in a multicultural and multi-religious environment and polity. Nkrumah had in his book, *Consciencism,* defined Consciencism as philosophical statement or ideology that contains "the African experience of Islamic and Euro-Christian presence as well as the experience of the traditional African society, and by gestation, employ them for the harmonious growth and development of that society." (Nkrumah 1964:70). For Nkrumah, the contradictions inherent in the post-colonial African experience of traditional religion, Euro Christian religion and Islam inheres good or bad depending on handling. Hence he argues that:

> social milieu affects the content of philosophy, and the content of philosophy seeks to affect social milieu, either by confirming it or by opposing it. In either case, philosophy implies something of the nature of an ideology in the case where philosophy confirms a social milieu; it implies something of the ideology of that society. (Nkrumah, 1964:57)

In Ali this quasi-ideological speculation is converted into reality as social and moral philosophy and ideology.

M. Chris Alli was born into a Muslim-Christian family, where the father was a Muslim and his mother a Christian, wherein there were no contradictions, almost all the offsprings bore Christians names and all including father and mother, shared and dined together, in all the Islamic, Christian and traditional festivities as and when they come by. He confessed and postulated thus,

> During *sallah* festivals my father went through all the rituals which I frequently and gleefully participated in. These include open field prayers, the slaughtering of rams for family consumption, the sowing and wearing of new dresses, *babariga* and accoutrements (new shoes, cap, etc.). The sharing of rams was a most joyful tasks as neighbours on the distribution list often gave the messenger some small tip to show gratitude and more so, as an expression of the invigorating mood of *sallah*. It was mainly during the eating that the entire family had congruence. As I can recollect, no one complained, everyone was happy. A lot even our immediate neighbours were lost to the joys of *sallah*, notwithstanding that they were entirely Christians (Alli, 2001:5).

Ali, in his moral and political philosophy elevate this family palate and union inferred from the philosophies of Islamic, Christian and traditional religions to an axiomatic conceptual setting for a multi-religions society. It is a constructionism because it is a picture of how these religions concepts can cohere and it is both a reductionism and nominalism because only concrete existence are held to be primary and real in his moral, political and military philosophy.

Utilitarianism

Utilitarianism and its socio-political impact on the average Nigerian and any ethnic nationality or group in Nigeria seems to be of serious concern to M. Chris Alli. He leveraged on the ethics of utilitarianism to envision the core values of Nigerian state. Utilitarianism is one of the most important contributions of English thought to ethics. Founded by Richard Cumberland in his book, *De leg bus nature*, it reached full expressions in David Hume's, *A Treatise of Human Nature* (1739), Jeremy Bentham's *A Fragment on Government* (1776) and, "An introduction to the principles of morals and legislation (1789), John Stuart Mill's *Utilitarianism* (1861) and Henry Sidewick's *Methods of Ethnics* (1874). Jeremy Bentham eloquently reflected utilitarianism's anti-metaphysical import in suggesting that apart from pleasure and pain moral terms have no other meaning whatever. He says that he is an adherent of the principle of utility

> when I measure my approval or disapproval of any act, public or private, by its tendency to produce pains and pleasures: when I use the terms just, unjust, moral, immoral, good, bad, as comprehensive terms which embrace the idea of certain pains and certain pleasures, and have no other meaning whatever (Beck 1979: 67).

M. Chris Alli readily agrees with Bentham and other utilitarian's that man ought to choose that which will produce the greatest happiness (pleasure) for the greatest number. The determination of moral acts is made in terms of the consequences they produce. For Alli, the core values of Nigerian state (a) are the ground norm for rallying all sections of people (b) aside from directing national ethics, they are the ideological subtract on which the nation is constructed (c) promote the enactment and enhancement of the collective will and sovereignty of the people over the state, the security and identity of its components and (d) ensure that the largest and smallest have access to opportunities in national affairs (Alli p. 1010). M. Chris Alli added extra value to classical utilitarianism by an overwhelming adherence to utilitarian orientation of John Rawls' Theory of 'Justice as fairness' and this he inexorably uses to address the complexities of Nigerian state and Federalism from both in and outside the calculus of Nigerian civil and military leadership.

Historicism

In his book, *The Federal Republic of Nigerian Army, The Siege of a Nation* M. Chris Alli attributed a lot of meaning and significance to space and time such as historical period, geographical space and local and foreign culture. There is an acute sense of history in his analysis of socio-political issues to the extent of saying that history determines stereotypes and immutable laws such as the colonization of Africa, military interventions, militarianism, political instability and religious bigotry. Reflecting on Historicism, he argues that the Nigerian nation since 1900 had been ruled by military and quasi-military personnel with the traditional militancy of pre-colonial authority (Alli, p. 162) and, "Before slave trade and colonization became the scourge of our historical experience, Africans had receded from the high pedestal of their great civilizations..." (Alli, p. 184). Alli's predilections for Historicism and historical anecdotes (I) have a hidden positivism because of his savvy for rules and stick adherence to set standards either in the constitution or in the military protocols and (b) are a pure historical response to radical pluralism by rational argumentation and critical theory i.e. self-consciousness of a process of emancipation and enlightenment (Bernstein, 1994:164-165) All in all, Alli's positivism and historicism is a critical science which has its ancestry not only in Jurgen Habermas critical theory but also in Kantian critical philosophy.

Liberalism

In the light of some basic theoretical framework of Alli's thought there are some basic liberal assumptions which are philosophically indispensible. The philosophical leads to the political. He is of the classical genre of Greek and Roman thought and the Enlightenment's liberalism in his recognition of man as a moral being. What he seeks for in the Nigerian project is an abiding framework that is both divine in nature and secularly positive. He appeals to natural law to answer questions of obligation, right and morality and explains individualism and individual right by an appeal to reason. He often argues that his career's driving force is "abiding faith in God, hard work and self-confidence" (Alli, p. 23), which presupposes natural law, morality and reason. On the question of liberal political right, he says, "it is really up to Nigerians to decide whether the people of Nigerian can collectively establish good governance through reflection and choice or whether they are forever sentenced to depend on habit and force for their political evolution." (Alli, p. 104). By implication or coincidence his moral and political liberalism is reminiscent of H.L.A Hart's liberal legal positivism and John Rawl's political liberalism. Harts identified some five meanings of legal positivism in contemporary jurisprudence: law are commands of human beings; there is no necessary connection between law morals , or law as it is and as it ought to be; the analysis of legal concepts is worth pursuing which should be distinguished from historical, sociological and moral inquiries into the nature of law; legal system is a 'closed logical system' in which correct legal decisions can be deducted by logical means from predetermined legal rules without reference to social aims, policies, moral standards and that moral judgments cannot be suggested or defended, as statements of facts can by rational argument, evidence or proof (Dukor, 2004:58). On the other hand, Rawls theory of justice is a prodigious attempt to construct a liberal theory of justice and make it acceptable to the world where the gap between the rich and the poor is increasingly assuming an alarming dimension (ibid.)

Neo-Liberalism
One and only one concept or analytic scheme which straddles all the notions, concepts, bodies, entities and empirical statements in M. Chris Alli's magnum opus is neo-liberalism. Neo-liberalism in economic and political term is a path finder and ace interloper in finding solutions to the excesses of vulgar liberalism, crude capitalism and false federalism. It is an idea referring to the nineteenth and twentieth centuries' laissez-faire economic liberalism, although, it is distinct from modern liberalism because it is a critical reflection on the former's failures in addressing

imperialism, neo-colonialism, injustice, inequality, ethnicism, racism. Neo-liberalism is an apt theoretical and practical response to the crisis of the post-modern world especially in Africa and Nigeria in particular with gargantuan socio political instability and underdevelopment. What Neo-liberal political and economic philosophy or logic should counteract, according to M. Chris Alli,

> is the logic whereby we can excuse and justify our incompetence by every conceivable reason, the most concrete that never fails to stick, is that we are a developing country, therefore, we should allow for instability in all ramifications. Our logic, quite rationally, is that the developed world of Europe and United States of America went through this phase over 200 years ago and Great Britain, perhaps, 300 years back. We then proceed to pump hands and pat ourselves on the back for killing and wasting less beings and resources in the year of our Lord nineteen hundred and ninety-nine, in times of grave crises (P. 139-140).

Neo-liberal thinking seeks to abolish all forms of inequality, injustice and poverty and strives to enthrone economic laissez faire freedom and liberty of individuals and groups against excessive power of government.

Federalism

Federalism is not only a major key word or concept in The Federal Republic of Nigerian Army. It is also a major paradox the book sets for itself to resolve in the Nigeria state. It can be simply defined as a system of government where there is a social contract among component units in a state: sharing and unifying their social and economic powers for the greatest good of each and every one of them. Appadorai defines it as

> a division of powers and double allegiance. It means, in effect nothing less than the surrender by the nation-state of part of its sovereignty. The minimum Federal subjects are defence and foreign affairs; other common affairs may or may not be transferred to the federal authority (Appadorai, 1975).

Federalism is indeed, one of those modern applications and employments of neo-liberal thought in checking the excesses of liberalism and in Nigerian case, M. Chris Alli castigated the Nigerian governments for destroying the principle and practice of fiscal federalism and democracy. According to him, "the origin of Nigeria's federalism is a reverse of the American system in both concept and truth." (Alli, 2001:104). For him federalism is equity and fairness.

Republic

A republic is a nation or nation-state whose democracy is either direct or indirect but ultimately derives its strength, function and authority from the people. All constitutional democracies are supposed to be republican system of governments, that is, peoples' government, for instance the 1963 Nigerian Constitution that forestalls the people's rights from the British colonial power in terms of a Nigerian President instead of the Ceremonial Governor-General who was an appendage of British monarchy is a republican constitution based on Nigerian people's sovereignty. From M Chris Alli's exegesis, republican rights and franchise hardly subsisted for the individuals and components nationalities that formed the Nigerian quasi-federation because of the misrule of the military and political class, hence the metaphor of the Federal Republic of the Nigerian Army. "Republican government derives its power from the people, and it rules by their consent" (Ogbinaka, 2002:149). For M. Chris Alli, republicanism is a ruse in the Federal Republic of Nigerian army and

> it is therefore through a recourse to a restructured federal system in which all component parts of the Republic can have a say in resource allocation, federal representation and federal power limitation that Nigerian can find space for genuine all-encompassing development. (Alli: 121).

Therefore, republicanism is accommodated gleefully in neo-liberal thought.

Post-modernism

One conceptual tool in M. Chris Alli's piece meal social engineering is the recognition of individuals and groups identities in multicultural and multi religious societies and values. This drive and passion is a postmodernist instinct which he reflectively asserted in the thinking that "the unending crises in Nigeria point to the need for the restructuring of the federation to install a balance of power of some sort, not a shift of power. Such a re-restructuring should be capable of providing competent leadership and alternative ideologies for political action, "politicking" (Alli, 2001:124). He also argues for "justice not force, political alternative not a one party state, compatibility of ethnic nationalities and not hegemonies and static unified structures...we need commercial patrimony, not majority conquest of resources." (p. 315)

By all standards he is a postmodernist thinker who believes in shared assets, ideas and values in a state and in the community of nations:

> Post modernism emerged in the late 1970s to capture the changed character of the science in the twentieth century which called into question the idea that the organized pursuit of knowledge has a unique and natural course of development that can provide the basis for the general improvement of humanity, typically in the form of rational statecraft (Fuller, 2007: 123).

Despite the temporal ambiguities of the concept of postmodernism all point to an ironic twist, whereby the future turns back into the past. Post-modern, therefore, has different strands of principles and corresponding adherents in response to the enlightenment tango. However, M. Chris Alli based on his Nigeria's post-colonial experience would agree with Iyortad and Richard Rorty that the Enlightenment has been given a fair run, so it is time to move onto something else (Fuller, p 1250) as against Stephen Toulmin and Jacques Darrida position that "the Enlightenment has been given a fair run and merits continued pursuit" (Ibid), the critical theorist (Frankfurt School) contention that "the enlightenment has not been given a fair run but desires to be" (Ibid.) and finally Bruno Latour and others who argue that "the enlightenment has not been given a fair run and for good reason it has never been in a position to govern the rest of the society. For Lyortad and Ali, therefore, systematic enquiry has become increasingly bold and free, yet the result has not been the coherent and unified world view that the Enlightenment promised (Ibid). This is the reason for Alli's neoliberal tinkering of Nigeria's federalism.

Nigerian Factor
Nigerian factor' is a conceptual scheme and normative idiom for social political and economic selfish actions in Nigeria. It is so tap rooted in the collective unconscious of the majority that it has become a factor in production, social and political relations, hence, it is systemic. It has displaced merit and becomes a standard for measuring the quantity and quality of corruption. M. Chris Alli first, periscopes it as a phenomenon and then analysed it with the science of phenomenology in order to explain its modus operandi and origin. For Ali it is a long term consequence of colonialism, imperialism and military rule in Nigeria but unique for Nigerians in the sense that Nigerian diversity of people has a weird way of rationalizing failure and weakness.

Big Three
The 'Big Three' concept in M. Chris Alli's articulation is a phenomenology at work trying to understand the political, social and economic interests and forces that shape policies and actions in Nigeria. Naturally and empirically speaking the Big Three is The Big Tribes inordinately influencing socio-political actions in Nigeria. These big tribes are Hausa/Fulani, Igbo and Yoruba about which M. Chris Alli summarized, in the words of Alhaji Maitama Sule, as follows:

> Allah wisely endowed different people with different talents...the Igbo are talented entrepreneurs, businessmen and traders, Yoruba's, he sees as administrators servicing the polity and the civil services as teachers and diplomats. He then goes for the nation's jugular by saying that the Hausa/Fulani have the gift of leadership and that this role should be their exclusive privilege in the Nigerian state, an exclusive birth right (Alli 2001:94).

Big Three created what M. Chris Ali calls the "triangle of fears" (Ibid). These fears also translate into political and economic forces that reinforce corruption in all ramifications including military rule which was skimmed by imperialist powers in favour of the Hausa/Fulani who accordingly remains at the influential heights of the military and political equation in the country. The Big Three is, therefore, a phenomenological term in Nigerian politics that explains how the minority and oil producing regions were maltreated and exploited for many years until they resorted to militancy and violent resistant as means of stopping state's inequity, injustice and culpable underdevelopment of the regions that produce the national wealth.

The reading of M. Chris Alli's *Federal Republic of Nigerian Army: The Siege of a Nation* is an introduction to a more rigorous analysis of thematic issues. In this symposium on siege philosophy, ideas reflecting the different background of the respective scholar-philosophers were on release like catharsis as they x-rayed the theoretical, ontological, epistemological, socio-political and ontic planks of the thought-provoking ideas and questions in General Mohammed Christopher Alli's *Federal Republic of Nigerian Army.*

The mainstream, penumbra and margins of the interlocking themes discussed in this symposium are collectively and severally reflections of similitude and ambers of theory and practice, military and national security, politics and development, unity and diversity, courage and honour, integrity and accountability as well as the question of conflict resolution in multi-religious, multi-ethnic and neo-liberal democracy and economy. The contributions to this anthology or symposium are twenty-first century eminent and contemporary Nigerian philosophers. The respective thematic issues they are grappling with are arranged according to three general themes as follows:

The Military and National Security
Ujomu, Philip Ugochukwu, M. Chris Alli, "Nigerian statist-Militarist Realism and National Security"; Balogun, Oladele Abiodun, "M. Chris Alli and the Politics in the Nigerian Army: A Philosophical Approach"; Aja, Egbeke, On M. Chris Alli's Morality of War."; and Ukhun, Chris "M.C. Alli On Security and Media Within The Context of Jeremy Bentham's Ethics".

Morality and National Question
Unah, Jim Ijenwa, "Moral Character and Holistic Development in M. Chris Alli"; Eboh, Ben Okwu, "M. Chris Alli and Moral Perspectives of National Question"; Uduigwomen Andrew F. and Udofia, A.,

Christopher, "M. Chris Alli and the Peril of Religious Exclusivism: Religious Pluralism As a Panacea."

Federalism and Philosophy of Development
Okoro Chidozie, "M. Chris Alli, Militocracy and the Crisis of Leadership in a Plural State"; Oluwagbemi-Jacob Dorothy, "The Matter of Justice and Equity in Nigeria: A reflection on M. Chris Alli"; Dukor Maduabuchi, "Neo-liberalism and M. Chris Alli's Hermeneutics of Federalism."

References

Ali, M. Chris Alli (2001) *The Federal Republic of Nigerian Army: The Siege of a Nation* (Nigeria: Malthouse Press).

Appadoriai, A. (1975) *The Substance of Politics* (Oxford, OUP)

Beck, Robert N. (1979) *Handbook in Social Philosophy*, (London, Macmillan).

Bodunrin, Peter (1989). "The Question of African Philosophy" in C.S. Momoh (ed) *The Substance of African Philosophy* (Auchi Nigeria, African Philosophy Project Publications).

Dukor, M. (2001)," Theistic Humanism; African philosophical tradition" in *Journal Of Indian Council Of Philosophical Research* vol. xviii, no. 3 July-Sept;

Dukor, M. (2005) "The Great Debate on Deconstruction, Reconstruction and Cognition of African Philosophy" in *Philosophia: Philosophical Quarterly of Israel*, Vol. 33, Nos. 1-4 Dec. (Springer)

Hountondj, Pauline (1989) "African philosophy: Myth or Reality" in Sophie Oluwole (ed), *Readings in African Philosophy: An Anthology* (Lagos, Nigeria, Masstech, Publications).

John Rawls (1997) "A Kantan conception of equality" in *Ideological Voices: An Anthology of Modern Politics,* eds Paul Schumacher, Dueight C. Kiel and Thomas W. Heilke (USA, McGraw Hill).

Kaufmann A. Walter (ed) (1956) *Existentialism from Dostoevsky to Sarte,* New York.

Lioyd and Marry Moran (1954), *Humanism.* (Washington DC, Humanist Press).

Nkrumah, Kwane (1964) *Consciencism*, (London, monthly review Press).

Oruka Odera Henry (1989) "The Question of African Philosophy "in Sophia Oluwole (ed), *Readings in African Philosophy: An Anthology* (Lagos, Nigeria, Masstech, Publications).

Philip Pettit (2000) "Rawl's people" in *Rawl's Law of Peoples; A realistic* (eds) Rox Martin and David A. Reidy (Blackwell Publishing, USA).

Rorty Richard (1979) "Habermas and Lyotard on Postmodernity" in *Habermas and Modernity*, (ed) Richardson J. Bernstein, (U.S. MIT Press).

Steven Fuller (2007). *The Knowledge Book* (Montreal- Ithaca, McGraw Hill-Queen's University Press).

Warner Rex (1958). *The Greek Philosophers* (London, Mentor Books).

The Military and National Security

Chapter 2

M. Chris Alli, Nigerian Statist-Militarist Realism and National Security

-Ujomu Philip Ogochukwu

Introduction

This chapter is a critical and analytical study of the ideas of M. C. Alli on Nigeria's military, especially the Army and its key doctrines and philosophy, within a statist- militarist realist social system. The problem is that in Nigeria, statism, which is a continuation of the ancestral Westphalia cosmology, suggests the predominance of the state and its emphasis on force, fear and might. This situation elicits negative values of domination, suppression, alienation, terror, intolerance among others. This trend is particularly pronounced in a poverty-stricken, violent, corruption prone, multi-ethnic and multi-religious society as Nigeria, which struggles with identity politics and citizenship issues. The main finding is that statist-militarism suffers both from a grandiose egocentrism and the emergence of modern threats that vitiate and demystify its functionality. Hence, the imperative of change; seen as the unbundling and revision of militarism, in favour of a more humane social architecture based on integrated human values such as dialogue, constitutionalism, self-regulation, reconciliation and social justice. This work basically recommends a more holistic pathway to security, peace and social order in Nigeria. The idea is that agencies and institutions should live by their core visions and values, as well as missions and mandates so all stakeholders or social members can play a role in the formation of a stable, viable and progressive society.

Before we go into a full study of the Nigerian army's philosophy of security and militarism as proposed to us by M. Chris Alli (2001), a preface or preliminary comment is required in order to put the central issues and nuances arising from his thoughts in proper perspective. The truth must be told that Alli's book is deep, well-written, thoughtful and highly critical in nature. He says that "this book is not an indictment of the military, of which I am a part. It is my perception of the conduct of my generation..." (Alli 2001:3). In fact I dare to say that this book ought to be a 'must-read' for every military officer in Nigeria today. We can glean from Alli's book that he is no doubt a loyal, suave and morally upright officer and gentleman. Interestingly, he comes across as a good family man, who equally grew up in a good family. His reports about his ancestry attest to these (Alli 2001:4-18).These are laudable human values. As a soldier, his records are straight forward and his achievements distinct. In fact, he celebrates the Nigerian soldier by saying "I found the ordinary Nigerian soldier intensely loyal to the state, to his superiors and to the cause." (Alli 2001:27).Without pre-empting the rest of the chapter, we may ask if truly the problem of betrayals and coups in Nigeria that Alli tells us about in his book represent positive military ideals and value?

According to Alli, "the nature and roots of corruption in Nigeria, our value systems, state structures, core values, tribes, the minority/majority tribes equation and the structure of the Nigerian society are some of the issues that can be extracted from the book." (Alli 2001:3). Be that as it may the focus of my chapter is to critically and systematically examine the security and militarist ideas exposed in his book with a view to add 'value' to the army. I intend to do this with a robust sense of fairness and balance as well as a commitment to the truth. So I shall offer more truths and perceptions about, through the lens of a citizen, a civilian, and as a friend of the Nigerian army (I have close relatives and former school-mates still serving therein). In the quest for knowledge of something, it is safer and better to go the empirical way, by finding out peoples' observations and perceptions about that thing. Like they used to teach us in the University of Ibadan- 'the empirical explodes the myths.' There is no doubt about the immense and irrefutable contributions of the Nigerian military, and especially the army, to the security and development of Nigeria. However, thankfully too, Alli, has in his book, told a lot of home truths about the strengths and weaknesses of the Nigerian military. He talks about the lust for material gains by the soldiers, politicization of the Corps by some ceremonial or 'political' soldiers, faulty and grandiose beliefs by some soldiers that the Nigeria army is the custodian of Nigerian unity. These are serious matters for deeper intellectual consideration. All of these issues cannot be trashed in this chapter, but a few of them will be addressed in the body of the work.

Simply put, I am highly convinced that Alli is a man of truth and will not shy away from hearing or reading the truth when it comes from other sources. In fact for the sake of fairness to all, some matters require further clarification. Firstly, the conscientiousness and loyalty of Alli is not surprising, when we notice that he supplies glowing reports about patriotism, sincerity and frankness of his superior officers - Buhari and Idiagbon (Alli 2001:59) - as well as his course mates or contemporaries in the army. He tries to balance and shed light on the rationale for their actions, especially in their public lives. But we are also aware that there are some complaints about aspects of the Nigerian military actions as professionals, especially during the civil war and subsequently, their expedition into political rule. There are concerns about the obedience to the rule of law in the style of these erstwhile military rulers who made draconian, retroactive and obnoxious laws stifling press freedom and more seriously, they made laws that were backdated to capture offenders retrospectively. This is not right under the rules of natural, moral or positive law.

For instance, Alli mentions in glowing detail the character and dynamics of the Nigerian Army's military expedition to the delta Igbo region of Nigeria during the civil war, but his report of that encounter is suggestive that the alleged misdeeds of the armed forces there is not confirmed. According to Alli, "then in Asaba, it was rife to overhear miffed discussions about the unbecoming conduct of federal forces in that environment. There were stories about how the natives were lined up in football fields and along the River Niger and shot without provocation." (Alli 2001:25). Alli's perception of the account does not seem to fully tally with those of people like Emma, *Okocha Blood on the Niger*, and others, who continuously, in writing, allege with credible facts and arguments that there was a genocide attack by the Nigerian troops against the Aniocha people during that war. This one example suffices to show that there are contested issues about the excellence and professionalism of the Nigerian army, even to this day. Also note, the more recent allegations against the Nigerian army about genocide at Odi in Bayelsa, Zaki Biam in Benue, the Shi'ites or IMNL in Kaduna, Bama and other citizens in parts of Borno, etc. If we are to be fair to all parties concerned such matters need to be brought to the fore inevitably, in line with the need for a critical narrative. Let us proceed to the next set of issues this chapter seeks to interrogate.

Prolegomenon to the Nigerian Army's institutional Role in National Security

Suffice it to say that the real value of Alli's ideas in this seminal book is to bring his personal experience in the Nigerian army to the fore, and more importantly to systematically and critically present the Nigerian army to the readers in a way that is easy to understand, even if we do not agree with all that Alli has to say. One other thing that comes across is that idea or image of 'exceptionalism' in the self-concept and purpose of the Nigerian army in relation to the Nigerian project. Here lies the core value of Alli's ideas in the book: The opportunity that Alli's work allows us, to have a meaningful conversation on the logical and empirical character and context of the Nigerian army of today, which is need of constant self-regulation for increased best practices, and an honest appraisal from all well-meaning Nigerians- home and abroad.

The philosophical beauty and epistemological significance of Alli's is that his thoughts allow us to interrogate the institutional foundations of the military profession especially, the Nigerian army that he so effectively represents. It is clear and indisputable that the Nigerian army is nothing other than an institution made up of men and women; 'human beings,' who innately, by virtue of being human, are not perfect. This is the truth. So it is not possible to understand, not to talk of re-thinking the army's role in Nigeria's security unless we conceptualize the idea of an institution and its institutionalization. Let us have a brief prolegomenon analysis and conceptual study of the idea and practice of the army of Nigeria through the concept of an institution.

What are the logical and empirical properties of an institution? This question can be divided into two parts that seem to be of relatively equal significance: First, is, what is an institution? Second, is, how are institutions formed? Every human society possesses institutions of different sorts: Political, economic, social, educational, religious, and cultural among others. Let us examine the first question. An institution is easily known by the values it upholds and defends. It defends these values deeply because inevitably, they are generally accepted by its members and who have thoroughly internalized or imbibed them. So an institution ensures that its members assimilate its core values, namely, a complex cocktail of duties, obligations, norms, expectations, relationships; meaning that there is a process of enculturation or institutionalization. Put simply, an institution is a carrier or driver of values; it is a value system (Johnson 1961:15, 16, 20 &21), or a system of values (McLean 2004: 209). Put simply, an institution is a purposive organization with a set of well-defined features. For an institution to be effective it needs to be capable of being institutionalized. Institutionalization suggests that the institution and all that it embodies have taken root (Ujomu 2004: 33).

Let us examine a second and more important question of the formation of an institution. An institution arises from the manner in which people or a nation arranges its values - what it desires, chooses, considers important or of interest. Such an institution needs to emanate from the people's freewill, voluntariness as well as innate and acquired abilities. A people's values arise from their behaviour, choices and experiences, thus the institution(s) arising thereof must possess the capability and ability to meet with the social expectations and needs of the people; to provide social order, directing principle and stability. So an institution is a signpost or mirror of the values of a people or nation; a product of choice and performance (McLean 2004: 209-212). Put simply, this institution must be reliable, viable and predictable in ways that are capable of responding to the needs of the people that formed it. This simply means that a person or institution cannot give what it does not have. So when we create institutions, we seek security, efficiency and continuity of the more general rules of human social living that the people have adopted and adapted. Yet in Nigeria, our institutions are not able to attain these goals of decision making for the common good of all. Rather, our institutions have been perverted, violated, hijacked and relegated, thus posing a threat to collective survival (Ujomu 2004: 31-33).

The truth remains that Nigeria's national security is threatened by the problem of inefficiency, collusion and despondency of its major institutions and structures as instruments of social action and rectification. This has ensured that the various governments and the state agencies have been unable to consistently and institutionally guarantee the adequate protection, peace and well-being of their citizens (Ujomu 2000, 2001a, 2001b, 2008, Ujomu and Olatunji 2013). The institution of the Nigerian army has a lot of good sides to it, but it also has some deficits that need to be highlighted. The Nigerian army has a foreign dominating culture or colonial history or cosmogony that inevitably adversely affects its character and relations to the citizens. Colonialism is the carrier of ancestral negative and inimical values such as; discrimination, segregation, apartheid, exploitation, oppression, dehumanization, 'might is right,' and disrespect for human dignity and human achievement. Alli experienced this first-hand and he reports that there were tensions between some British military trainers and their Nigerian counterparts such that he said and I quote: "I explained without equivocation that I totally reject any notion, openly or subtly expressed suggesting that a Nigerian lieutenant colonel was under any circumstance equivalent to a British major." (Alli 2001:55). Also, Nigeria's crisis of multi-religiosity and multi-ethnicity makes the army to be continually partisan or tainted by these disruptive variables. It becomes clear that to rethink the identity and personality of the Nigerian army, we need to go deeper into the theory and knowledge of the idea of security.

A philosophical foundation of security

From a layman's viewpoint, Alli talks about his cherished philosophy of life to be "faith in God as the beginning of wisdom and human purpose" (Alli 2001: 84). Put simply, but teleologically, he believes in divine providence as the determiner of thoughts, actions and destiny. So we may hold minimally that philosophy is the study of God, man and nature. From the era of the masters of antiquities such as Plato, Machiavelli, Hobbes, Bentham and others, the study of security has remained a dominant part of the concerns of philosophy and philosophers. This era is not different. So we can develop a philosophical foundation of security when we focus on philosophy as something unique and different from other kinds of knowledge such as Science. Some benefits of philosophy may not be practical or immediate, the way you can see the road that an engineer has built or the loaf of bread that a baker has made. A lot of the benefits of philosophy are concentrated on the development of people's minds and thoughts. The power of philosophy is targeted at changing the human mind - the way people think so that they can have clearer ideas and hence create improved ways of achieving more productive action. Philosophy "is deeply rooted in human life" (Stace: 1937: 316), generally using the mind to generate thought and the body to perform actions. Viscount Samuel (1956:199) holds that "men's actions are governed by their ideas: right ideas lead to good actions and good actions bring welfare: wrong ideas lead to bad actions and bad actions bring suffering and disaster." The effect of philosophy is to improve in the quality of the thinking, imagination and knowledge of the people. Philosophical thinking gives an opportunity to be critical, to broaden the mind so that we can rationally justify positions held, and determine choices concerning the fundamental questions of life, as well as our answers to them.

The security of philosophy is based on the fact that philosophy holds that no topic is immune from discussion. Every issue needs to be critically examined in order to establish what is right to accept or reject. Philosophy encourages openness and tolerance as well as the need for us to allow alternative ways of viewing the world. Philosophers try to provide answers to questions with aim to break down a lot of bad reasoning, stereotypes and prejudices that arise from our living in this world. According to Francis Bacon in his theory of "Idols" he notes that human nature is captured by the idols:

> The idols of the Tribe have their foundation in human nature itself, and in the tribe or race of men. The idols of the Cave are the idols of the individual man. For everyone (besides the errors common to human nature in general) has a cave or den of his own, which refracts or discolours the light of nature; owing to his own proper and peculiar nature (Bacon 1972:92).

In the quest to alter or change the behaviour and experience of man, the demands of philosophical training are discordant from the natural tendencies of human nature. Human nature in most cases seeks to be egoistic, harmful to others, intolerant, anachronistic, oppressive, disobedient to the rule of law, emotional and disdainful of the rules of logic, objectivity and sound reasoning. The nature of the human being creates a two stage problem that reveals the weak point of man universally and then shows the weak point of each particular man. Such limitations are tied around the categories or parameters of race, intelligence, ethnicity, religion, sex, gender, beliefs, values, institutions, culture, traditions and class or caste among others.

Some philosophical ideas are required for the security of philosophy and also for the philosophy of security. Let us simplify a few of these ideas. Pragmatism is more than the fact truth is what is useful or workable to us. More importantly, it is the reference to the 'habit' of something or an institution. The habit of a thing is seen in its behaviour and experience, which reveal its logical and empirical properties, or to put it simply, its essence and essentials. To seek for the above qualities, is to try to understand the nature of a thing or institution as it evolves primordially or by nurture. So naturalism is mainly the quest for the true features or nature of something or an institution. One way to contact the nature of something or institution is to observe its behaviour. The study of overt behaviour is called behaviourism. Put simply, it means that my identity is shown by my actions; 'I am what you see me do.' This is known as the evidential approach which is based on the observational or empirical knowledge. The things I do are my functions or tasks. Functionalism is the idea that the society is like the human body that is made up of many active and mutually interdependent parts, and that the infirmity of one part may affect the smooth functioning of other parts.

The classical idea of security and controversies about the meaning of security

There is no single idea or definition of security. It is an evolving concept with many nuances and intrigues lurking in it. The idea of security is well known as a 'slippery slope.' So there is a more serious logical question about: Whether any particular typology of security, be it militarism, realism, statism, idealism or whatever, can claim to have an epistemic or even a moral high ground in the discourse? Hence, the idea of security suggests so many different things to different people. Every meaning carries its own deeper connotations. According to Makinda (1998:282) "security is generally regarded as a 'contested concept' because it does not have a clinical definition." It is not just that but that also the idea of security is fundamental to human existence and it is a carrier of value, culture and prestige. Thus it is a battlefield of ideological contention. According to Sandlers (1997:5), given that "modern threats to security are complex and assume myriad forms: thus, the notion of security needs to be rethought." As such, we can employ the notions of hard and soft in simplifying a sense of complexity and controversy underlying the idea of security.

Despite this flexibility in the definition of the idea, Ochoche (1998: 105) maintains that "security for all entities, organizations and especially nations is a first-order concern." The concern for the security of a nation is undoubtedly as old as the nation-state itself (Brown 1982:21). The central feature in the quest for national security is the concern for national survival (Brennan 1961:22). National security is the concern for the desire and capacity for self-defence (Ray, 1987:248-249), or as the preservation of the borders of a state (Goldstein, 1999:79), as the confrontation of threats to peace in the society (Hare, 1973:86-89) or even as the avoidance of conflicts, confrontations and the preservation of the lives of people in the society (Africa Research Bulletin, 2000:13931-55). The modern army is central to national security of a state. This state-centric idea of security is a legacy of Westphalia treaty of 1600s. Westphalia was nothing other than a logical and empirical shift from the old monarchic and emperor based socio-political system, to the formation of the modern state as a carrier of national and political values. So due to the essential feature of sovereignty of the state system, it became all the more necessary for the state to have a modern army to protect its government, territory and perhaps citizens from external and internal enemies. This focus has shifted slightly to a broader view of security, whose conceptualization goes far beyond the role of an army of soldiers. This is a wider dimension of security.

Furthermore, Lester Brown and others, argued that survival and military might is not all there is to security. Security and peace in the contemporary era are threatened by worldwide problems such as; international terrorism, over-population of human beings, food scarcity, unemployment, pandemic diseases, poverty, inequality, unemployment, environmental issues, etc., (Brown 1978:47, UN Panel Report 2005: 595-

596, Ferguson 2006:7). So there is also the focus on the attainment of peace and progress of individuals, groups and the society (Ujomu 2001a:176, 2001b, 2008). this It must be noted that real or perceived threats to national security "may have an internal or external dimension" and for many less developed countries LDCs, of which Nigeria is one, national security is manifestly endangered by external threats (Deger and West, 1987:3-5). Thus we have a wider context of the security imperative. Thus O'Brien (1995:100) argues that security is more than just safety from the violence of rival militaries, it means the absence of violence whether economic, sexual or military. Alli notes that some of the greater threats to security emanate from "the condition of Nigeria...a Nigerian nation in which the forces of ethnicity and theology take centre stage in a triangular struggle among tribes." (Alli 2001: 87&86). Let us return to the military dimension of security.

Some key typologies of a statist- militarist conception of security

The classical idea of security

The classical idea of security is the oldest definition of security and is linked to the Latin word '*securitas*'. This refers to "tranquillity and freedom from care or the absence of anxiety upon which the fulfilled life depends" (Liotta 2002:477). This suggests a lack of hindrance or restriction and a sense of harmony and a stable undisturbed sense of purpose and attainments. This definition is idealistic and utopian and thus unsatisfactory given the long history and plethora of security concepts, threats and solutions prevalent in the world today.

The Realist or State centric realist perspective

The state-centric realist view of security is the dominant idea of security since after Westphalia. It is explained by Ayoob (1984:41):

> the term security has traditionally been defined to mean immunity (to varying degrees) of a state or nation to threats emanating from outside its boundaries. A nation is secure to the extent to which it is not in danger of having to sacrifice core values. By security we mean the protection and preservation of the minimum core values of any nation: political independence and territorial integrity.

It means that "nations like individuals must predicate their relationships on given well-conceived and properly defined precepts and norms. Such values and value-systems are the ground norm for rallying all sections of the peoples." (Alli 2001:101). This is the most common and prevalent view of security in the modern era. However, Hoogensen and Rottem (2004:158) have offered the clearest possible reason why we must move away from the realist view of security. They observe that "state security is essential but does not necessarily ensure the safety of individuals and communities." The world has grown so complex that statist-realism can no longer cope with present day security challenges. So to respond to worldwide security concerns, the entire world has moved on to regional and global level solutions that are beyond and individual state(s).

The idea of security dilemma

This is a form of security that depends on the consequential fluidity of the power balance among competing and contending states in the international arena. To clarify issues, Messari (2002:416-417) describes a security dilemma as that process by which

> as a consequence of this condition of international anarchy, states are permanently arming themselves in order to protect their borders. Through this states aim at self-protection. However, the unintended consequence of pursuing such a policy is to create a feeling of insecurity among one's neighbours. Thus one state's effort to ensure its own security becomes a source of insecurity for other states.

So it is possible for a state to simply and genuinely desire to protect its sovereignty, but such an action may be misconstrued or perceived by another state as a threat. So that other state then takes more threatening actions purely with the motive of defending its own sovereignty. This means that while the reality can be different from appearance or perception, yet both of them are equally consequential. This security dilemma is a complicated and dialectical process that can lead to convolution and instability in international affairs. According to Roe (2001:103) "the security dilemma has the capacity to say something important about the responsibility of those actors involved." Therefore, Roe (2001:104) proposes a qualifying classification, namely, "a categorization of the security dilemma into three types: 'tight', 'regular' and 'loose'."

The Third World perspective on security
There is a Third World dimension to, or perspective on, security. This global South or hemispheric view of security, as Ayoob (1984) has rightly observed, can be summarized in the statement, "Despite the rhetoric of many Third World leaders, the sense of insecurity from which these states suffer emanates, to a substantial extent, from within their boundaries." Since "it is these regimes, and their bureaucratic and intellectual hangers-on, who define the threats to the security of their respective states, it is no wonder that they define it primarily in terms of regime security rather than the security of the society as a whole" (Ayoob 1984: 42 &46). This is the linchpin that helps us to understand the reasons for the state's formation of an army and its uses. If the threat to a third world state comes from within, then the rulers have no choice than to use the military to protect themselves. Hence the primary focus personal and regime security of the government cannot stand side by side with the view of an army that desires to be nationalistic and representative of national unity. Put simply, such an army will either be partial to vested dominant interests or it will be traitorous by betraying the rulers it was designed to protect. Or it will simply take over political power and go outside its core mandate. This is the dilemma of the Nigerian army.

Statist-Militarist realism and the high politics of "hard" security
A further conceptual framework of the 'high politics of security' (Akpan 2008: 184-186) requires us to do some simplifications and clarifications on the notions of statist- militarist realist conception of security as done below.

High Politics
Let us examine the meanings of high. Let us start from the basics. The idea of high may have to with things that are up there, abstract, senior, distinguished, extraordinary, advanced, esoteric, cryptic or hidden, elite or special. This list is by no means exhaustive. Specifically, it seems that high in this sense has to do with matters affecting the state, national security especially top secret, cryptic or sensitive issues about logic,

causality and architecture of security. The exemplar or epitome or archetype of high security is the statist realist militarist typology or cosmology.

So the logical implication of the above is that the high politics of security has to do with the building up of a set of dominant values which include 'fear and might' (Akpan 2008: 184-186), force, psychological intimidation, (Ujomu 2008) command and control of decision making affecting the collective, but not always in their interest, unleashing of violence as a first resort, a mono-logical way of thinking and approach unbending view of reality, selective humanism based on an aura of superiority, inequality and inequity, debasement and dehumanization of others who do not belong, aura of born to rule or the raw power of the arches or archon, a display of arrogance and impunity, a tendency to secrecy and lack of access to information, the reinforcement of the structures of hegemony.

Hard

The idea of 'hard' as used in security refers to the use of core offensive strategies such as military force or defensive strategies such as customization and reinforcement of buildings and so on as security measures. The concept of hard implies fixity, solidity, concentration, compactness, decisiveness, entrenchment and direct impact of elements used in ensuring security. There has been a modernization of the design and structure of buildings through the 'target hardening process' reinforcement of their core and exoskeleton leading to increasingly safer physical infrastructures and improved security architectural design. In the area of aircraft technology there is a focus on the construction of long range capability machines, reinforced cockpits and other technological on- board equipment. Put simply at the individual level a person can embark on hard security or harden the security of his home or house by building and raising the fence, constructing burglar proof devices among others. A country can harden its security by increasing the number, variety, deployment and equipment of its armed forces, reinforce the national defence architecture. When something is hardened, it ceases to be flexible, fallible- open to correction or improvement. This tendency can be very dangerous.

Statism

The statist view sees the State as the centre of the universe; rights, burdens and benefits are to be defined and distributed by the state and its agencies. The state retains control over all the domains of life political, economic, military and educational. It exercises a prominent majority power in quantity and quality over all other sectors in the society; private or civil society. Any country like Nigeria, that runs this system of government runs a statist society or statist-corporatism.

Realism

The realist view asks us to see things or people the way they are actually, the way they appear to us or present themselves to us in this real life of individual experience. A thing is the way it is, so deal with it the way it offers itself to you. For instance, human nature is the way it is; egoistic, difficult and unpredictable at best. So we need to manage it that way and make the best of the situation by looking for pragmatic or practical solutions that can work in real life. Realism or the insistence upon military power as a political theory or instrument of security suffered a two-pronged defeat: firstly, the problem of the ascendancy of a greater military power over another leading to spiralling conflict, arms races, genocidal violence and eventually the mutual decline or expiration of the combatants. This is what we mean by a security dilemma, a process by which

> states are permanently arming themselves in order to protect their borders. Through this, the unintended consequence of pursuing such a policy is to create a feeling of insecurity among one's neighbours. Thus, one state's effort to ensure its own security becomes a source of insecurity for other states (Messari 2002:416-417).

Militarism

The militarist view sees every issue and its solution in terms of a military solution through the acquisition and deployment of arms and ammunitions, otherwise through the use of military power. Alli uses the idea of the army training modules to explain militarism "at the Depot, as a greenhorn, stark recruit, they...panel-beat you into a voiceless obedient machine. At the Defence Academy for officer cadets they...give you a gunboat military education...they refine your character" (Alli 2001:52). The potentials of current theorizing for liberation and transformation facilitate better insight into security analysis providing a new theoretical basis for the understanding of the security problem. Seen from a historical perspective, it is clear that natural security paved the way for militarism or militaristic security. The increase in human populations and the generally lower levels of awareness of the rules of wider cosmopolitan habitations heightened the spate of wars and conflict among men. This age ushered in the trajectory of militarism; which depended on the "active use of military force for political purposes and in defence of national interests." (Blau and Goure 1984:13)

All through human history, it has been shown that mere militaristic power will never be, and has never been enough in the long-term guarantee of national or human security. Militaristic security therefore smacked of a rigid deterministic motion towards the intensification of the amassing of military weapons, which could only be overcome by a greater amassing of weapons. The logic of militarism was apparently a faulty one, depending strongly upon force and the appeal to force and the illusions of power that have consistently heralded the defeat of great civilizations. The tracks of militarism were seen clearly in the rigidity, fear, arrogance, secrecy, domination and haughtiness that heralded that peculiar vision and form or stage of security theorizing. The features of militarist viewpoint were defined by the indomitable preference for order, efficiency, utility, form and power. Finally, we may say

> that recalcitrant conservatism, in any form it appears on the intellectual and socio-political landscape, needs to be repudiated. This is because it cannot be allowed to block the development of new knowledge, creative theorizing and the alternative futures that it might encourage (Ujomu 2008).

Nigeria's Statism, militarist-realism and a "hard" approach to national and human security: an empirical account

Let us examine the 'hard' approach to Nigerian security through the doctrine and operations of the army. Without doubt, the view of Peters (1983:115) is illustrative of Nigeria's security policy. According to Peters, the ultimate aim of Nigeria's national security effort is to protect it from attack, whether direct or indirect. But to get to the stage where it is possible to adequately determine the structure of the armed forces, there must be, one, a policy that reflects stated national objectives, and two, a national security management capacity that can cope. It is not enough to provide the armed forces with long-range military capability, without a clear-cut strategy as to how these forces are to be deployed and used. This policy statement exhibits some deficiencies. Such a restrictive militaristic conception of security cannot lead to the desired form or level of social and economic advancement required by a country confronted by diverse socio-cultural challenges among which is pervasive violence and terrorism. This policy is not only limited in its scope and method, but it is also prone to perversion (Ujomu 2008). Alli informs us that "...northern emirs had reservations over the appointment of another Christian to the command of the strategic 1st Infantry Division...At this time, the Nigerian Army was steamily enmeshed in politics." (Alli 2001: 74 & 75).

The Nigeria Army's singular mandate is to preserve the internal stability and external integrity of the country. In Nigeria, the force structure or security architecture is predominantly statist-militarist. The core military defence organizations that have the responsibility for key departments of national and human security are: The armed forces- Army, Navy, Air Force, comprising the Divisions, Battalions and Brigades and then the Counter terrorism squad (CT), Northern Joint Task Force (JTF or N-JTF) operating in the north east and north central Nigeria, Southern Joint Task Force (JTF or S-JTF) operating in the entire south-south of Nigeria, (STF) special task force operating in the middle belt, (IS) internal security operating in most volatile parts of the Niger Delta such as Ogoni land.

The intelligence agencies - Nigeria Intelligence Agency (NIA), Defence Intelligence Agency (DIA), Defence Intelligence Services (DIS), State Security Services (SSS) or Department of State Security (DSS), Directorate of Military Intelligence (DMI), Special Services Office (SSO), The Presidency, Office of the National Security Adviser (O-NSA), Intelligence community (IC), Joint Intelligence Board (JIB). The Nigeria National Guard (GD or N-GD) an embedded all-pervading group of soldiers from all the forces brought together and trained as GD but dispersed by the Abacha regime into the Police, SSS, army navy and air force waiting to be recalled (see The Nation Newspaper series in the references). It should be noted that the Nigeria National Guard GD or N-GD proposed headquarters in the Sambisa forest of north-eastern Nigeria was later taken over by the boko haram terrorists and other sundry criminals terrorizing that part of the country. But it should also be noted that despite reports but residents that some boko haram terrorists still roam around that place, the Nigerian military has stridently claimed that these nuisances have been dislodged from there.

Some weak points of the 'hard' or militarist approach to security in Nigeria

The army's 'hard' statist realist militarist approach to security in Nigeria suffers due to certain debilitating weak points. Alli identifies the "morass of grabbing for power and office at all costs and, second, the blind pursuit of materialism in the forces." (Alli 2001:69). He also talked about "the dog eat dog, cat and mouse intrigues which had become the bane of staff work in the corridors of power" (Alli 2001:72), and "the usurpation of civil power and the sacking of properly constituted governments" (Alli 2001:184) as the Nigeria army's Achilles heel. There are other major shortfalls but let us pick a few of these for discussion.

Negative perception and distrust of the force(s)

The security forces seem to generally suffer an image or perception problem that has to do with the contradiction between the way they see themselves and the way other stakeholders in the society see them. This perception is highly negative, having repercussions on behaviour and experience of the forces. The army suffers this problem to some degree, but the Nigeria police suffer it the most. Put simply, the problem of perception has so much do with the ability of the forces to learn skills and apply logic in the security domain so as to perform efficiently and creditably for organizational and social benefit. The relationship between the security forces and the majority of harried and harassed citizens has been one of cat and mouse game. In Nigeria, people do not seem to wish to have anything to do with these forces due to their highhandedness, apparent ignorance of social and security dynamics, overbearing nature and cruelty. The army exists within a Nigerian nation which has not confronted effectively, the critical task of national reconciliation. Many within the Nigerian polity are demanding for greater autonomy, benefits and recognition for their peoples or regions within the country. This situation has adversely affected the army's performance as a neutral and professional body.

So we can agree with Ifeka (2000:122) that the lack of trust between the rulers and the ruled in Nigeria ensured that there was an obstruction to more effective utilization of the national army for the purpose of development at all levels of social existence. Furthermore, we can say that the absence or lack of operation of some core social values such as, trust, co-operation, compassion, justice, tolerance, etc. among the different institutions and interests in the society, ensured that the various levels of national government could not effectively manage the nation's resources for the overall security, peace, prosperity and well-being of all. Citizens withhold information from the security forces and generally prefer to give information to the media, and try to resolve all matters and disputes out of court and without the knowledge of law enforcers where possible. This is the current trend, though effort is being made to change the situation. Despite this, the reality of mistrust is palpable and unassailable. There is the alienation of the state agencies in the vigorous pursuit of commutative justice. In adopting the internal security option, we stress "activities collectively undertaken by security agencies towards the restoration of peace and stability." (Yusuf 2003:36).

Inadequate manpower and lack of best practices
There is a more serious logical problem which has deep consequences for collective security. Compared to the high population of Nigeria put at about 160,000,000 million people, the numbers of the core military available in the security work force appear grossly inadequate. The statistics as at 2012 are; 371,000 Policemen, 130,000 Army, 15,000 Air force, 18,000 Navy (Adebakin and Raimi 2012:15). The security men and women have been depleted by persistent attacks and killings by terrorists, armed robbers, kidnappers, assassins, sub-regional ethnic militias, foreign Fulani cattle-rearers, civil disturbances and other causes of mortality or fatality common to these professions. Yet is should be noted that more young people are being recruited into the forces almost on a bi-annual basis. One major problem here is that if recruitment into these forces is to be increased, then there needs to be a sustainable way of

paying their salaries. Should these forces go into large scale agriculture? Will that be in line with their primary assignment? Will there be no conflict of interest or distractions? These are legitimate concerns. This is a problem because the Nigerian economy is traditionally currently agrarian and mono-logical depending on primitive farming and crude oil exports. More so due to massive corruption, the economy is having a downturn. Though, it must be said truthfully, that the situation of agriculture- animal and crop farming has improved significantly in the northern and southern states like Kebbi, Taraba, Benue, Yobe, Adamawa, Jigawa, Sokoto, Cross River, Edo and Delta, among others, yet, Nigeria, is still not out of the woods because, it still spend a lot on importation of food.

Still on the challenges facing the Nigerian military, there is the accusation that the government even refused to take some warnings about the activities of some of these terrorist groups seriously. Here the case of the Eggon militia called Ombatse becomes instructive. The Nasarawa state government of Nigeria has alleged that the federal government of Nigeria under President Jonathan did not do enough to heed the warnings about the activities of the Ombatse hence this laxity and levity led to the killings of 63 policemen and 10 officials of the SSS (The Nation Newspaper Friday September 13, 2013:6). This is a grave accusation that strikes at the heart of the Nigerian problem. In Nigeria, 'the military, which appeared most constitutionally and professionally suited to fulfil the task of providing security, has played a particularly negative role in the maintenance of national security. Thus, a large body of security forces, cannot guarantee Nigeria's quest for national security since much of the insecurity, conflicts and crisis that happened in the country from the 1960s were in fact due to the actions and omissions of these same security forces' (Ujomu, 2000:38). Alli agrees with this point when he says "unfortunately, the military have fundamentally induced more insecurity in the polity since colonial times" (Alli 2001:181). The weak points of the men in uniform have been identified as disobedience to the rule of law through extra judicial killings, maiming, torture, arson, destruction, looting, etc., (Editorial of *Tribune* newspaper 2005:10).

There were also serious problems of military complicity in creating atmosphere of terror, terrorism and instability in the country due to political and economic self-interest. The Nigerian military saw its role in national security from the angle of their own personal interest and professional ambitions (Oladiran and Adadevoh 2008). The situation of national and human security was so bad that the death-squad-type of killings by army undercover units became a popular trend. Some people earn their living from this security racket. For example, Brigadier-General Ibrahim Sabo (Rtd.), the boss of the Directorate of Military intelligence (DMI) during the Abacha regime in Nigeria, noted in a press interview that in these governments (Babangida's and Abacha's), a lot of intrigues were brought to play (Oladiran and Adadevoh 2008). These people would create a problem 'and then go and report to the system and thereafter ask for a specific amount of money to quell it. It is selfishness, if somebody has been getting money under the name of security by faking situations of insecurity and thereafter, get imaginary suspects to deal with'. Similar points have been made by Albert (2005: 49-51). The above statement clearly illustrates how the military use the excuse of security to minister to their personal needs and create security problems internally (Oladiran and Adadevoh 2008).

Fifth column or internal treachery and external betrayal
There is also the issue of indiscipline, betrayal and treachery within the forces. Alli confirmed this in his work. Do we have a Fifth Column (traitors) in the Nigerian military? On Friday, 13 September 2013 some 105 Nigerian soldiers of the MN-JTF reconnaissance patrol were ambushed along the Baga-Maiduguri expressway after an aerial bombardment failed to take place. On August 4th 2013 a group of 20 Nigerian soldiers were also ambushed by terrorists at Malam Fatori. All of these may have seemed to suggest the presence of fifth columnists or insider-betrayal within the military formations and hierarchy as well as laxity through a failure of intelligence to uncover Boko Haram's backers and sources of weapons. The most damning evidence of a military-based collusion with the Boko Haram can be easily seen in the case of Umar aka Kabiru Sokoto who was arrested in a Governor's Lodge in the company of a serving military officer.[1] The problem of compromise and criminal

---

[1] Agekameh in *The Nation* newspaper Wednesday December 18, 2013:21, *The Nation* newspaper Wednesday December 25, 2013:21, Editorial in *The Nation* newspaper Wednesday December 11, 2013:19.

infiltration of the highest levels of government by core subversive elements has been noted to be a key threat to Nigeria's national security. Recently, attention has been drawn to the fact that "many people with criminal antecedents occupy strategic positions in various Federal Government Ministries, departments and agencies." [2]

Conflicts of leadership role and Intra-service or inter-service rivalry

There was no consistency in the definition of roles of the intelligence agencies among Nigerian military regimes. For example during the military era in Nigeria there were issues about the dominance and role of the state security services SSS. During the regime of general Babangida who created the SSS, this organization was the primary clearing house of all intelligence and its head was the coordinator of the activities of the other intelligence agencies. However, during the regime of general Abacha when the chief security officer (CSO) to Abacha major Mustapha held sway, the SSS was relegated to the background and intelligence agencies created parallel communication channels for themselves, often sending conflicting messages directly to the Presidency. There was evidence of a serious problem of coordination, jurisdictional confusion, counter- productive competition and grand standing during the totalitarian rule of Abacha (Babatope 2005:149-150). This tendency is not peculiar to Nigeria. In the case of Britain in Northern Ireland, police-military relations were confused with respect to conflicts over policy focus, mission and action. According to Brewer and others (1996:62-64) "poor communications and a lack of trust between the police and the army added to the difficulties of the security forces during the strike."

More specifically, years of military rule ensured the weakening of the police and then later even the military itself under some stratocracy and its many dictators of different hues. The eventual hate, acrimony and disdain emanating from this brew spawned the inter service rivalry that we have today. Thus we have a problem of basic human and institutional relations that can only be solved by increased inter-force co-operation, modern training to enhance professional and technical competence,

---

[2] Editorial in *The Nation* newspaper Friday December 27, 2013:19.

intensification of training and academic programmes to keep these forces very busy and thus less prone to diversionary, debasing and needless violence. Also the military barracks in particular, and under a civilian government need to be moved further away from the zones of civilian populations or cities to prevent unnecessary military and civilian conflicts.

There is a tendency to poor intra and inter military and paramilitary co-operation for action and active sharing of information. This politicization, arrogance, territoriality, divide and rule, domination and favouritism of one organization over another by the political and security elite has compromised security and aggravated conflicts, violence and instability in the country. With specific reference to Nigeria, let us offer some striking examples of the consequences of the ineptitude, politicization and rivalries between the forces. We have contention between; the police and the state security SSS or DSS, the police and the army and air force, the police and the civil defence, the navy and the army and air force, the police versus the ethnic militia groups, as well as the citizens versus the institutionalized security forces. These disputes have together made collective security a nearly impossible task to achieve. This situation pushes us to realize that we cannot afford to ignore or underestimate the balance of power within, and between the security organizations that currently suffer from deep fractionalization and politicization (Fayemi and Ball 2004:11).

As recently as December 21, 2013, there is evidence of a lack of harmony, restraint, co-operation and discipline between the police and army as witnessed in a clash between the Paiko police station and 31 artillery brigade in Minna, Niger State, Nigeria.[3] Thereafter the army basically denied invading the police station offering so many different excuses. In all, it seems that the continuation of ego-tripping, power show, extrajudicial violence, high-handedness, detention and killings by the police still serves as a basis for inter-service conflicts and an undermining of the existing but tenuous national security architecture.[4]

---

[3] Orintunsin in *The Nation* newspaper Saturday December 21, 2013:59
[4] Orintunsin in *The Nation* newspaper Monday December 23, 2013:9

Records from the PEDEP 2003 Annual Report on Violent Conflicts in Nigeria (ARVCN 2004) informs us statistically and descriptively of clashes between the security services in the year 2003. Nigeria Police and Nigeria Prison Service 1, Nigeria Navy and Youths 7, Nigeria Police and Civilians 6, Nigeria Police and Nigeria army 3, civilians to civilians 101, out of which 25 were ethnic militia clashes, 23 were clashes between youth gangs. These clashes have not abated. In July 2005, there was a clash between the Nigeria Police and the Air Force leading to the loss of many lives and a probe was set up to investigate the shameful event (The Punch 9 July 2005). Unfortunately, even as at October 2005, there were still disruptive and violent clashes between the Nigeria Police and the Nigeria Army leading to massive human and material destruction.[5] To appreciate the theoretical implications of these statistics let us now use some examples to further buttress our point.

There is incontrovertible proof of the difficulties in inter-security service co-operation in Nigeria leading to colossal human and material losses for government, state institutions including the security forces and generality of the citizens and foreigners in Nigeria. It is quite tragic and also on record that there were cases where the SSS or DSS gave pre-emptive information to the police and other security organs, who, in turn did not seem to do enough to contain the eventual situation of insecurity that erupted. The Maitatsine episode can be used as an example of this problem of discordant focus and commitment. The costs of allowing such dispositions and groups to thrive can be overwhelming. Of special importance to our claim of the sectarianism or closed community is the indictment of the security forces. According to Falola (1998:160) one major reason for the powerful surge of this closed community is that "there had been negligence on the part of the police and the National Security Organization for their failure to stop the sect from building such strength. Both the police and the security agents had been unable to effectively coordinate their activities to be able to handle the sect."

Another example will suffice, in respect of the Kaduna riots of February 2000, the NSA National Security Adviser found it difficult (for

---

[5] See *Nigerian Tribune* 31 October 2005, *The Vanguard* October 5 2005, *The Vanguard* October 6 2005, *The Comet* October 5 2005, The Guardian October 5 2005, *ThisDay* newspaper October 6 2005.

unclear reasons) to act to pre-empt or manage the crisis, "despite reports by the State Security Services SSS. The SSS had noted the imminent danger" (Abimboye 2000:14) but those who ought to have cared failed to read in between the lines and take effective counter measures to foil the Kaduna crisis. Still on the Kaduna crisis of 2000, the lack of co-operation and ego trip of the military and paramilitary forces created a situation detrimental to the society and its members. There was a discordant assessment of the crisis situation by the army and police. It is on record that the then Kaduna state Police Commissioner CP refused military assistance even when all the facts suggested that he should have jumped at the offer. Thus "even when the GOC general officer commanding, 1 Mechanised Division of the Nigeria army in Kaduna reportedly inquired about the situation, the police boss was said to have replied that everything was under control" (Abimboye 2000:15). This example shows that the army is not always at fault in some of these situations.

The Army's role in security and the security of the Army: towards a holistic approach to national development

Alli informs us of the mandate of the army that "it is a soldier's moral duty to ensure mission accomplishment at all times...We must without equivocation, affirm that the soldier's sense of sacrifice is incomparable, and rightly so" (Alli 2001:30). This seems to be a utopian estimation. The concepts of sociality and stakeholder are central to the clarification of the 'hard' and 'soft' aspect of security. At the highest levels of government there seems to be a predominant view that civilians may have a place in the war on terror in Nigeria. The nature of civilian involvement requires clarification. The office of the NSA national security adviser is requesting more effective communication between the security agencies and the civilians in the areas of operation basically. This raises issues about a new conception of the stakeholder or contributor to national security. The office of the NSA is also focusing on new developments in weapons and anti-terrorism technologies.[6] There is a concern for more integrated security training for the military and security services working for the

---

[6] Yishau in *The Nation* newspaper Wednesday December 18, 2013:3

government of Nigeria (Chukwu in *The Guardian* newspaper Thursday August 22, 2013:3).

To this effect, the military through the GOC 81 Division has commended the role of the media in security asking practitioners to collaborate with the armed forces to build a secure and stable Nigeria.[7] The Nigerian military has suffered heavy causalities at the hands of Boko Haram, the most pronounced being the December 2nd 2013 attacks that destroyed an air force base, army barracks, police stations, helicopters and jet fighter bombers as well as killing hundreds of civilians and soldiers and their families. Also destroyed were petrol stations, fuel tankers, trailer parks, motor parks, private houses, etc. (*The Sun* newspaper Tuesday December 3, 2013:1).

At the level of industrialization through the use of local technology the PROFORCE, an armoured manufacturing company, has linked up with DICON (Defence Industries Corporation of Nigeria) and has embarked on the mass production of all grades of armoured machines; APC armoured personnel carriers, armoured security boats, bullion vans, etc.[8] All of these are with a view to curb the excesses of armed assaults on vehicles bearing high value targets- human or otherwise. Recall that banks have been the target of armed banditry and terrorists in the last years. There has also been an intensive development of the unmanned aerial vehicle UAV programme of the Nigeria air force leading to the development of the Gulma UAV which was unveiled by the president of Nigeria Goodluck Jonathan. The drone will be used for national achievement in indigenous technology, surveillance, intelligence gathering and combating crime as well as promoting infrastructure and human capacity development.[9]

The Nigerian navy has also gone towards the acquisition of surveillance technology as a way of combating sea-based terrorism or piracy. The focus is on building automated camera surveillance towers with high frequency radios on the high sea to monitor and curb crude oil theft on Nigerian waters. The technology is called Regional Awareness

---

[7] Onozure in *The Vanguard* newspaper Wednesday December 11, 2013:46
[8] Adebanjo in *The* Nation newspaper Wednesday December 11, 2013:47
[9] Akowe in *The Nation* newspaper Wednesday December 18, 2013:7

Maritime Capability Area of Responsibility, Forward Operating Base (RAMC, AoR, FOB) is a means for checking piracy for hundreds of kilometres of maritime space.[10]

Some of the more recently embraced paradigms of security analysis and planning that Africans utilize emanate from most parts of the world especially Europe. So these ideas face the challenges of blending into the specific cultural nuances and social proclivities of African societies. Though the idea of security suggested so many different things to different people, meaning that it was a 'contested concept,' yet the idea of security was seen to be fundamental to human existence. It conveyed values, culture and prestige and was a battlefield of ideological contention. We rethought the notions of hard and soft terms of simplifying that sense of complexity and controversy underlying the idea of security. We drew attention to the problem of agency or the human factor as a threat to security theory, knowledge and practice especially in an African setting. These challenges show that in the area of the military action for national security, only a creative joint action for physical security and the creation and sharing of intelligence can make the required difference in the quest for security for a less developed society that is critically deficient in human and material capacity utilization, epistemic inspiration and evolving technology for sustainable security management, inter-service security co-operation and social control.

Security will be possible only when people can be genuinely free to proffer useful alternatives to dominant ideas, to create zones of freedom where ideas, values and institutions will legitimately contend for rational supremacy in the public sphere. There is a need for a space where constructive ideas and interpretations of social reality can be given priority. This is the more significant in a developing society where it is increasingly obvious that those rulers who should be the repositories of inspiration, do not yet, have the kinds of capacity and imagination truly needed to move society forward. There is a need for devolution of powers and responsibilities to persons, institutions and agencies that can produce results. There must be a way to identify or create opportunities for society

---

[10] *The Nation* newspaper Saturday December 21, 2013:5, Odiegwu in *The Nation* newspaper Sunday December 22, 2013:7

to benefit from the more excellent elements of its human capital and resources. The problem is not really with the quality of alternatives, but with the often myopic and laughable pupation and encysting of the urgently needed critical and reconstructive mind-set of the African state. This closure and occlusion ensures that the state in Africa is essentially not open to ideas, unable to create sources of ideas, and worst of all is unable to generate its own positive ideas for full and future development.

The Nigerian army's commitment to excellence is a special challenge. It embodies a combination of outstanding good character and optimal advanced skills and vast innovative experience. According to Alli the Nigerian soldier, over the years, "has been hardened by the shortcomings of a disoriented officer-leadership" (Alli 2001:27). Thus the demand for personal and institutional excellence is an irrevocable condition of enduring social and aesthetic change in a developing society because individuals, groups and institutions have hitherto hidden under the veil of social anonymity induced by an abetting ethnicity, religion, corruption and organizational inefficiency, to perpetrate all kinds of evil and misdeeds. At the level of societal excellence, education is one of instruments for attaining excellence. Excellence will result in higher productivity because "education is used as a screening device so that the high returns may be the result of better educated people getting the best jobs" (Atkinson, Baker and Milward 1996:190) and giving the best performances or excellent outputs. However, those few who are hardworking and forward looking will make the difference for the rest of society.

Education in the northern Nigeria is not as encouraging as the performance in the south. This may be a reason why so many northerners opt to join the Nigerian military especially the army. Seton-Watson (1977: 348) holds that the West and the East both had a much higher level of education and modern skills than the North, and both were largely Christian, while the North was mostly Muslim. Cultural and religious factors that have given rise to the differences in educational status, values and attainment among the various ethnic groups in Nigeria has been emphasized by Helen Kitchen (1962:364-365) This generally lope-sided situation of education among the Nigeria ethnic groups has not really changed significantly since the nation's Independence. Rather it has worsened due to the perversion, over politicization and under funding of the Nigerian educational system prevailing over the years. A bulk of those who have occupied significantly positions from which they could have effectively and positively influenced the education policies of the country (but did otherwise), were themselves from the northern ethnic groups which were the most backward in the issue of education.

Excellence, which spans the moral, intellectual and institutional, must be institutionalized through the strategies of rewards, incentives and opportunities that should be based on merit and desert within the bounds of equity. The basis of this demand is simple. The technocratic spirit, which currently rules the world, is the spirit of excellence for optimal productivity. The future survival of people will depend on this quality taken as a socially accepted norm. Hence excellence must be encouraged at all levels and anyone undeserving of reward must not be favoured to the detriment of the deserving. Any society that neglects this value does so at its own peril. Let us have some recommendations.

Final Comments and Recommendations

We shall end this chapter with some philosophically motivated recommendations that may go a long way to improve the quality of the self-concept, doctrine and professionalism of the army. It must be stated that some of the recommendations are already being implemented, yet it is important that these options are emphasized as the pathways for the future development of the army and for better service to the society that it exists in.

The Nigerian army needs to see itself as a team player in the Nigerian project, so that it can take its proper place in the social and political order.

The Nigerian army needs to be true to its essence and nature: It should concentrate on its primary vision and value, commitment and concern, mission and mandate. This seems to be the only way that we can truly be able to evaluate its performance and evolution in the scheme of things. Alli holds that "the soldiers' role in the political environment and defined in the constitution of the land should be respected" (Alli 2001:85).

Also the Nigerian army needs to develop a robust sense of history and destiny that makes this institution and its members to look beyond today, and do things that will stand the test of time. The Nigerian army needs to be able to sincerely, say 'sorry' when it makes mistakes deliberate or otherwise. This is the hallmark of integrity, honour, trust and respect for self and others.

The Nigerian army needs to follow the rule of law, guiding civil-military relation: this means abiding by its own regulations, obeying constituted authority and the courts, as well as respecting the social rules of working with, and among the civilian populace. The Nigerian army needs to embark on regular security sector self-regulation and reforms in order to become more professional and protean - capable of evolving in line with the exigencies of the times.

The Nigerian army needs to re-think its role in peace time, because defence is capital intensive and a great consumer of national resources (men, land, materials and funds). So the army needs to focus more on wealth generation by outsourcing and collaborating with others in its areas of comparative advantage and expertise; medical, engineering, agricultural, education, search and rescue, humanitarian work, international assignments, etc.

The Nigerian army needs to market and export some of its laudable values to the rest of the Nigerian society; discipline, obedience, prestige and functionalism.

Finally, we end this chapter with a recommendation from Alli on the Nigerian army's enduring central task, which remains, to pursue relentlessly "the battle for the hearts and minds of the population as well as their physical security" (Alli 2001:30).

References

Abimboye Demola. 2000. "The failure of Obasanjo's men" *The News*.Vol.14. no.10.13, March. pp.12-21.

Adebakin M.A. and Raimi L. 2012. "National security challenges and sustainable economic development: Evidence from Nigeria." *Journal of Studies in Social Sciences*. Vol. 1 no. 1. Pp. 1-30.

Africa Research Bulletin.ARB. 2000. Nigeria 1st-30th (April)

Akpan Wilson. 2008. Review Article: Rethinking Security in Nigeria: Conceptual Issues in the *Quest for Social Order and National Integration* by Dapo

Adelugba and Philip Ogo Ujomu, eds. [Dakar, CODESRIA, 2008. x plus 162.] *African Sociological Review.* Vol. 12.No.2. Pp.184-186.

Albert, Isaac Olawale. 2005. "Terror as a political weapon: Reflections on the bomb explosions in Abacha's Nigeria" *IFRA Ibadan Special Research.*Vol.1. pp. 37-56.

Alli M. Chris. 2001. *The Federal Republic of Nigerian Army: The Siege of A Nation.* Lagos: Malthouse Press.

Atkinson Brian, Baker Peter and Milward Bob. 1996. *Economic Policy.* London: Macmillan.

Ayoob, Mohammed. 1984. "Security in the Third World: The Worm about to turn "*International Affairs.* Vol. 60.no.1. pp. 41-51.

Babatope Ebenezer. 2000. *The Abacha years: what went wrong?* Lagos: Ebino Topsy publishers.

Bacon Francis. 1972. "The Four Idols" in John Herman Randall Jr. Justus Buchler and Evelyn Shirk edited. *Readings in Philosophy,* (New York: Barnes and Noble). pp. 91-101.

Ball Nicole and Fayemi Kayode. 2004. *Security Sector Governance in Africa.* London: Centre for Democracy and Democracy.

Blau, Thomas &Goure Daniel. 1984. "Military Uses and Implications of Space" *Society,* January/February. pp. 13-17.

Brennan, Donald. 1962. 'Setting The Goals of Arms Control' in D. Brennan (ed) *Arms Control, Disarmament And National Security.* New York George Brazillier.

Brewer John D, Guelke Adrian, Hume Ian, Moxon-Browne Edward and Wilford Rick. 1996. *The Police Public Order and The State.* New York: St Martins Press.

Brown Lester. 1978. "The Real Threats to World Peace." *Current.* No. 200.February. P. 47-49.

Brown, Lester. 1982. An Untraditional View of National Security in Reichart American Defense Policy. Baltimore: John Hopkins University Press.

Deger, Saadet and West Robert. 1987. *Defence, Security and Development.* Edited. London: Frances Pinter.

FalolaToyin, 1998, *Violence in Nigeria.* Rochester: University of Rochester Press.

Ferguson Yale H. 2006.The crisis of the state in a globalizing world, *Globalizations.*Vol.3. no.1.pp.5-8.

Goldstein, Joshua. 1999. *International Relations.* New York: Addison Longman.

Hare, R. M. 1973.*Applications of Moral Philosophy* (Los Angeles: University of California Press).

Hoogensen, Gunhild and Rotten SveinVigeland.2004 "Gender Identity and the Subject of Security" *Security Dialogue,* vol. 35, no.2. pp. 155-171.

Ifeka, Caroline (2000) "Conflict, Complicity and Confusion: Unravelling Empowerment Struggles in Nigeria After the Return to Democracy" in *Review of African Political Economy* no. 83.

Johnson Harry. M. 1961. *Sociology: A systematic Introduction.* London: Rutledge and Kegan Paul.

Kitchen, Helen. 1962. "Nigeria" in *The Educated African: A Country by Country Survey of Educational Development in Africa.* New York: Frederick A. Praeger.

Liotta, P.H. 2002."Boomerang Effect: The convergence of National and Human Security," *Security Dialogue.* Vol. 33.No. 4. pp. 473-488.

Lodge, Juliet. 1995. 'Internal Security and Judicial Co-operation' in Juliet Lodge. Edited. *The European Community and The Challenge of The Future.* London: Pinter.

McLean George F. 2004. "Institutional Patterns in Social Transformation," in George F. McLean and Robert Magliola and Joseph Abah. Edited. *Democracy and Values in Global Times.* Washington . D.C.: Catholic University of America. Pp. 207-225.

Makinda, Samuel M. 1998. "Sovereignty and Global security." *Security Dialogue,* Vol. 29, No. 3. pp. 281-292.

Messari, Nizar. 2002. "The State and Dilemmas of Security: The Middle East and the Balkans," *Security Dialogue* Vol. 33, No. 4. pp. 415-427.

O'Brien, Robert. 1995. 'International Political Economy and International Relations: Apprentice or Teacher?' in John Macmillan (ed*)* *Boundaries In Question :New Directions In International Relations.* London: Pinter.

Ochoche, Sunday A. 1998."The Military and National Security in Africa in Hutchful Eboe and Abdulaiye Bathily. Edited. *The Military and Militarism in Africa.* Dakar: Codesria. P. 105-127.

Oladiran Olusegun and Adadevoh Irene. 2008. "Cultural Dimensions of the national Security Problem" Professor D. Adelugba D and Dr P. Ujomu. *Rethinking Security in Nigeria: Conceptual Issues In The Quest For Social Order And National Integration.* Dakar: CODESRIA. pp. 95-117.

Peace and development Projects (PEDEP). 2004. Annual Report on Violent Conflicts in Nigeria 2003. Lagos: PEDEP.

Peters, S.B., 1983. "National Security Management in Nigeria," *Nigerian Journal of International Affairs.*Vol.9, no.2.

Ray, James. 1987. *Global Politics.* 3rd Edition (Boston: Houghton Mifflin)

Roe, Paul. 2001, "Actors' responsibility in 'Tight', 'regular' or 'Loose' security Dilemmas." *Security Dialogue.*Vol.32, No.1. pp. 103-116.

Samuel Viscount Rt. Hon. 1956. 'Philosophy and the life of the nation.' *Philosophy.* XXXI. (118): 197-212.

Sandlers, Todd. 1997 *Global Challenges: An Approach to Environmental, Political and Economic Problems.* Cambridge: Cambridge University Press.

Sani Shehu. 2011. "Boko Haram: history, ideas and revolt" *Constitution.* Vol. 11.No.4. December. Pp. 17-41.

Stace W.T. 1937. "The place of philosophy in human culture" *Philosophy.*Vol.12. pp.302- 316.

The Comet Reporter. 2005. "Guns boom on 'day of madness' in Lagos" *The Comet.* Vol.6.no.2222. Wednesday, October 5. pp.1-2.

The Guardian newspaper October 5, 2005.

The Guardian newspaper Thursday August 22, 2013. p. 3.

The Guardian newspaper Tuesday December 3, 2013. pp. 1, 2, 39

The Nation newspaper September 13, 2013.

The Nation newspaper October 6, 2013.

The Nation newspaper Friday October 11, 2013. p. 47.

The Nation newspaper Wednesday November 6, 2013. p. 23.

The Nation newspaper Thursday November 7, 2013. Pp. 2, 5, 6, 8, 57.

The Nation newspaper Friday November 8, 2013. pp. 6, 25, 30, 31, 56.

The Nation newspaper Thursday December 5, 2013. Pp. 4, 5, 6, 7.

The Nation newspaper Wednesday December 11, 2013. pp. 19, 34, 37, 47, 48.

The Nation newspaper Thursday December 12, 2013. pp. 17, 36.

The Nation newspaper Friday December 13, 2013.

The Nation newspaper Saturday December 14, 2013.

The Nation newspaper Wednesday December 18, 2013. pp. 3, 5, 7, 21, 64.

The Nation newspaper Saturday December 21, 2013. pp. 4, 5, 56, 59.

The Nation newspaper Sunday December 22, 2013. pp. 5, 7, 76.

The Nation newspaper Monday December 23, 2013. pp. 5, 9, 10, 28, 29, 33, 36.

The Nation newspaper Wednesday December 25, 2013.

The Nation newspaper Friday December 27, 2013.

The Punch. Friday, July 9. vol.17. no.19,122. pp.1,2&7.

The Vanguard newspaper October 5, 2005.

The Vanguard newspaper October 5, 2005.

The Vanguard newspaper Wednesday December 4, 2013. Pp. 9, 19, 46.

The Vanguard newspaper Wednesday December 11, 2013. p. 46.

The Vanguard newspaper Friday December 13, 2013. p. 40.

The Vanguard newspaper Tuesday December 24, 2013. pp. 11, 13, 15.

Ujomu, Philip Ogo., 2000-2001 "Ethics and National Security in Nigeria: Critical Issues In The Search For Sustainable Development". Voice. Millennial Edition Major Seminary of SS Peter and Paul. Ibadan. No. 39. pp. 38-40.

Ujomu, P. O, 2001a, "Cultural Relations, Human Communication and The Conditions For Intercultural Relations: A Critique of Anta Diop and Kwasi

Wiredu", in H. Igboanusi (Ed), *Language Attitude and Language Conflict In West Africa.* Ibadan: Enicrownfit. Pp.165-188.

Ujomu, Philip Ogo., 2001b, "National Security, Social Order and the Quest for Human Dignity In Nigeria: Some Ethical Considerations," *Nordic Journal of African Studies* Vol. 10, No.2. (November).Pp.245-264.

Ujomu P.O. 2004. "Democratic Institutions, Participation and the problems of social engineering in an African nation-state," *Perspectives on Democracy and Development in Post-Military Nigeria.* Kunle Ajayi and Bonnie Ayodele. Edited. Ibadan: Julius and Julius. pp.30- 54.

Ujomu P. O. 2008. "The Bounds of Security Theorizing: Envisioning Discursive Inputs For The Rectification of a Postcolonial Situation" Professor D. Adelugba D and Dr P. Ujomu 2008. *Rethinking Security in Nigeria: Conceptual issues in the quest for social order and national integration.* Dakar: CODESRIA. pp. 5-56

Ujomu P. O. and Olatunji F.O. 2013. "The value of human life and a philosophy of national security for Nigeria: some theoretical issues." *Annales Philosophici/ Annals of Philosophy.* Vol. 6.No. 1. June.Pp. 47-67.

UN Panel Report. 2005. "Poverty, Infectious Disease, and Environmental Degradation as Threats to Collective Security." *Population Development Review.*Vol.31. no.3.September. Pp. 595-600.

Waston, Hugh Seton (1977) *National and States.* London: Methuen.

Yusuf Ki Major 2003, "Rudiments and Roles of the Military In Internal Security Operations" *Defence Newsletter.* January –March.

Chapter 3

M Chris Alli and the Politics in the Nigerian Army: a Philosophical Discourse

-Oladele Abiodun Balogun

Introduction

The classical representation and mandate of the Nigerian Army in defending the territorial integrity of the Nigerian state through professionalism and political neutrality is, in recent times, being seriously threatened by both professional politics within the Army and the enticement of external politics. Sequel to democratic rule in Nigeria, the Army is increasingly experiencing ethical tensions within its fold in the form of structural corruption, elevation of mediocrity, morbid quest for political power by retired military officers and involvement in partisan politics by in-service officers. The dismal orientation and distrust being generated by 'military in politics' and 'politics in the Army' are damaging to sustainable democratic governance and philosophically self-annihilating for the Nigerian Army. Chris Alli's narrative intervention on the political intrigues in the Nigeria Army deserves some further philosophical interrogation. This article, therefore, critically expounds the concept of politics in the Nigerian Army as seen in Chris Alli's discourse. On the strength of Plato's characterization of the military and the virtues surrounding the military profession, this chapter exposes the antinomies in Alli's narratives on political and apolitical Nigerian Army.

The Nigerian Army is a professional institution rattled by divisive politics, morbid tenacity for power and high-level manipulations. Political intrigues occur within the official institution of the force and in the l adventure into political life. While the immediate interest of this paper is not to examine the internal politics in the Army, an excursus into the external participation of military officers in partisan politics shall be attempted. Externally, it becomes so critical that the lure of position and class materialism occasioned incessant coup and the tendency to foist a military president on the nation. Major General Chris Alli (rtd.), in his *The Federal Republic of Nigerian Army: the Siege of a Nation*, attempts a graphic narrative of this issue. Focusing on this work, this paper examines the dimensions, implications and possible solutions to military in politics as x-rayed in Alli's corpus. An attempt is made in exposing the logical contradictions in the militarization of politics in Nigeria's democratic space, as demonstrated by the existential language and narratives of Ali's narratives

Ideas of Politics and Philosophy

Politics is a multi-faceted word. Thus, one should be very careful in any attempt to give it a definition. Generally, it is the activities, art or science of government or governing. To Jeffrey Rudolf (2014: 36), "it is the methods or tactics involved in managing a state or government. It is the methodology and activities associated with running a government, an organization or movement." Maxwell substantiates the nuances of politics when he writes, politics is the science or art of government; the regulation and administration of a nation or state for the preservation of its safety, peace and prosperity (Maxwell, 2000: 43). In a narrower sense, politics is an art or vocation of guiding or influencing the policy of a government through the organization of a party among its citizen - including, therefore not only the ethics of government but also the schemes and antiques of political parties.

While politics involves rational plan on how to get power, retain power and manage resources, it equally involves social intrigues to gain authority or power. It entails strategies and diplomacy between people or organization in the bid to acquire and retain power. From a wider viewpoint, politics is associated with the governance of a country and other activities aimed at improving someone's status or influence within an organization.

Though, politics is a complex term, Philosophy has more conceptual complexity. But to avoid excessive verbiage, Philosophy is a systematic reflection, an organised logical insight into the issues of life. As aptly put by John Herman Randal (1963: 19), "Philosophy is the criticism of the fundamental beliefs in any man's great cultural enterprises, science, art, religion, the moral life, social and practical activity, when some new idea or some altered experience has impinged upon them and generated intellectual tension and maladjustment." The view of Randal shows philosophy as a dynamic act that generates an interface between issues and reason. "It is systematic critical comprehensive and uncompromising in method. It probes into the fundamental cause of things. It is the study of the ultimate nature of existence." (Garmonsnay and Simpson 1969: 527).

Chris Alli has ventured into a serious narrative in his book, *The Federal Republic of Nigerian Army*, but this chapter applies the systematic and logical tool of philosophical discourse to examine the cogency of this narrative and the intellectual worth of the book. It brings out the basic presuppositions of Alli and the logical contradictions in his psychology; it reviews his recommendations and provides philosophical grounding for the military institution in Nigeria.

Dynamics of Power and Politics in the Nigerian Army

The armed force is a crucial component of the political sustenance of any nation, but the complexity of modern politics now makes it difficult to tie the army down to a definitive role. But, as expedient as military incursion into power may be, it has been arbitrarily misused by the Nigerian Army. As Chris Alli point out:

> My conclusion would be that the military's protracted stay in power was on error of judgment...it should have confined its energies mainly to supporting civil power strengthening and protecting political structures and democracy. It should have limited its emergence to short and sharp intervention, not lasing for more than six months for new election to take place (Alli, 2001: 311).

With the above expression, Chris M. Alli eventually expresses his mind-set on the rationality of military intervention in Nigerian politics.

A clear look at the above shows that the military as a regimented structure has its own role within the administrative structure of the state. Ali regards one of these as protecting political structures (p. 311). They are to defend that nation from invasion, implosion and aggression. This is their duty. Plato, like Alli, delineated a specific role for the military, so that, there will not be unnecessary usurpation of power and distortion of the idea of justice in a state. As stated by Plato:

> Justice is the requirement we laid down at the beginning as of universal application when we founded our state, or else some form of it. We lay down if you remember and have often repealed that in our state, one man was to do one job, he was most naturally suited for...justice consists in minding your own business and not interfering with other people (Plato, 1974: 204).

Plato is simply saying that just as we have three parts in the human soul, there are three classes of people in the society. These are "the guardians (rulers), the auxiliary (soldiers) and the artisans (masses)." The guardian is to guide and govern the state, the duty of the auxiliary is to defend the state while the artisan (masses) have the duty of providing the material and economic needs of the state (Omoregbe, 1999: 162). On this note, the military regime being in full control of the state, is an aberration.

As sound as the above may be Chris Alli delves into the peculiarity of the Nigerian situation to justify the rationality at least circumstantial of military rule, but this should be corrective, short and sharp. Alli brings out a Machiavellian idea of politics in his book. In his analysis of military rule, the sustenance of military rule is fuelled by Machiavellian politics and distortion of military hierarchy. A soldier who is to stay in power needs horses (boys) who are ready to carry out his whims and caprices. The hierarchical structure of the service was assaulted by the encouragement of a 'boys' culture by which younger officers are given access and privileges far more than their ranks and experience" (Alli 2001: 193). This phenomenon resulted in the phrase, 'IBB Boys', 'Abacha Boys' - a kind of personality cult at the expense of the ethics and tradition of the military profession (Alli 2001:193). A system of this nature brings about a tough security, special guys, round the leader and they are ultimately concerned with protecting the interest of the leader, even at the detriment of the entire state. Like boxer will say in the Animal farm, "Comrade Napoleon is always right". Thus, Mr. General is always right before his myrmidon.

Ali is emphatic on his point that "the intervention of soldiers in power definitely brings about a rupture of military hierarchy." The military became a vehicle to clique and oligarchic power. Junior officers could walk up to the Commander in Chief, expecting anything from a brown envelop, a million naira cash to a brand-new car. It is to consolidate the security of the leaders (Alli 2001:193). "A ruler should do everything possible to preserve himself in power and ensure the stability of the state. He is entitled to use any means to attain this end. It is the end that counts; the means used to attain it is unimportant" (Omoregbe 1999: 192). "He should not deviate from what is good, if that is possible, but he should know how to do evil, if that is necessary" (Machiavelli, 1981: 101).

Part of the good-evil of Machiavelli's philosophy which the military class adopts is extreme dictatorship. Such autocratic leadership silences opponents and keeps the ruler long on power. In his x-ray of Abacha's regime, Ali mentions, "The sign of a mindless and brutal dictatorship." According to him,

> the signs of a mindless and brutal dictatorship were manifest and only a violent and turbulent medium could rid the nation of General Sani Abacha's cancerous place in polity (Alli 2001; 177). He has turned the security forces and agencies into personal Gestapo, willing to do his evil without blinking. The masquerading political class was in league and ruins buoyed by a blind pursuit of self-interest (Alli 2001; 177).

He built some boys round himself and they were ready to quell any opposition.

Another idea is gagging or muzzling of the press. While pondering on the coup of 1999 aimed at unseating Abacha, Alli notes that the incorporation of pressmen into the conspiracy by the regime was designed to intimidate the media and public (Alli 2001; 177). Beyond this, some perceived critics were also silenced. In Ali's remark:

> Sani Abacha had successfully silenced or intimidated even our respected senior retired generals who lays claim to statesmanship into a loud silence. Many had been shamelessly compromised by the pursuit of mammon and highly rewarding offices. Some highly placed ones basked in the splash of all currencies which a small circle of his

co-looters, local and external, had limitless access in a vortex of obnoxious thievery (Alli 2001: 177).

Thus, with reference to Nigeria Army, no military ruler can be termed a saint. They rely on unethical strategies to retain power.

In his exploration of the phenomenon of coup d'état in Nigeria, Alli notes that no coup plotter is without a selfish mandate. In his definition coup d'état is a behavioural pattern of actions, conspiratorial in nature, by which an individual or groups with vested interest seek to change by violent overthrow the status quo." (p. 96). In furtherance of this, Alli argues that "in Nigeria's experience, the motivations have been personal ambition, tribal, ideological, hegemonic and regional imperative."

On page 177, Alli's use of the word "hegemony" strikes my attention. Though, hegemony has diverse meanings, yet, in its simple rendition, one can say that

> it refers to a social situation in which a certain social group or an alliance of certain social groups have a total social control of authority over other social groups, not as a result of direct force or by direct imposition of ruling ideas but by winning and shaping consent so that the power of the dominant classes appears both legitimate and natural (Hall, 1977: 74).

In the same vein, Anthony Gramsci characterizes the state "as the entire complex of practical and theoretical activities with which the ruling class not only justifies and maintains its dominance but manages to win the active consent of those over whom it rules. Thus, the state embraces the private apparatus of civil society" (quoted in Irele, 1996: 7).

There is a northern military hegemonic class (as remarked by Chris) which in quest for power, co-opted other forces to stabilize there regime (all military regimes). While most coups have been conceived and executed by Northern and Middle-belt officers who manned the operational terrain, they have been led without exception by Northern senior officers with Northern mentalities. Three coups have been led by Southerners. All these attempts failed. Alli specifies these:

- Ifeajuna/Nzeogwu 1966

- Mukoro, Guazo Orkah 1990
- Phantom Diya's Coup 1997

All these coups failed (p. 182)
The coups led by Northerners include:
- Gowon/Murtala 1966
- General Murtala 1975
- Buhari/Babangida 1983
- Babangida and Boys 1985
- Abacha's Walkover 1993 (Alli 2001:182)

All Northern coups succeeded. Why? There is a hegemonic order in the north that makes this easy. "There is no pan-Nigeria hegemonic order, and this is because the various ethnic political elites are too divided and given to soulless pursuit of their selfish interests." (Irele 1996: 12) When military hegemony is foisted on a nation, the disadvantaged class at times, cave in. The reason is not because "their human consciences repudiated the impropriety of the acts; but because they were simply disadvantaged by the real politick of the time and by the poverty of their own power resources." (Nwankwo 1990: 41). This is one of the reasons for the long-term military rule by Northern members of the army. The adventure of soldiers into power is an open existential space where unfolding of the self can be realized through any means.

Politics in the Nigerian Army: a philosophical discourse

The Nigerian army is a dynamic entity. It is enriched in internal politics and external manoeuvring within the larger political space of the nation. Surely, it has gone beyond the regimented order of Plato to a situationistic apparatus to settle order or balance political force. Alli shows that the Nigerian Armed Force is both professional and highly political. While Alli extols the professional integrity of some soldiers, he aptly points out that the force is besieged by unethical forces or act. For Ali two factors have contributed tremendously to undermining the moral tone and professional ethics of the officer corps in particular and therefore the army in general. What are these factors? Alli's response is as follow:

> One was a seeming blitzkrieg into the morass of grabbing for power and office at all costs and the second, the blind pursuit of materialism in the forces with no holds barred particularly within the last decade. It has become almost inconceivable that individuals can make valuable contributions to the growth and development of any organization if they are not at the apex. (p. 69)

The core of this citation is that the Nigerian army is notorious for corruption. The prevailing spectre of corruption in the society has permeated the force. Thus, professional integrity is frowned at, while mediocrity is elevated. One crucial point that Alli must note is that the society or the environment permeates the human spirit and determines the direction of action to a very great extent. This is one of the centre piece of environmental determinism. Young soldiers cannot but be influenced by the action of the top brass. More so, action of even self acclaimed principled soldiers become situationistic. Alli mentions General Ishola Williams, Colonel Abubakar Umar, etc. (2001: 237), as circumstantial moralists (who would slide in and out of this position depending on circumstances). With specific reference to Sani Abacha, Alli made it obvious that financial inducements and other gifts were used to lure perceived rebels: "A free flight to Abuja and a workless day and two prospects for welfare or brown envelop large enough to massage respective family anatomies for a while." (Alli 2001: 237). Thus, corruption is used to enhance legitimacy of regime.

Corruption is a politically deployed phenomenon to enhance military perpetuation in power. In the absence of a moral basis for government and consequently, its lack of legitimacy or authority, the leader could only sustain himself through a manipulative style of rule. The state becomes an avenue for the attainment of wealth and status, rather than an instrument for the creation of the conditions of freedom which are required for human survival (Oladipo, 1998: 113). Besides, the army is highly manipulative. The pervasive greed in the society also permeates the spirit of the soldiers. Some callous elements of the civil population were often exploiting their closeness or association with some service personnel to exert severe penalties on their victim who often may be innocent but lack sufficient clout to protect their civil liberties (Alli 2001: 75). This is a profound violation of professional ethics and an adventure into brazen injustice. Within the rank and file of the Army, posting is political.

Religion and ethnicity are factors that also play crucial role. Alli referred to when he was supposed to be promoted as commander of 1st infantry Division but politics deprived him of this portfolio. According to him,

> General Salihu Ibrahim told him that Christian officers were commanding the other three divisions and that Northern Emirs had reservations over the appointment of another Christian to the command of the strategic 1st Infantry division. Their sensitivities had to be recognised and therefore he was offering me the office of the Director of Military Intelligence (Alli 2001: 75).

Thus, competence is shared aside to enhance ethno-religious representation. More seriously, the position was given to another Christian Brigadier Halilu Akilu. This shows that reference to Northern displeasure as mentioned above is a political contrivance to pave way for Akilu. "It was a sleek design to patronize someone else, also a Christian, who conceivably could not be appointed if I remained within the formation for lack of seniority." (Alli 2001: 75). This is politics.

Another political dimension to military politics is the use of evasive speech to enhance self-perpetuation in power. For instance, in a dialogue between Babangida and Chris Alli on when the former would leave power, the response was terse and vague. He said, he would think about it in due course.

Politics of a hegemonic order as practised by the members of the armed forces will only birth a revolt. Thus, in the 1993 General Election, majority of the members of army voted for M. K. O. Abiola in anticipation of a better working condition. Yet, the election was annulled. General Ibrahim Babangida, as Chris Alli reported, said the annulment was inevitable. Why? "The state was owing Chief Abiola, so many billions of naira and that letting him run the federal government would be tantamount to subletting the national treasury to his whims" (Alli 2001: 236). This argument cannot be translated to a categorical imperative of the Kantian order: "It is a place of mafia ethics - if you must lie, be brief. If you can't win, make the price of your enemy's victory exorbitant; if you can't win by fighting fair, fight foul; agreements are made to be broken." (Dukor, 2003: 362).

Concluding Remarks

A critical applause of Alli's magnum opus, *The Federal Republic of Nigerian Army: The Siege of a Nation*, is in order as he has ably penned the unknown intrigues of power-play in the Nigerian Army. From his analysis, one can see that even soldiers are political, which contrasts with the apolitical mandate of the military institution. However, the political embroil of the Nigerian military is in consonance with Aristotle's view that man is a *homo-politicus* (a political animal). Although the author of the text under study seems to belong to the Plato's school of thought on justice within a nation, he is not a Platonist to the core. This is because his opinions at times oscillate. It must be noted that all men are existential beings. Soldiers are men; therefore, soldiers are existential beings. They, in pursuit of self-realization and correction of perceived anomaly, can venture into the political space. Alli does not deny this outright but argues that it must be a short intervention.

Within the confine of situationism, military intervention in civil governance cannot be dismissed. Corruption, electoral manipulations, indiscipline, etc., are issues that call for immediate intervention especially when civil regime tends to be unconcerned. But there is a seeming paradox engendered by the politics of the Nigerian Army: they become more sophisticated in those crimes they alleged the civilians of committing when they get into power, using material gratification and positional bribery.

General Buhari was ousted for his tough disciplinarian stance by a cabal who ordinarily ought to perform better but relapsed terribly into the doldrums of complex corruption and morbid tenacity for power.

Adventure into politics by Nigerian army is an unravelling of a deep existential quest for self-fulfilment by some. Existentially, man is nothing. He is always becoming, and the phenomenon of frequent coup has further opened a vista of opportunity to coupist. Thus, military politics in the nation is an outcome of existential craze for self-fulfilment.

A good reading of Alli's text shows that there is a subtle diarchical order between the civilian and the military. Corrective regime and an order of balance which the army is fond of using to justify its claim to political power is questionable:

> The military as part of the society gets involved in the vices for which in most cases civilians are overthrown. Sometimes military political office holders are more corrupt than the civilians they overthrow. Any time the military is in government, its needs and welfare are seriously relegated (Alli 2001: 262).

This is a paradox in Alli's work.

It must be noted that when the military ventured into political life, intrigues and diverse manipulations come in. The Gwadabe and General Diya's coups brought the concept of set up to the fore when Diya demanded that Bamaiyi should also be tried, "he insisted that the Chief of Staff was the mastermind, planner and instigator of the coup." (Alli 2001: 306). In a nutshell, coup d'état undermines the ethics of the Nigerian Army. It brings about the use of trump charges to silence perceived enemy.

Finally, the Nigerian Army is a politicized institution that must be quickly redeemed. Chris Alli's analysis is fundamental to a pragmatic over-haul and re-structuring of the Nigerian Army. If this is not done, the Marxist's idea that "every stage of human development contains its own seed of destruction" (Peter 1943: 84) will certainly prove to be correct. Although Alli argues for a short intervention where circumstances necessitate, he must understand that political stability is ballpark. Commendable as his work is, it is an eye-opener to the political intrigues of politics and the military. He writes with finesse. However, a philosophical incursion into his thought brings out palpable contradictions especially on coup and military leadership in Nigeria.

References

Ali, M. Chris (2001). *The Federal Republic of Nigerian Army: The Siege of a Nation* (Lagos: Malthouse Press Limited)

Century Dictionary (1994). (London: Century Press.)

Garmonsuay, G. N. (1969). *The Penguin English Dictionary* (London: Penguin Books)

Irele, Dipo (1996) "Rupturing the Hegemony" in Sola Olorunyomi (ed) *Current Viewpoint* (Ibadan: Hope Publications).

Machiavelli, Niccolo (1981). *The Prince* (England: Penguin Books)

Maduabuchi, Dukor (2005). "The Relevance of Philosophy and the Corporate World" in A. O. Echekwuba and P. Iroegbu (eds) *KPIM of Morality* (Ibadan Spectrum Books).

Maxwell, J. (2000). *Political Philosophy* (London: Routledge).

Oladipo, O. (1998). "Modernization and the Search for Community in Africa," in O. Oladapo (ed) *Remarking Africa* (Ibadan: Hope Publications).

Omoregbe, Joseph (1999). *Ethics: A Systematic and Historical Study* (Lagos: JERP)

Plato, (1994). *The Republic.* 433 a - e. Trans by Desmond Lee (London: Penguin Books)

Randal, John (1963). *How Philosophy Uses its Past* (Columbia: Columbia University Press).

Rudolf, Jeffrey. (2014). *Idea of Politics* (London: Nestle Press).

Chapter 4

On M. Chris Alli's Morality of War

-Egbeke Aja

Introduction

The chapter articulates Alli's morality of War as solution to conflict from his book: *The Republic of Nigerian Army: the Siege of a Nation*, and thence, observes that he decided to be part of the solution to the Biafra/Nigeria conflict by joining the Nigerian Army. Therein, he noted with regret that the Nigerian Army battle-cry: "To keep Nigeria one…" was no longer the focus of the war on both the Nigerian and Biafran sides. Reviewing literature on approaches to discussion on morality of war, the chapter observes that neither the utilitarian nor the proportionist views about the morality can stand up as objective ways of answering the question of the morality of war as solution to disputes. Nor is the position of moral nihilists tenable. For Alli, therefore, the weapons of war are moral only if used in such a way as to respect the traditional rules concerning just and unjust methods of pursuing a war, namely, maintaining the distinction between killing combatants. The chapter concludes that though Alli adopts the combatant/non-combatant distinction in his morality of war as solution to conflicts in war not a rewarding means to settling disputes.

M. Chris Alli was born to Mallam Alli Adakwo Alaburah and Mrs Rebecca Ojumori Nanashe Abayomi both of royal families who lived after migrating from Lokoja, in the bustling market town of Onitsha. Mallam Alli was a Muslim while Mrs Nanashe Rebecca Ojumori was a devout Christian. This union, I think, had much impact on the personality of young Chris Alli. More so, as the story goes, the union in marriage was supported by the late Obi of Onitsha, Obi Okosi I, a revered Onitsha monarch with whom Chris's father quickly, established cordial and rewarding relationship. Furthermore, that Mallam Alli spoke Igbo, Hausa, Yoruba, Fulfude languages and Igala dialect fluently served as social and cultural assets for M. Chris Alli to acquire and exhibit leadership potentials in his military career.

M. Chris Alli served in various capacities in the Nigerian Army. More importantly, he served as Chief of Army Staff (December 1993 - August 1994) and participated in the Federal Troops campaign that led to the capture of Onitsha by the Nigerian Army. Given his family background, educational career and military experience, he had ample opportunities to be a true Nigerian. He was focused early in his youth with an unquenchable desire to join the Nigerian Army. His experiences before joining the Army and when he served as an officer of the Nigerian Army spurred him to write *The Federal Republic of Nigerian Army: The Siege of a Nation* in 2001 after his retirement from the Nigerian Army. This text captures what he felt were the problems with both the Nigerian Army and the Nigerian state project. And he gladly stated in the book:

> Finally but paradoxically, good fortune smiled on me in 1967, when the Civil War took the nation by storm. Biafran troops had just invaded the Mid-West Region, the seeming underbelly of Nigeria and the nation's vital resources were a factor in the invasion. I contemplated my situation in the Air Force and drew blank. It was clear to me that I might just end up knowing the happenings of the Civil War from history books and not from personal experience (Ali, 2001: 22)

Alli had no passion for a career in the Air Force; rather his focus was the Army. He had confidence that he could lead in war and finally he realized his dreams when on 22nd October 1967, he completed the six-month officer cadet training and was so commissioned. That is to say, he enrolled as a combatant in the Nigerian Army with the ambition to be part of the solution to the Biafra/Nigerian conflict. The foregoing, I think, served as the building blocks that informed M. Chris Alli's morality of war as solution to conflicts.

It is important to note that in *The Republic of Nigerian Army: the Siege of a Nation*, Alli did not explicitly articulate what, in this write-up, I refer to as his morality of war. Mine is an attempt to tease out his concept of morality of war as solution to conflicts such as the Nigerian/Biafra

War. So, I offer a minimum conception of the concept, morality as used herein:

> At the very least, it is the effort to guide one's conduct by reason - that is to do what there are the best reason for doing - while giving equal weight to the interests of each individual who will be affected by one's conduct (James,1986:11).

Understandably, when an aggression is on an individual level, the moral issue of self-defence may be simple enough. But when a conflict assumes a national or group proportion, as was the case with the Nigeria/Biafra conflict the problem of defence assumes a much more complex character. Because of the methods and weapons used in the war, the conflict had become a "total war". Consequently more people became involved and more destruction inflicted on both the people and their properties.

Hence, there is the need and tendency to differentiate between combatants and non-combatants affected by the actors on both sides of the war. This, however, makes defence against an aggressor group much more delicate. For, how can Nigeria defend its unity against a secessionist group and still maintain a distinction between the combatant and non-combatant segments of a war-torn area? How can Nigeria defend itself adequately or fight for its unity and still maintain its national solidarity? Who is a combatant and who is a non-combatant in a war situation? In this chapter, a non-combatant is a civilian who is not actively engaged in the military pursuit of a war; whereas the combatant is actively involved (Manuel, 1985:190-191). The above questions and other issues concomitant with the war agitated the mind of M. Chris Alli as the battle cry of Nigeria was "To keep Nigeria one, is a task that must be done". The greater the destructive potentials of weapon used by both sides of the war, the less discriminating actors in the conflict were. And at the point Chris decided to be part of the solution of the conflict, the war theatres were so devastated that as a professional soldier, Chris Alli was forced to reflect on the conduct of the war. And as he rightly observed, at the sector Onitsha, at which he fought and commanded, the war had developed far beyond the demands of any single known military target - all in the bid to keep Nigeria one. In his words,

> The consequences of Biafran forces over-whelming the South could engender the break-up of Nigeria into Southern and Northern or whatever names each would choose; conceiving the war as a counter-action, stemming genocide or the mindless slaughter or continuing killing of Igbos in some parts of the country had become less compelling as the reason for the war. Secession was becoming a reality. It was time for me to join the war on the Federal side in spite of my Biafran sympathies (Alli: 24).

As a professional army officer, M. Chris Alli well knew the implications of resorting to war as a solution to a conflict. What is his morality of war as a solution to the Nigeria/Biafra war? Why join the Federal side knowing the ill-effects of war? We have been able to distil this from his text after a brief examination of discussions of morality of war by some philosophers.

On Approaches to Discussions of Morality of War

Discussions of morality of wars often take one of two approaches: (1) the Utilitarian and Natural law/Proportionalist treatment of the morality of war (Mill 1985: 110-117); and 2) the natural law theorists or proportionalists.

Utilitarian and Natural law/Proportionalist

This approach exemplified by the teachings of Jeremy Bentham, maintains that there is one ultimate moral principle and that it is "the Principle of Utility". This principle, according to Bentham requires that whenever we have a choice between alternative actions or social policies, we must choose the one that has the best overall consequences for everyone concerned; or, as put it in his *The Principle of Morals and Legislation*, the principle of utility is meant that principle which approves or disapproves of every action whatsoever according to the tendency which it appears to have to augment or diminish the happiness of the party whose interest is in question or what is the same thing, in other words, to promote or oppose happiness (Bentham, 1986:80) Furthermore, one of Jeremy Bentham's followers was James S. Mill - a distinguished Scottish philosopher, historian and economist whose son, John Stuart Mill, became the leading advocate of utilitarian moral theory. Thus the Benthamite movement continued unabated even after its founder's death. In his Utilitarianism (1861), J.S. Mill presents the main idea of the theory as follows:

> First, we envision a certain state of affairs that we would like to see come about - a state of affair in which all people are as happy as they can be: So according to the Greatest Happiness Principles...the ultimate end, with reference to and for the sake of which all other things are desirable (whether we are considering our own good or that of other people), is an existence exempt, as far as possible from pain, and as rich as possible in enjoyments. (Ibid.)

Simply stated, therefore, the primary rule of morality is to act so as to bring about this state of affairs in so far as that is possible. That is to say, the end of human action is necessarily also the standard of morality. Hence, the utilitarians usually talk about weighing the evils of wars against the good that such a conflict might achieve. If more good than evil would result, and if no other alternative will produce a greater balance of good over evil, then it is moral to engage in any form of war or conflict; otherwise it would be immoral.

2) The natural law theorists or proportionalists. This is also referred to as "just law" theory. They talk about or are concerned with the proportionality of the goods and evils that would result from embarking upon any form of wars. For them, "the lives and other basic goods that wars would destroy indirectly must be proportional to the basic good that would be achieved directly". Hence, the proportionalist's arguments take two conflicting forms - (i) the evils of waging a war are so grave that they cannot possibly be worth the achievements of any political objectives no matter how desirable; (ii) Some political objectives are so important that they outweigh even the risks of waging any war.

Those who take the first position commonly focus on the massive numbers of the people that might die as a result of any forms of war. They also take into consideration the large economic, social and environmental damage wars would inflict on a people. On the other hand, they are those who claim that some political objectives are important enough to risk even such massive losses experienced in wars. They often focus on values such as liberty, democracy, equality, happiness and so on. The exponents contend that these values are so important that it is worth risking even any form of war in order not to lose them. In other words, for them, "Better dead than red" - or as Nigeria put, "To keep Nigeria on is a task that must be done". That is, the quality of certain form of life is so undesirable that it is better to die than to live and see humanity subjected to them. Logically stated, they argue that:

i) The morally right thing to do on any occasion is whatever would bring about the greater balance of happiness over unhappiness;
ii) On at least some occasions, the greatest balance of happiness over unhappiness may be brought about by war;
iii) Therefore, on at least some occasions wars may be morally right.

This brief exposition of the disagreements concerning the relative value of the evils of war in any human society are instructive. They are neither accidental features of the utilitarian nor of the proportionalist approaches to the discourse on the morality of wars. They are pointers to the inherent dangers of the Nigeria/Biafra war and to all such discourses with regard to war in general (Manuel, 1985:183-184). These approaches proceed by asking whether the potential losses inflicted during wars are worth the potential gains. It is a common knowledge that there is no objective way of determining the answer to the question. This is because wars are fought for a variety of intangible, controverted and immeasurable values such as liberties, equalities, honour, stability and so on. So to talk about objective way of determining the worth of war will be exercise in futility. This is because "any claim to the effect that a certain objective of a war is worth more or less than costs of waging the war must be based on the subjective preferences of the groups making such a claim".(Ibid). I conclude, therefore, that there is no objective way of answering the utilitarian or proportionalist question. On this note, one is forced to reject the utilitarian, the natural law and the proportionalist theses at evaluating the morality of wars, say, Nigeria/Biafra war.

3) A third approach which I consider more despairing is that of "moral nihilists" which is also referred to as the "realist approach". The realist thesis is that the use of any form of weapon in wars is not immoral because morality does not apply to the conduct of wars. In fact, the most important premise of this approach is based on the idea that "Wars are fought between groups or nations and nations exist in a Hobbesian state

of nature". Nations, the exponents maintain, exist in a world in which there is no force powerful enough to guarantee that they act morally towards each other. In the absence of a guarantee, no nation or group can expect that other nations or groups will temper their actions by moral restraints. Thus seen, any nation that does restrain itself by morality, will be at a grave disadvantage. This school of thought concludes, therefore, that no nation or group can be expected to put itself at a disadvantage by imposing on itself the restraint of morality. Consequently it is meaningless to evaluate the actions of nation or groups including the use of any form of war as solution to conflicts (ibid.).

Against this viewpoint, we argue that it does not follow logically that in war situations a group's action or that of another are not subject to moral principles. For example, morality requires that in normal circumstances, one is not to attack or kill one's fellow citizens. But when one of these citizens is attacking one as an armed robber, morality allows the attacked to defend herself by counter-attacking or even killing that fellow citizen. That is to say, "what moral principles require in one set of circumstance is then different from what they require in other circumstances." So, if the unity of a state is in constant danger of disintegrating, it may be morally justified to take measures to ensure its unity; including resorting to war. This, by no means implies that moral principles no longer apply in such a hostile situation. On the contrary, our recognition of the legitimacy of defensive measures in hostile situation, such as war, shows that we can and do evaluate such measures from a moral point of view.

Furthermore, it is mistaken to claim that we exist in a world in which there are no forces to enforce and ensure that nations/groups act morally. Observably, humans clearly do not exist in a Hobbesian state of nature. There are strong psychological and social forces operating upon humans that ensure that we will generally adhere to morality. We are, in effect, subject to morality and so also are acts of groups or nations. Humans knowingly and intentionally bring these about in their acts including their wars with each other.

4) Having critically examined the above three approaches to the discourse on the morality of war and having found them inadequate in justifying the use of war in settling conflicts, we are forced to seek for as

alternative. From my reading of The Federal Republic of Nigerian Army: the Siege of a nation, I imagine M. Chris Alli being in the same need for an alternative. This, I think, he found in the moral basis of the combatant/non-combatant distinction. Simply stated, the principle states that "In war, it is morally permissible to attack and kill enemy combatants, but it is wrong deliberately to kill non-combatants" (Ibid: 190). This position is distilled from assertions and condemnations made by the author on the pages of the text. And our vocation is to, with our philosophical microscopes, make them explicit and explicable.

The basis of morality of war in M. Chris Alli: the combatant / non-combatant distinction

The invasion of the Mid-West Region was the precursor to M. Christ Alli joining the Nigerian Army. He had self-assessed himself and came to the conclusion that his situation in the Air Force would not enable him realize his ambitions as a military officer. In order to ensure that the Mid-West Region and indeed the South did not fall into the hands of the Biafran troops he joined the war in the Federal side. That is, he consented to be a combatant in response to his training in the Nigerian Defence Academy. As he informs his readers, they were reminded time and again that sooner than later they would go into real combat confronting Biafran soldiers. He was engaged in the River Niger crossing operation and of that operation he reports that the crossing operation tolled heavily on the Nigerian forces in the dismal level of casualties in lives, morale and material. It had a devastating effect on the morale of Federal troops of the Second Division (Ali: 24). The author was more concerned with the loss of men and materials on the Federal side for any such loss on the part of the Biafran forces, would be salutary. If my interpretation is correct, it stands to reason that M. Chris Alli, though not rejecting the utilitarian approach and the other approaches in their entirety opted for the distinction between the combatant and non-combatant approach to discussion on the morality of war.

By this choice, it is my considered opinion that to him weapons of war are moral only if used in such a way as to respect the traditional rules concerning just and unjust methods of pursuing a war. Paramount among these rules is the one that rests on the distinction between killing combatants and deliberately not killing non-combatants. And military tradition holds that in war, even in war of defence, it is morally permissible to kill combatants and immoral to kill non-combatants. Since Biafrans who were not actively engaged in the military pursuit of the Nigeria/Biafra wars were non-combatants and therefore not military targets. But alas, as the author regrets:

> Then in Asaba it was rife to overhear miffed discussion about the unbecoming conduct of federal forces in the environment. There were stories about how the natives were lined up in football fields and along the River Niger and shot without provocation. Some of those so mortally executed included defenceless children, women, girls, boys and adults (Alli: p.25)

The tales were repulsive and bewildering so much so that the gallant Alli contemplated desertion as a second lieutenant. Those acts belied the pretext that the Federal Forces were fighting to keep Nigeria one. But events on ground showed that they were "just slaughtering the Igbo". Given the author's family background, civic consciousness and Christian faith, he could not reconcile the actions of the troops to the avowed aims of the Civil War. It is pertinent to note that the author was not appalled because of the large number of Biafran forces crushed by the Federal forces with their superior war machines. Instead, his concern was with the civilian casualties - the non-combatants.

And in respect of his colleagues - the Nigerian combatants, Alli feels that "It is therefore derogatory, poor regard for human life and dignity and a statement of our incompetence at records and manning that, till date, Nigeria still talks about the Unknown Soldier and proudly displays in moments to that effect".(P. 27) Instead of the current practice, he suggests that as a concept, these can be monuments dedicated to officers and soldiers identified for velour and courage and also for campaigns, battles and operations. And more explicitly such monuments can be dedicated to "Our Fallen Heroes, etc." (ibid), Yet lives have been lost, though, as combatants.

Objections to the combatant/non-combatant distinction as the basis of morality of war in M. Chris Alli

Having tacitly rejected the utilitarian and the approaches discussed earlier as nothing more than national or group preferences, parts of M. Chris

Alli's text gives us a sense that he goes more for the moral significance of the combatant/non-combatants distinction as the basis of his morality of war. What is the basis of this distinction and why does it matter in a war such as the Nigeria/Biafra war? From the Asaba saga, the difference between a combatant and a non-combatant in any war is rooted in the difference between an assailant who is, say, attacking my life and a bystander who does not pose such a threat. Suppose that one evening an enemy of mine begins shooting at me on my farm that is completely deserted with no one around except a woman carrying a child. In such a situation, the right to self-defence justifies my killing the assailant if this is the only way I can save my life. But I am not justified in killing the innocent woman and her child since neither of them posed a threat to my life. The moral distinction between the assailant and the bystander is built into the principle of self-defence. And this can be explained by appealing to the Kantian principle of treating a person as an end and not as a means. (Kant,1969:15).

To treat a person merely as a means is to treat the one in a manner intentionally designed to achieve my own purpose without any regard for the person's own rational choices; while to treat a person as an end, if I understand Kant, is to treat the person as if the one has freely and rationally consented to be treated so. Given this interpretation and understanding, the deadly attack of my assailant violates Kant's principle insofar as my assailant, in attempting to achieve his/her own purposes treats me as I had not consented to be treated. When I repulse his attack, I do not violate the Kantian principle because in attacking me the assailant knew that I might attempt to defend myself and nonetheless he/she consented to enter into the attack. My assailant, therefore, may be taken to have consented to a situation in which he/she would be making her/himself subject to a counter-attack. I do not wrong the attacker when I counterattack for I then treat him/her as he/she had consented to be treated.

The innocent bystander and her child on the other hand, have not given any similar consent. If I kill them, I would be attempting to achieve my own purposes without regard for their freedom of choice. I would, therefore, be using them merely as means and would be violating the Kantian principle. For Kant, "Morality consists then in the reference of ends possible" (Ibid: p. 62) The above scenario and interpretation of the right to self-defence is, I believe, the intuition that underlies the combatant/non-combatant distinction - the approach of choice to M. Chris Alli. The combatant has implicitly consented to bear the brunt of the counter-attack of the enemy. The non-combatant cannot be taken to have given a similar consent. So, to kill the former in a war does not violate the Kantian principle; whereas killing the latter clearly does.

If our analysis is correct, and if our understanding and interpretation of the Kantian principles is acceptable, then we can appreciate why it has always been a traditional rule of war that it is immoral indiscriminately to kill a non-combatant. But we know that using wars to settle conflicts will ultimately result in the killing of non-combatants - civilians who are not actively engaged in the military pursuit of a war as was the case in Nigeria/Biafra war.

There are obviously objections and brief replies to our thinking and that of Chris whom we supposed to be for the non-combatant/combatant distinction. It stands to reason that there is a correlation we have made between being a combatant and giving consent. Contrary to that it could be argued that combatants sometimes could withhold their consent. Chris in his text testifies to this as follow:

The Biafran accusations against the genocidal motives of the Federal Forces seemed so real and substantiated. It seemed like a time of passage of passion when ordinary humans descended to the level of savages, yet they proffered and proposed honourable intentions. In agony, I contemplated desertion even as a second lieutenant with all its unsavoury imponderables (Alli: 25)

Admittedly, this could have been seen as professional misconduct and liable for court-marshal. The stories of soldiers running way from the fires of the Boko Haram in the Northeast of Nigeria are rife. Such 'combatants' are forced to be combatants against their will - without their consent, that is. In the same vein, being a civilian does not preclude one from consenting to and actively participating in a military pursuit. This objection assumes that we equate being a soldier with giving consent to participating in a war, say, Nigeria/Biafra war. Yes, of course. However, all we are claiming is that being a soldier, through training, is a prima facie evidence that one has consented to fight a war when called upon to do so; while being a civilian merely implies the absence of such prima facie evidence. Although consent should be construed as one defining characteristic of a combatant, a person's military status should be treated as merely prima facie evidence of such a consent. But it is clear that regardless of our mental gymnastics regarding the lines we draw between those who consent and those who do not consent, any use of wars to settle scores certainly result in killing and injuring members of the non-combatant groups, namely children, pacifists, etc., etc.

A second objection is that the distinction ignores the citizen's responsibility for the acts of the rulers of their group or nation. All the members of a group, critics may claim, are collectively responsible for the acts of that group's government or leadership. And by virtue of this, collective responsibility demands that each citizen must share in the burden of the government action, just as each shares in its benefits. If this is granted, the argument goes, there are therefore no innocent non-combatant. Little wonder the Federal Forces maintained that "A rebel is a rebel no matter how small." Though a propaganda, it fuelled mindless slaughter of Biafran civilians.

This criticism faces a fundamental difficulty given its major premise which is questionable. Why should membership of a group or nation make one morally responsible for the acts of its government? We may support the premise by adopting the so-called "organic theory of the state (Manuel: 190-191) by which we are saying that, analogously, a nation is just like a living organism with its citizens as the constituent parts. So, just as we attribute to whole organisms what each of its part does, so also can we attribute the acts of a government to the citizens as a whole. A critical look at the analogy reveals that today no one will find this organic theory of the state acceptable. The citizens of a state are autonomous individuals; they can think, live and choose independently to the group in a way that will utterly be different from the parts of the organisms. Thus seen, the organic theory, which is analogous, is so deficient that it cannot be taken seriously.

As a last ditch attempt to counter the above objection, one might adopt a social contract theory of the state by maintaining that by becoming members of a state, all citizens agree to accept responsibility for the acts of their government (including going to war) in return for the services the government renders to them (Somerville and Santoni:205-2013). A major flaw in this argument is that it is based on an unacceptable fiction. For, most citizens never made such voluntary agreements to belong to a state.

Furthermore, a third attempt could be made by appealing to the "principle of fairness". Simply stated, since all citizens accept the benefits provided by their state, in fairness, they must also accept its burdens including responsibility for its pursuit of wars. Like the other arguments, this is obviously false too. The mere fact that one accepts a benefit from a group or government, that does not in any way make one morally responsible for the acts of that group or government. For instance, that my university promotes me in rank, I do not become morally responsible for the criminal acts of its administration, nor shall I take credit for the wise activities of the administration. In sum, the main problem with these theories is that they misconstrue the notion of moral responsibility. "One is morally responsible only for what one knowingly or negligently brings about or helps to bring about or fails to prevent through one's own intentional actions and omission".(Manuel p.191) The theories fail to appreciate these.

Conclusion

From the foregoing, our analyses, discussion and observations especially vis-a-vis M. Chris Alli adoption of combatant/non-combatant distinction in his morality of war as solution to conflicts, point to the fact that war is not a rewarding means of settling scores. Whatever method of justification, be it utilitarian, proportionalist, realist or combatant/non-combatant distinction, the unintended consequences of war are bound to occur.

References

James Rachael, (1986), *The Elements of Moral Philosophy*, (New York: Random House)

Jeremy Bentham, (1986), The Principle of Morals and Legislation, cited in James Rachel's, *The Elements of Moral Philosophy* (New York: Random House)

John Somerville and Ronald E. Santoni, *Social and Political Philosophy: Reading from Plato to Gandhi*, (New York: Anchor Books),

Manuel Velasquez, (1985), "The Morality of Using Nuclear Weapon" in Manuel Velasquez and Cynthia Rostenkowski, eds *Ethics Theory and Practice*, (Englewood Cliffs, N.J. Prentice-Hall, Inc).

Mill, J.S. "Utilitarianism" (1985) in Manuel Velasquez and Cynthia Rostenkowski, Ethics Theory and Practice (Englewood Cliffs, N.J.: Prentice-Hall, Inc)

M. Chris (2001) *The Federal Republic of Nigerian Army: The Siege of a Nation*, Lagos (Malthouse Press Ltd.).

Immanuel Kant, (1969), *Fundamental Principles of the Metaphysics of Ethics*, tr. Thom Abbott, (London: Longman, Green and Co. Ltd)

M.C. Alli on Security and Media within the Context of Jeremy Bentham's Ethics

- Christopher E. Ukhun

Introduction

As referenced by Christian (2009), Bertrand Russell is said to have claimed that "everyman, wherever he goes, is encompassed by a cloud of comforting convictions, which moves with him like flies on a summer day." Clearly, Russell words resonate in M.C. Alli's narratives on national security and media. The thrust of this work is an expose of Alli's convictions that the media has a crucial and unfettered role to play on the question of national security. In doing this, he adopts a moral or philosophical stance discernible in Jeremy Bentham's ethical theory – utilitarianism, which strives for the greatest happiness of the greatest number of people. By this, Alli announces himself as a patriot with philosophical insight and clout needed to liberate his people from tyranny, oppression, ignorance, retrogression and annihilation. Indeed, his disposition in this regard is genuinely suffused with utilitarian fragrance.

Anyone can be a philosopher, certainly, not everyone is a philosopher. Admittedly, a perspectivistic understanding of who philosophers are can be gleaned from the fact that they are people who tenaciously and consistently try to make sense of the puzzling absurdity we call the human conditions…they try to discern the root causes of distress, despair, pain, stupidity, joy and meaning of our being human. For two and a half millennia, Christian (2009), the works of Socrates,

Plato, Aristotle, Thales, Pythagoras, Rene Descartes, Immanuel Kant, J.J Rousseau, Jeremy Bentham, John Stuart Mill are expressed in this endeavour in which numerous and ordinary people lack capacity. Believe it or not, in every historical epoch there are men of positive and restless spirit ardently concerned about phenomena which threaten our common humanity or enhance those which enrich our lives. With alluring intellectual and philosophical insights, M.C Alli enunciates the quintessential issues of national security and media within the Nigerian polity. This is not without his moral disposition and the Benthamic moral content for development. These moral contents and dispositions, covertly or overtly, actually pull his narratives together.

Synopsis of Bentham's Ethical Theory

What we present here is synoptic and compact. This means that the essential, critical and central strands of Bentham's ethics would be posited; acting as a foundation of M.C Alli's philosophical survey of security and the media.

In his influential book, *Introduction to the Principles of Morals and Legislation*, the cardinal objective for Bentham is to reveal aspects of human nature which for most people, was unknown –resulting in moral insensibility and its attendant oddities. Perhaps, for Bentham, the refusal to bring to the awareness of human beings the "master" ethical principles, which propel and guide their actions for meaningful life would be an opposition to their natural responsibility. A re-enactment of Bentham's claim is indicated in Paul Russell's article, *Strawson's Way of Naturalizing Responsibility*. Russell (1992) maintains that for Strawson, "no reason of any sort could lead us to abandon or suspend our reactive attitude. That is to say, according to Strawson, responsibility is a given of human life and society, something which we are inescapably committed to."

Jeremy Bentham believes that the turmoil in his time in England was consequent upon the inconsistency of the English Law, its complexity as well as its inhumanness, to its foundation on the moral feelings of "sympathy" and of "antipathy". His argument is that the laws of all nations should be rationally based, not emotionally based on what appeared to him to be self-evident principle of the greatest good for the greatest happiness. 'This is the principle of utility which is the most reasonable guide to individual morality, nature and public policy.' The principle of utility is the arrow head of the two sovereign masters nature has placed on mankind, pain and pleasure. It is for them alone to point out what we ought to do, as well as to determine what we shall do'. On the one hand, the standard of right and wrong, the chain of causes and effects are fastened to their throng. They govern us in all we do, in all we say, in all we think, every effort we can make to throw off our subjection, we serve but to demonstrate and confirm it, Dewey and Gramlich (1961). So, if what we do or say does not diminish pain and increase the greatest happiness for the greatest number of people, then it has no utility value; it is immoral.

Bentham was not oblivious of the fact that there have to be a way to measure or evaluate the utility of what we do or say. What then logically followed was the enactment of the "felisic calculus", thus, he sought to establish an external standard, mathematically calculable, whereby to measure the legislator accomplishment. His contention was that he had made legislative reform, not of "caprice" or of unenlightened benevolence, but of logic, Bronowski and Mazlish (1960). The fabric of felisic calculus includes: intensity, duration, its certainty or otherwise, propinquity, and purity.

Without doubt, Bentham's philosophy attracted dithyrambic receptions or criticism in many philosophical circles. This is expected given that no human idea is infallible or unassailable. As Gorman (1987) has said, "reversibility of any philosophical conclusion is always a possibility." However, the views against Bentham are not within the purview of this work, but it suffices to say without equivocation, that human interest and welfare are pivotal to his philosophy. That is why his advocacy centred on how individuals, communities and governments should conduct themselves. The idea is to secure human dignity, rights, freedom, happiness and above all, survival, which is the first inexorable law of nature.

National Security

As a prelude to Alli's discussion on national security, a jungle or forest panorama might make his point more illuminating. As presented in *National Geographic Wild* or *Discovery Channel,* there are alarmists in the jungle, the cry or scream of a bird or monkey on a tree top most of the time, signifies danger. It blows the cover of a predator, which allows animals to run for cover and safety. A careless, feeble and inattentive pray gets consumed by the predator. In the jungle, high premium is placed on security- a logical warrant or precedent to the propagation and survival of the species. Even within lower animal kingdom, security is a *conditio sine qua non* for survival; it is a serious business.

For Thomas Hobbes, the advocacy for an absolute monarch to mitigate the state of nature in which life was solitary, poor, nasty, brutish and short was indeed, a praxis for security and survival. Right from prehistoric times to the present, for all living things, particularly humans, security has always been a desideratum for the sustenance and continuation of human civilization. Security remains within the ambit of variables of human historical process and progress. This point is lucidly corroborated by Oyeweso (2012) by his assertion that:

> in spite of the recent focus on security and development, the promotion of human security had been a major concern of different societies in historical times, not to say the least, the protection of human lives and properties is one of the bed rocks of any pre European and African societies. States are mostly saddled with responsibility of maintaining law and order in the society.

Before we have a sense of Alli's specific idea of national security and what motived his advocacy in this matter, it is pertinent to hazard some discussions on national security. Olayiwola (2013) argues that for "decades, the term national security has meant, by and large, - military security". In reference to Roman J., this meaning has increasingly been called into question. According to Olayiwole, "the question of national security is not merely a question of the Army and Navy. We have to take into account our whole potential for war, our mines, industry, manpower, research, and all the activities that go into the normal civilian life". Also referenced by Olayiwole (2013) is Walter Lippmann who opines that a "nation has security when it does not have to sacrifice its legitimate interests to avoid war, and is able, if challenged to maintain them by war."

According to the *International Encyclopaedia of the Social Sciences*

(1968), National security is said to be the ability of a nation to protect its internal values from external threats. In addition, the opinion of Amos Jordan and William Taylor are cited. For Olayiwole, both agreed that "national security, however, has a more extensive meaning than protection from physical harm, it also implies protection through a variety of means, of vital economic and political interests, the loss of which could threaten fundamental values and the vitality of the state." In the case of Charles Maier, according to Olayiwole, national security "...is best defined as the capacity to control those domestic and foreign conditions that public opinion of a given community believes necessary to enjoy its own self-determination or autonomy, prosperity and well-being."

From Obasanjo's view (2011), "security is about freedom in all its ramifications; emotional, economic, social and cultural well –being. Hence we take on board the issues of economic security, food security, health security, environmental security, personal security, cultural security among several others."

Alli (2001) argues that:

> within the Nigerian melieu, national security as a condition or situation can be defined as the safety of the state and all its components. A state is safe when its territory is not violated, its sovereignty is not threatened, its wealth is not plundered, its citizens can conduct their legitimate business in peace...A proviso to the above is that anything contrary to these essentials threatens national security, understandably, any hostile act or acts in support, which place the population at risk either through occupation or projection of armament, or disallows the population to the resources of our territory, and the right to maintain our cultural or multi-cultural institutions or values, are manifestly an affront on national security. *Ipso facto*, external intervention, passive or active, which is likely, in peace or war, to turn the territory into a focus of international tension or in wider war threaten national security. The very intention conceived in speech or in written word constitutes a threat to state security.

According to Alli, Funmi Olarunshakin's "calabash conceptualization" or metaphor of national security is a vivid illustration. She remarks that, "security should be all embracing and may include personal security and freedom from danger and crime, freedom from fear and anxiety, food and financial security, freedom from disease and a general feeling of well-being."

From the plethora of perspectives on national security, certain elements are consistently apparent which knit all the views together –it is all about national or state survival, with human beings as the focal point. In consonance with Bentham's moral passion, Alli's articulation of national security reverberates the philosophical underpinning of human community, survival and development.

Alli's description of national security at once, shows that he does not see it as a mere abstraction. Specifically, he sees it in teleological term. If this is the case, what are the variables, better still, what are the intervening variables which can sustain national security? In this regard, the media is fingered as a critical factor.

To start making any real connection between the two as Alli attempted to do, to grasp the meaning of media becomes paramount at this point. Surprisingly, not many people know what the media represent. Sometimes, this problem becomes compound when the concept becomes reducible to pluralism, that is that, the concept draws in many interpretations from different perspectives. Naturally, this leads to intricate confusions and perplexities. The conception of the media by Alli (2001) is in the acknowledgement that:

> the media appeals through the press; pamphlets, leaflets, newspapers and magazines; pictures, drawing, cartoons, posters and photograph, broadcasting, radio, and television otherwise called electronic media, stage and literature, political theatre, cabaret, political literature and song, film which includes documentaries, news read and movies. In aggregate, they perform three basic functions, namely, to inform, to educate, and to entertain.

In the words of Alli, all these provide the recipes for "idea formulation which form the wheels for mobilization within the state." The above deposition provides a broad spectrum analysis of the media. This is helpful, for it reveals the difference between the press and the media. Sometimes, people confuse the two concepts, whereas, the press is embedded within the larger framework of the media. Enahoro (1990) expresses the tenability of Alli's definition of the media by insisting that the journalist (mass media) is

> the watch-dog of the public, his role is like that of a dog that is kept to guard a house and who gives warning of the approach of intruders or invaders. The role of the journalist in this regard is to watch over the interests of the people and bark if and when these interests are threatened. He is the crusader for social justice, public morality, civil liberties and human progress.

For more emphasis, Enahoro refers to William Rivers in order to give credence to his assertion. In this regard, Rivers opinion is that,

> the mass media serve as the bulwark of the citizens against tyranny of the majority, the intoxication of power, the grinding oppression of authority and the mindless exploitation of the underprivileged, by the privilege, specifically, the mass media, particularly the print media have a clear and unshrinkable duty to criticize and appraise the occurrences of the moment.

What appears to be profuse in these viewpoints regarding the media is that it protects, entertains and educates in any given environment.
Arising from the above, we are in a position to come to Alli's serious concern about the relationship between the media and national security. Alli is good at showing the relevance of the media to national security which promotes development. This is in line with Omoera and Aiwiyo (2017) thinking that, "...the media can help to prioritize societal issues including security and sustainable development issues in a human community such as Nigeria." Before doing this, he delves into history, citing many critical reflections on the importance of the media by philosophers, and world leaders. Indeed, excerpts from the Bible are points of reference too. In spite of this importance, he reveals that history is replete with attempts made to stifle the expression of ideas for the protection of self and group interest.[1] We appreciate this first and important step taken by Alli. It introduces and shows us the weight of his thesis. This is in agreement with what the philosopher Epicurus has said,

---

[1] Pages 150-151 of his work capture this.

the very first stage of every task is the most important; it gives a direction and reveals the mind-set, vision and mission of the individual.

In our globalized and insecure world, no nation including Nigeria can afford to be complacent, docile and insensitive. The media, through its contents or roles of education, information and entertainment can help get a nation out of these fixations of docility, complacency and insensitivity. Consequently, the rational question to ask in this regard is whether in the Nigerian polity, has the media been able to play its proper role? To answer this question, Alli, first of all, has to remind us about the power of the media or press. For him, it can make or mar; its positive and destructive powers are enormous. With much gusto, Alli (2001) declares that,

> no human in situation has such all-pervading potentialities for good or evil, perhaps, only with the possible exception of unfettered military autocracy of the Nigerian experience and coloration. As the short-lived regime of Generals Buhari and Idiagbon illustrate, the media often revels uncontrollably in its importance and arrogates to itself the status of a king-maker in the polity, they tend to believe that, being king-makers, they, can unmake the king. It is under this kind of scenario that they came into conflict with the military in 1984. It resulted, through Decree 4, 1984 to the precipitate rustication of two journalists of the *Guardian* newspaper, precipitating and providing good excuse for the realization of General Ibrahim Babangida's consuming ambition to rule Nigeria.

Added to the above, it is in recognition of the importance and power of the media that makes it to occupy the Fourth Estate of the Realm. Obviously, the media or press has the power. It is for this reason that we talk about the "power of the press". But has it used the power to defend or protect the citizenry or assisted in national security and development? A reflection on colonial experience in Nigeria would be helpful here. What ensued between the media and the colonialists is described by Ukhun (2017) when he argues that,

> The invading and pervading colonial rule came with its encumbering oddities. Such resulted in stifled aspirations of the people; liberties and human rights were sacrificed on the altar of colonial interest. In the striking maze of denial and confusion agitation for self-rule or in depend

ence became a natural consequence of colonial panorama. Nationalism took the centre-stage, but the nationalists could not fight a stubborn monster with the spine of a weakling. They had to adopt a potent force of propaganda though the press.

In this epic situation, we remember the *Daily News* published by Herbert Macaulay, the *West African Pilot* published by Dr. Nnamdi Azikiwe, the *Tribune* published by Chief Obafemi Awolowo. There were the platforms upon which independence was realized in Nigeria.

Thus, Ukhun (2017) further explains that,

> A critical assessment of the role of the media in colonial Nigeria invites a positive nod. This is in virtue of the end which justified the means. The "end" "means" relationship was not just a mere re-enactment of Machiavellian philosophy, which is sometimes coloured with negativity, it was an "end" "means" relationship fixated on pragmatic or utility value or moral principle of survival. After all, the press perceived that it would have been immoral to be moral in an immoral society designed and put in place by the colonialists. How could the press moralize with the colonialists with immoral intentions? Indeed, one could make bold the assertion that the media won for Nigeria, independence devoid of bullets and blood.

In post-colonial or post-Independence Nigeria, which was doted by military rule and occasional democratic pretensions such as that of Alhaji Shehu Shagari, what truism could be inferred from the relationship between the media and national security? To answer this question, Alli's observation provides the premise, perhaps, for an objective assessment of the post-colonial media national security connection. In his words, "in Nigeria, we are redeemed by the fact that anyone can establish and run a newspaper, publishing house or news media. This is one of the hallmarks of Nigeria's relative press freedom and the resolve of the press empire." As a matter of fact, this liberty is not without the official secret Art of 1962 which provides legal restriction on the media and to help sustain its life. Courageously, in this atmosphere, the press or media in its reportage, has provided valuable service(s) that added value to national security in economic, political, social, health and international issues. For instance, "Chief Obafemi Awolowo cried blue murder over the degradation over the Nigerian economy under Alhaji Shehu Shagari's government in 1982"

(Alli 2001). Amongst others, the reportage on the chocking and chiselling corruption and terrorism is a refreshing reminder of the enhancement of national security by the media. Its role in matters of national security has been appreciable.

Paradoxically, the press or media has had it challenges in the Nigerian polity. It should be said of Alli, uninfluenced by professional contagion, pin-pointed the military as a "Trojan horse" in its unflinching attempt to stifle the press in one form or another for the propagation and protection of regime interest. In other words, the military sees national security purely from an egoist stand-point- a deviance from utilitarian morality advocated by Alli.

He insists that, "it is evident that the men in green have come to see national security in the light of regime protection or survival." Expectedly, given this mentality of the military, the interests, methods and approaches of the media and military to national security issues would conflict or clash at one point or another.

Hence the epiphenomena of this clash of interests are intimidation, harassment, obnoxious treatment, and sometimes death –with journalists usually being the victims or recipients. Alli (2001) graphically adumbrates military mentality in this fashion saying:

> ...successive military regimes would throw up laws that not only constrain the press in the interest of security, but also whittle down individual liberties and often right to life. If the liberty of the press cannot be brazenly abridged through decrees, they can be invalidated by other means. It can be achieved by ambush through value-added tax; sale of newsprint; the press council, or outright closure or bare faced gangsterism, murder and arson.

Even though the

> way military regimes marked the political landscape of this country is perceived as obstructionist, the media, whether in military era or democratic accident or incident in Nigeria, it cannot be completely insulated from its failure on matters arising in respect of national security. Conspiratorially, and by Dukor's (2003) estimation, the media has allowed itself to be hijacked by the power-that-be for blatant

partisan propaganda subverting established institution and upstaging persons who could have claims to sobriety and probity.

Also consistent with Dukor's view, it is safe to say that with the Nigerian journalist, his profile easily gives him away daily – not too educated, lacks the power of analysis, "the grappling need for daily survival" is his bed-fellow, etc. This profile plainly has implications for national security.

Conclusion

Alli's comments on national security and the media provide enduring and "penetrating analysis" of what can be achieved in terms of the relationship between the two barring all problematics. This analysis is particularly a reflection of his genuine desire to preserve a country he served with passion. Within the context of Bentham's utilitarian ethics, his thesis "reaches a deeper level of moral requirement" needed for the greatest happiness to be the slogan for the greatest number of Nigerians. Like Socrates who drank the hemlock and died for the enthronement of truth and justice in his society, Alli was prepared to "bite the bullet" to allow Nigerians "bloom past all predictions"; preserving the integrity and sovereignty of the nation so that the efforts of our present and past heroes will not fizzle into will-o-the-wisp.

References

Alli M. Chris, (2001) *The Federal Republic of Nigerian, Army: The Siege of a Nation*, Lagos: Malthouse Press Limited

Bronowski J. & Mazlish Bruce (1960), *The Western Intellectual Tradition*, US: Dorset Press, U.S.A

Christian James L (2009) Philosophy: An Introduction to the Art of Wondering, (Tenth edition), California: Wadsworth Cengag Learning

Dewey E Robert & Gramlich Francis. W. *et al.*, (1960), *Problem of Ethics*, New York: Macmillan Company

Dukor Madubuachi (2003) 'The State and Media in Africa " in Maduabuchi Dukor *(ed) Philosophy and Politics: Discourse on Values, Politics Power in Africa*, Lagos: Malthouse Press Ltd.

Enahoro A.U (1990), 'The Nigerian Journalist: A Praise Singer or a Watch –Dog' in R.A. Akinfeleye (ed) *Media Nigeria: Dialectic Issues in Nigerian Journalism*, Lagos: Bodmarch Press

Gorman J.L (1987), "Philosophical Confidence" in *Moral Philosophy and Contemporary Problems*, Evans J.D (ed.), Cambridge: Cambridge University Press.

Obasanjo Olusegun (2012) "Leaving No Nation Behind: Enhancing Human Security in Africa through Partnerships and Cooperation" in *Human Security in Africa Through Partnerships and Cooperation*, Obasanjo Olusegun & Mabogunje Akin. L. *et al.* (ed), *Abeokuta*.

Olayiwola O. Abdur-Rahman (2013) "Media and Security in Nigeria" *European Journal of Business and Social Sciences (2:9)*

Omoera Osakue. S & Oluranti Mary Aiwuyo (2017) "Curtailing Security Challenges and Strengthening Democratic Spaces in Nigeria Through Media Inventiveness" *The Humanities and the Dynamics of Africa Culture in the 21st Century*, Ukhun Christopher E. *et al.* (ed), Cambridge: Cambridge Scholars Publishing.

Oyeweso Siyan (2012), "Enhancing Human Security in Africa in a Changing world through Partnerships and Co-operation: What Can We Learn from History?" *Human Security in Africa through Partnerships and Cooperation*, Abeokuta.

Ukhun Christopher. E (2017), "The Media, Corruption of Language and Democracy in Nigeria," *Journal of Educational Research*, 13 (1), Institute of Education Ambrose Alli University Ekpoma

Morality and National Question

Chapter 6

Moral Character and Holistic Development in M. Chris Alli

-Jim Ijenwa Unah

Introduction

Three considerations will animate discussions in this essay on Major General M. Chris Alli. These considerations are: (i) the fact of ethnicity not being a factor in social and intercommunity relations in Nigeria in the early days of political independence from Great Britain (ii) the imperativeness of early moral character training under a master disciplinarian, in the school system, in a sustained manner, as pivotal to the full blown capacity development of the human person, and (iii) a confirmation of the Ika (African) aphorism that "Somebody makes somebody to become somebody."

Alli's thought-provoking book prescribes early childhood character training, unrelenting rigorous mentoring of young people and a consistent demonstration of concern, care and discipline for the growing person as absolutely fundamental for holistic human development. Getting it right, training individuals to take school work seriously and to combine it effectively with supportive enterprises and daily chores is certainly the way to go for both the individual and the society in order to secure a future of responsible adult life for the individual and egalitarianism for the state. All of these background orientations were to prepare M. Chris Alli for a fruitful military career, his subsequent disillusionment with a failing military culture that confused its role with those of the civil order; a situation that turned the entire social order and state structure into a military command structure and a unitary state disguising as a federation; a politically wayward anomaly that has destroyed the social, cultural, economic, political and moral fabric of the Nigerian society.

The Gist of Alli's Book

From the narrative of the family background and early childhood of M. Chris Alli, beautifully detailed out in *The Federal Republic of Nigerian Army: the Siege of a Nation*, we are furnished with the information that the factor of one's place of birth or tribe was not an issue in Nigeria at a time, in the history of the country. This perspective is vividly portrayed and conveyed in Alli's early school experience in Onitsha, a gateway commercial town in the South-Eastern part of Nigeria. The author of the book, under study, Major General M. C. Alli, speaks for himself and captures the scenario in the following words:

> From all appearances, individuals were seen in the light of their personal relationships with each other. The concept of tribe had little or no relevance even when it was clear that your neighbour may sometime lapse into some other language in addition to the local one (Alli, 2014: 7).

Earlier on, the point had also been made that his coming from a Muslim and Christian parentage which necessitated being given a Muslim name Mohammed Baba Alli at birth, did not constrain him in later adopting a Christian name—Christopher-- which was his baptismal name, and even much later taking on another Christian name Emmanuel. What this goes to show, according Alli's narrative, is that religious bigotry and fanaticism, which nowadays prevent people from seeing what is good in the faith of the other, was also not an issue in Nigeria of Chris Alli's early childhood. Evidently, this dual religious heritage was to prepare young Alli for the complexity of social existence in his adult life Nigeria; in which religion, whether Islam or Christianity, has become an instrument of manipulation, oppression, denigration and destruction of the other and, conversely, a strategy for favouritism, nepotism and corruption of power (Ibid. pp.4-5).

Similarly, this perception of cosmopolitanism in Alli's early life was positively aided by the fact that his father had a liberal, non-fundamentalist, view of Islam. Unarguably, this liberal orientation on religious life by Alli's father made to accommodate a Christian wife which later impacted on the children's attitude to life; thus, enabling young Alli to have an enhanced understanding of the essence of religion, which Nurudeen Alao enthused is to enable each person to realize the divine in him, to be his brother's keeper, and to eradicate all evils in society (Alao, 1988:).

This ambience of religious understanding in which Muslims and Christians exchanged gifts and pleasantries during religious festivities provided a wonderful background for a social culture of artistic integration of foreign religions embedded in the African communalistic orientation of reciprocal solidarity and the value of shared existence (Unah, 2002: 145-147). This early positive signs of social and religious harmonious interrelationships of Nigerians runs counter to what Alli describes as religious bigotry, fanaticism, intolerance and fundamentalism; which now ruins every attempt to promote peace, understanding, and genuine national unity in modern day Nigerian society. This new and strange phenomenon, Alli avers, has taken a firm grip of the life-line of all Nigerians and the component ethnic nationalities (Alli, p. 5). As he says, this phenomenon of fundamentalism, has truncated the people's social status, privileges and access to social goods and benefits. It has now destroyed the fabric of the Nigerian state in the new wave of insurgency and terrorism; which he blames on the rivalry amongst the big three tribes, blind greed, and social parasitism, now threatening the foundation of the country's cohesion and sovereignty.

All of this reinforces the perspective that there was sufficient room for artistic and pragmatic integration of the various ethnic nationalities and diverse religions in the country; in such a way that Nigerians could coexist happily, without undue rivalries, mutual distrust and antagonism; a fabulous development wantonly destroyed by the military introduction of unhealthy unitary structure that fuelled and exacerbated inter-ethnic discord and divisiveness. The crises ravaging the Nigerian State, he says, is the product of unbridled greed, military parochialism, miscalculations and over-centralization of political power; which was an unthinkable disgrace, in the Nigerian setting of Alli's childhood that he nostalgically cherishes as the golden era of his country's unity and days of bouncing gaiety.

Imperativeness of Early Character Training

Thus, in a bid to adequately prepare Chris Alli for a well round future of responsibility, his father who hailed from the Northern part of Nigeria had to send him to an Igbo man, a school teacher noted for rigorous training and discipline of younglings under his watch. The man's name is Mr. Okafor, who doubled as Ali's class teacher and character trainer. It must be emphasized that, sending Chris Alli to Mr. Okafor's house was not because Chris Alli's parents lacked the financial capacity and material resources to fully cater to his wellbeing but rather, for him to imbibe sound and excellent missionary school education under the management of tested Reverend sisters, and also to be closely watched by an acknowledged disciplinarian in the person of Mr. Okafor. As could be seen in the text, the presence of committed and dedicated Reverend Sisters as teachers in the Convent,

> ...guaranteed excellent results; both academically and in the pupil's character formation (p.8).
> The above except aptly agrees with the theory and conviction that a sustained and systematic moral character training is absolutely necessary to prepare children for the future.

While in Mr. Okafor's house, Chris Alli effectively and adequately combined his academic mission with some domestic servant's roles. This he discharged conscientiously and diligently, even when he was not being paid for his services, but for the mere fact that Mr. Okafor presided over his mentorship processes. While in Okafor's house, Chris Alli as a young lad of 8 years, was strong, energetic and hardworking; although this was a character he began to manifest while he was with his own parents back home; thus, giving a leverage to the Igbo adage that a chick that would grow to a cock could be spotted the very day it hatches. This is also to support the perspective that while rigorous character training is crucial in preparing children for an adult life of responsibility, nature appears to embed elements of strong character traits in some humans who would become outstanding in the pursuit of authenticity.

However, as it is to be expected, Chris Alli equally tasted his own portion of the bitter pills of master-servant relationship, as it then appeared to him. As a student, Chris Alli engaged in some activities which later impressed some life-principles on him. One of these activities was his involvement in school farming programme which instilled in him the fundamental principles of sowing and reaping, dignity of labour, the quality of labour; which implies that you do not reap where you did not sow. From this activity, Chris Alli came to the conviction that for anyone to expect to reap where he did not sow is dubious morality. This sort of conviction should be integrated into school curriculum as part of the character traits to be taught to correct the character flaw and anomaly in the children of today who struggle to partake of the perquisites of accomplished adults; which deprives them of the requisite incentives to aspire higher, and thus leading them to a life of short-cuts, drugs, robbery and kidnapping.

No doubt, Alli's family which combined the mixture of Islam and Christianity greatly influenced Chris Alli's belief in God and the doctrines of the Holy Bible (see p.84). This also contributed to forming his attitude towards life in general. One of the many Christian beliefs which Ali held strongly to while growing up is the power of God and His supremacy in the affairs of man, *deus ex machina*. Thus, he believes in all the principles of the word of God and believes that the family too is the greatest gift God gave to man on earth, and that we must hold it firmly and do everything possible to protect, preserve and promote its sanctity as a place of permanent relationship, source of succour and strength (Ibid.p.84). Furthermore, Ali believes in pluralism as a right approach to religious matters. Thus, he maintains that "each religion is only of the many paths to one universal Almighty God. Any belief system to the contrary, is politically-motivated ethical posturing." (p.85) This conviction of Chris M. Alli is re-inforced in the story told by Professor Nurudeen Alao, a former Vice Chancellor of the University of Lagos. The story goes thus that there was

> ...an old Sufi tale involving four fellow travellers—a Turk, a Persian, an Arab and a Greek—who had an argument as to how to spend the last coin left with them.
>
> According to the tale, the Turk asserted "I would purchase Uzum with

the coin." The Persian retorted, "I want angur." The Arab wanted *inab*, while the Greek insisted on purchasing *stafi*. A multi-linguist over-heard them and intervened claiming that if he was given the coin he would meet the preference of each of the fellow travellers.

The multi-linguist went and bought a bunch of grapes. The Persian jumped at the bunch saying "It is my *angur.*" "It is my *uzum*" said the Turk. "It is my *inab*", said the Arab. "It is my *stafi!*" remarked the Greek. The four soon realized (thanks to the wisdom of the multi-linguist) that they all had the same preference expressed in different tongues. The four shared the grapes, and were pleased with one another ever after (Alao, 1988: vi-vii).

The point made in this story is that there is something common to all religions which is desired by all genuine religionists. The difference in the religions essentially is the approach and linguistic imprecisions. The relevant multi-linguist which is Chris M Alli in this instance is the one who can identify the procedural differences and linguistic ambiguities, and reveal what is common to all religions. The objective of all genuine religionists lies in "making each man his brother's keeper and of eradicating all evils in society" (Ibid. vii).

Most importantly, he believes that man, not God, is the product of his ambition. Man is what he makes of himself (ibid). Here, Alli strikes the existentialist cord and joins in their patrimony and fraternity. Existentialists hold the view that human beings, in the last analysis, are the architects of what they become in life. While there are noticeable moments of divine intervention in the affairs of men, right from creation, humans are the ones who make and unmake themselves, by the training they receive, the choices they make and the company they keep. No human being, on the existentialist orientation is allowed to invent excuses for himself. Humans are totally free to define their essences having found themselves compelled into existence. Finding oneself in existence is the only choice he does not make; all other choices are contingent upon his being. Human beings are free rational and irrational beings. They are free to decide and make themselves what they will be. No human being can run away from choosing, deciding and acting. Action is what characterizes and defines a person. The nature of human freedom is such that when a person refuses to choose, the refusal is a choice already made, the refusal to decide is a decision already taken, and the failure to act is an act already performed. And this inalienable freedom to choose, decide and act is accompanied by a heavy burden of responsibility (Sartre, 1977: 63-67). No human is allowed to choose, decide and act and transfer responsibility for his choices, decisions and actions to another moral agent. Choosing, deciding and acting and the responsibility for all these go hand in hand. As they say, burden and benefit go together. Neither God nor Satan is responsible for what we choose to be. Alli's life loudly proclaims that we cannot legitimately invent excuses for our failures and that we must take responsibility for them. It is this orientation that fires Alli's imagination to detest indolence, mediocrity, parasitism and unmerited privileges.

Consequently, as a believer in hard work and meritocracy, he frowns at the practice whereby citizens' opportunity to gain access to jobs, admission into schools, et cetera, are decided on the basis of the state of origin, religious inclination and quota system. As a matter of fact, Ali was a victim of this practice too at a point in his academic development and career. Thus, he strongly believes that partly responsible for the sorry state of the Nigerian state, is the habitual practice of rewarding mediocrity at the expense of merit. No nation ever rose to world citizenship through patron-clientism, an undue reward, and primordial promotion and gratification system. By this conviction, Ali seems to envisage the Nigeria State where the opportunity of a Nigerian child to exhibit his or her God given talent and educational abilities will no longer be a factor of tribe, religion or on the basis of favouritism and nepotism. This, to him, is the only sure route to create an egalitarian, strong and just society where the people express a sense of belonging to the state and are willing to sacrifice their all towards the general good of the state.

Come to think of it, how could one explain a situation where a child whose parents had resided in a particular region or state for decades, and happens to be the only state that child had grown up to know as his own place of birth; then at a time when the child decides to seek for a certain opportunity in that state, he is then reminded that his parent are not from that state; the child again decides to go back to his parents' supposed state of origin to seek for another opportunity and he is again reminded that he is not known to the community, and that he wants to reap where he did not sow, even though he is an indigene of such a state. This is the dilemma of the indigene-ship, state of origin and quota system which Ali agonizes about and is very critical of. Accordingly, he equally envisages a political structure that allows for self-determination of the component units where hard work, value-creation and strategic competitiveness will become the hallmark of inter-ethnic interaction; a culture of wealth creation that would enrich both the centre and the federating units of the country; thus, announcing the obituary of a monocultural, rent-seeking and rent-collecting, feeding bottle, self-impoverishing and wayward federalism; and the introduction of an egalitarian Nigerian State in which individuals or the citizens can fully realize their potentials. It also envisages the eventual emergence of equilateral education system which this writer intends to design, develop and propagate and which allows for merit to blossom while equally providing for the less intellectually gifted to be educated.

Power and authority, Alli believes, are transient. For this reason, he says we must use it to capture human respect, affection and endearment so that when we leave office or at death, good things will be said about us. One remarkable character that distinguishes Alli is his strong commitment to a course. In fact, he believes that "a man, who has nothing to die for, is living a worthless life." (p.85). To form a right attitude towards life, he believes that the mind must be trained to overcome all forms of threats, deprivation and degradation, and transcend over darkness (ibid). As such, he imbibed such virtues as "truth, neighbour over self, honesty over deceit" (ibid), and for the human society to flourish, he believes that moral suasions and temperance are ideals which must be treasured and pursued vigorously.

Another salient issue which the author raises, and which captures our own persuasion that for society to be holistically developed there must be a sustained and systematic moral character moulding, is his notion of "the Nigerian factor". This he defines as a "euphemism for operating outside the laws or rules or seeking to moderate them. It is a twister of norms and laws guiding officials and non-officials in the conduct of affairs...its greatest articulation lies in its propensity to dilute principles, laws and order, rules, regulations (p.135). This factor, the author says, accounts for increasing dilution of security values in many

Nigerians' daily transactions and equally accounts for the sorry state of our development. It has increasingly gained permanent residency in the mind-set of Nigerians to the extent that no matter how sound or of good intent a government policy may appear, there would always be that distrust in the minds of people concerning the workability of such policy. One of the dangers of the Nigerian factor as implied by the author is that it sacrifices all values at the altar of compromise. Even government officials and state actors also join in making sure that what works elsewhere is aborted in the Nigerian system. In short, this term can simply be described to mean that things are not what their names imply in Nigeria, that is, there is also the Nigerian skewed brand. When a meeting is slated for 3 O'clock, for the Nigerian factor, it is either something before 3 O'clock or something after 3 O'clock. It can never be the exact time. Exact time is seen as abnormal.

Alli's Early life Experience and Lessons for the Roles of Parents

What could issue from Alli's early life experience is the role of parents in child's upbringing. The later events that played out in the life of Chris Alli could be largely attributed to the rigorous early trainings he received both from his direct parents and the master-parent. This aptly agrees with the views of J. C. Ryle on child character training. In his seminar paper, "The Duties of Parents", founded on Proverbs (22:6), which says "Train a child in the way he should go, and when he is old he will not turn from it." With this, Ryle x-rays a comprehensive guideline for child character training.

How to Train a Child

A child is not to decide how to be trained. He or she is to be trained in accordance with what is right and proper for him to do in the wider context of what is right and proper to do. The task is placed squarely on the shoulders of fathers and mothers in the light of what would conduce to the greater good of society. Training is to enable a child to adjust properly in society. So, the thought of the other, consideration for others, should occupy an important place in proposing a curriculum for child education, both at home and in school.

Parents as Role Models

In Ryle's interpretation, parents should use what they do as examples for the child, as children tend to learn more from what they see than what they hear. Examples, they say, are the best precepts. You should not say one thing and do differently and expect to be taken seriously by the child. It is wrong and socially very dangerous to teach a child what you cannot practice; unless there is a good socially beneficial reason to do so, which should be followed with good explanation.

Avoiding over-indulgence

Continuous dialogue and communication with the child is the way to demonstrate and convey love and affection, never by over-indulgence. The scriptures are replete with the devastating consequences of over-indulgence with children. Parents must jointly and firmly correct the children whenever they go wrong. The counsel, "spare the rod and spoil the child" must be taken seriously and applied whenever the need arises. This was the experience Chris Alli under-went while in Mr. Okafor's house. Mr Okafor, a disciplinarian to the core, never failed in whipping Alli into line with the right conduct. In fact, Chris Alli has this to say about Mr Okafor:

> On many occasions, for one infringement or the other, Mr Sylvester Okafor, either as home-master, or school-master, would unhook his ever-ready, unfailing cudgel which hung menacingly over his town's almanac on the wall and proceed to teach either one or both of us lessons in house-keeping or school work...Mr Okafor left indelible imprints on my life (p.9).

Inculcating Time-consciousness

Children are generally lazy and slothful. It is the duty of the parents to constantly remind the child of the appointed time for his or her chores and assignments. Even when they complain of parental disturbance in their affairs, the parents must insist that children perform their tasks at appropriate time.

Ika Supportive Economic Solidarity

From the practice of child rearing through mentoring by disciplinarians and parental discipline to systematic and sustained moral character training in school, Chris Alli's life journey could well be summed up in the Ika aphorism that "Somebody makes somebody to become somebody." In the pre-colonial African communal setting, the moral education of the child was not the assignment of parents alone much less was it the job of formal school teachers alone. Children's discipline and moral character development was the concern of entire communities; as members of the group strove to produce communities of cultures of moral values and integrity. Corporate child upbringing in which members of the group took part in correcting and straightening up any young person found wanting in good moral conduct was the vogue. There was solidarity in the way every member of the clan made the affairs of the growing child their preoccupation. This practice of caring for other people's children so that they too, in return, would care for your own children when you are unavailable summarizes the Ika theory of supportive reciprocal solidarity, which was a general characteristic of pristine African societies; from which Chris Alli benefited and thrived admirably.

An important dimension of the supportive reciprocal solidarity is its application to the economic life of the African. It was almost practically impossible to find a man in abject poverty because he could not attend to his farm project. The not too strong and the weak found support in the collaborative spirit of the community expressed in organized rotational labour force which took turns attending to the farm projects of the members. This supportive economic solidarity of the members of the African community made loitering or begging an unthinkable disgrace.

Socially, if a man's fortunes were adversely affected by sudden calamity, such as famine and drought, members of his clan, his work team or rotational labour force helped him to bounce back. And this is because as the saying goes, *umune ububon ani ububo daru ali*, literally stating *that ububon*'s kinsmen do not allow *ububon* to fall flat to the ground. They practically lend support to each other. These moral relics of the African past should constitute the basis for rebuilding modern African societies. Thus, Alli's work identifies and points to a systematic moral character training for the African child to prepare him for a future of ethically sound and responsible leadership of his household, his business and the institutions of state and society.

These are the reasons why sustained and systematic moral character training for holistic development is imperative if indeed we hope to build an equitable, just, merit-driven and peaceful society.

Conclusion

Chris M. Alli's early childhood training, his experiences of inter-ethnic relations at the inception of nationhood immediately after the attainment of political independence from Great Britain reveal the ingredients of personal moral rearmament and holistic development of a multi-ethnic, multi-cultural, plural society such as Nigeria. It describes a state of affairs in which the phenomenon of convoluted ethnicity, inter-ethnic mutual antagonism and unhealthy rivalry was never noticeable in inter-tribal interrelationship in the country. The factor of ethnicity deliberately exploited and manipulated by power seeking politicians and religious bigots and fanatics had not always been noticeable in the Nigerian State—it was at a time alien, and almost unthinkable! That was the narrative of the country where people nowadays could never imagine that it was possible for a child of northern birth and origin to be trained and mentored by a south-easterner. Yet, it happened and it was part of the circumstances that made the all-round development of Chris Alli a reality.

More than anything else, Alli's upbringing and character training point to the need for an early, rigorous, systematic, and unbroken moral character development of the Nigerian child both for his or her own benefit and the over-all good of society. It also emphasizes the overarching importance of human support system and human solidarity in the collective health and wellbeing of society. Man's cooperation and solidarity with his fellowmen is what makes man more human, more accommodating and more supportive of his fellow humans.

References

Alao, N. O. (1988). General Introduction: Designing Peace, Tolerance and Understanding in *Nigerian Studies in Religious Tolerance*, vol. iv. Eds. C. S. Momoh, E Onuoha and T. El-Miskin. Lagos: John West Publications.

Alli, M. C. (2001). *The Federal Republic of Nigerian Army: the Siege of a Nation*. Lagos: Malthouse Press Limited.

Ryle, J. C. (2017). "The Duties of Parents", available @www.biblebb.com//files/parents.htm (1985 updated), accessed 22/5/2017.

Sartre, J.- P. (1977). *Essays in Existentialism.* Secaucus, New Jersey : The Citadel Press.

Unah, J. I. (1997/98). Bantu Ontology and its Implication for African Socio-economic and Political Institutions, *Journal of Oriental and African Studies.* (Athens Greece), pp. 133-147.

Chapter 7

Chris Alli and Moral Perspective of National Question

-Rev. Fr. Prof. Ben Okwu Eboh

Introduction

My procedure here is first and foremost to beam a search light on the life and background of the man, M. Chris Alli, the author of an interesting book titled *The Federal Republic of Nigerian Army: the Siege of a Nation*. The author took pains to examine the role of Nigerian Army in governance in Nigerian state. Firstly, it is necessary to say a few things about the author's family background and upbringing, particularly how it relates to religious tolerance. Secondly, I will attempt to examine the point of birth of Nigerian state and its challenges and prospects. Thirdly, there will be need to discuss fully the role of the Nigerian Army in the political development of Nigeria. Fourthly, it is important to evaluate the moral decadence in the Nigeria state and its citizens. Fifthly, we search for a way forward for the Nigerian state by advocating the enhancement of the moral strength and character of our leaders. Sixthly, if Nigeria is to be developed it must grow from material and moral aspects of development. Finally, a short conclusion sums up the work.

I happened to come across a number of books written by military men about military government in general and in particular Nigerian civil war. Most of the writers naturally pursued their narratives from their own point of view and their standard point. I don't need to quarrel with any of such books that I read with keen interest. The point is that of all books of that category, I was delighted with the work of M. Chris Alli titled, *The Federal Republic of Nigerian Army: the Siege of a Nation*.

What attracted my attention to the work was not only the title of the book but also the personality of M. Chris Alli.

I could not resist adding a voice and value to what Chris Alli has done in his excellent work and so I decided to evaluate the National Question from moral perspectives so as to know where Nigeria is heading to.

The man, M. Chris Alli

I consider M. Chris Alli to be a man of many parts. My mind tells me that he is "an open page" of a kind of person. He is a kind of a person who is ready to call a spade a spade. His background story shows me that he is a person, whose YES IS YES and whose NO IS NO. I saw in him a kind of person who is eager to put things right in the Nigerian Nation. He has a strong character and he knows his limitations. M. Chris Alli is a visionary from his childhood.

I would like to limit myself to only his family background upbringing which has much bearing to his religious life and moral behaviour that the nation needs in my consideration. I want to take for granted his childhood development and experiences as a school boy to the stage where he finally found himself in Army and he made a name there. I decided to use the parents of M. Chris Alli family life as a case point to illustrate how religious tolerance can influence family growth and development of a nation. I am more inclined to reflect on the nature of the family of M. Chris Alli than any other part of his early life for an obvious reason. He is a product of mixed marriage. His father was a Muslim, Mallam Alli Adakwo while her mother, Mrs. Rebecca Ojumori Nana she was a Roman Catholic Christian both of the royal origins in their respective rights and they lived a very happy family. According to M.Chris Alli mixed marriages affect not only the couple's attitude but also that of their offspring when they are confronted with the positive and negative shades of the Nigerian tribal experience (Alli, 2001:p. 4). Furthermore, he says that Sometimes, these can be a blessing, providing very strong bridges between communities. Though, when there is a passage of emotions - deadly emotion - nothing in the Nigerian integrationary process really counts. A mixed marriage frequently helps to shape your understanding and responses to the larger Nigerian tribal situation. It builds bridges, breaks boundaries of religion, language, class and cultures (Ibid).

It is of note that, in their mixed marriage, all the children are Christians without exception and even when their father made an attempt to win them over to Islam it was not possible. However, from time to time, M. Chris Alli, though, innocently, accompanied his father to the mosque for payers and his mother to her prayer in the church. As a matter of fact, during Sallah and Christmas festivals, the Moslems and Christians exchange invitations at both festivals and everyone used to be happy. One can say that this stage of cordial religious relationship among religions in Nigerian state was at its stage of innocence until advent of Fundamentalism and things fell apart. That is how it would have been in Nigerian state had not a third religion surfaced into Nigerian socio-spiritual dictionary called fundamentalism. In the words of M. Chris. Alli,

> fundamentalism is amorphous, self-regenerating and all pervasive; sometimes, even deity has to be qualified by it, as well as life after life. This new and strange phenomenon has taken a stranglehold on the lifeline of all Nigerians and component tribes. It frequently demarcates our individual social status, privileges and access to public good. Often, it finds expression in the world-wide terrorism, aviation hijacks, holy war, arson of places of worship, intolerance and calculated provocation. It could be anything but compassion, love and justice. The combined forces of religious politics, tribalism or ethnicism and the rivalry amongst the big three tribes, blind greed and parasitism constitutes the scoundrels that have turned Nigeria history into a chronicle of a spectacular turbulence. (Ibid)

As a soldier and as a man of good conscience, M. Chris Alli was not comfortable with the way the Federal Republic of Nigerian Army was going about the issue of religion in Nigeria state. He foresaw the harm the religious bigotry and fundamentalism would do to Nigeria and Nigerians.

M. Chris. Alli, could not overlook the Federal Republic of Nigerian Army's action on religious matter and he had to open up what the Nigerian army is doing secretly in these words:

> in 1986 the Federal Government secretly sent a powerful delegation led by a cabinet Minister to a meeting of Islamic states under the

umbrella of Organization of Islamic Conference (OIC) at which Nigeria's flag was flown presumably as an observer... it was manifested in the deepening of government's definition of Islamic identity with the secret induction of Nigeria into the Organization of Islamic Conference by General Babangida in a questionable and covert circumstances. Furthermore, he projected Islam a religion under siege, in desperate need of coverts and introduced a governmental, parochial behaviour that sourced dissension and dichotomy. The nation is yet to recover from the wounds and the undue-politicization of religion in Nigeria (Ali. P. 120).

This information from M. Chris Alli is a manifestation of his religious upbringing and strength of character. Most human beings will not be bold to say what they saw as evil for fear bad consequences.

It is obvious that The Federal Republic of Nigeria Army is responsible for where we are today about religious crisis in Nigeria. In the *Sunday Punch* newspaper of 8 November 1998, the Secretary to the Federal Military Alhaji Gidado Idris was reported to assert with glee atop his high pedestal that 'it is generally agreed that Nigeria, not having a state religion is none the less, far from being a classical secular state" (p. 127). He goes on: "Religion and the Nigerian State are learning to adapt and co-exist...One is tempted to ask if Nigeria is far from being a secular state, then what is it? It is certainly not a Christian, Moslem or Animist State" (Ibid)

The important point I want to raise here is that if Moslems and Christians had kept the pace of their cordial relationship among them, as one could see in the exemplary family of M. Chris Alli, Nigerians would not have been having religious intolerance which has become a divide in Nigerian polity. The advent of the fundamentalism is one of the greatest problems of today's Nigerian state.

As a thorough going Roman Catholic Christian, Alli's view on religious intolerance is that "it should not exist for any reason whatsoever and he believes with due respect to all theological standings and posturing, that each religion is only one of the many paths to the one universal Almighty God" (p. 128). And therefore, for purposes of peace and harmony, every religion should pay great attention to his/ her own religion and respect other people's religion and faith. It is obvious that if every religious denomination remains faithful to its religious morality the interference in other peoples' religious morality should not exist. If every citizen follows strictly to the religious morality of his or her Religion and faith, peace should reign supreme in Nigerian state.

I want to conclude my impression of the life of M. Chris Alli. I see him as a man of great integrity, a true Christian of great faith and an honest human being. And he is above all, in my calculation, a role model for Nigerians and in particular the Nigerian Army. He loves the Nigeria state. In spite of all odds, he still dreams of Nigeria as a great nation.

The point of Birth of Nigerian state

The birth of "Nigeria" was problematic because instead of coming out through the head it decided to come out with both legs. Only one God knows how Nigeria came to be. Nigeria was born at seventh month of pregnancy instead of the normal ninth month. Efforts were made to rescue the seventh-month baby called "Nigeria" in hands of British colonialists. In short, Nigeria was not born at a platter of gold.

The amalgamation of the Northern and Southern protectorates in 1914 by Lord Fredrick Lugard came to be what is called "Nigeria". And it was neither a blessing nor a curse in disguise. This ambiguity was as a result of British selfish interest in favouring one part of the colony, precisely the Northern protectorate for purposes of commercial trade. According to E. Anowai "Nigerian state forcibly came into existence and many ethnic groups have in one way or the expressed disenchantment with the unjust political structure and have been longing for a change and proper re-organization" (Anowai, 2014:73). It was clear that all was not well with the amalgamation. It is pertinent to note that the then Prime minister of Nigerian, Sir Alhaji Abubakar Tafawa Balewa in 1952 in a speech in the Northern House of Assembly stated that "since the amalgamation in 1914, British Government has been trying to make Nigeria into one country, but the Nigerian people are different in every way including religion, custom, language and aspiration. The fact that we are all Africans might have misguided the British Government" (Balewa 1972). In addition, the then leader of the Western region, Chief Obafemi Awolowo expressly stated that "Nigeria is not a nation. It is a mere geographical expression. There are no 'Nigerians' in the senses as there are 'English', 'Welsh', or 'French'. The word Nigeria is merely a distinctive appellation to distinguish those who live within the boundaries of Nigeria and those who do not." (Awolowo).

In short, the point of emphasis is that the idea of amalgamation was never consensual. The parties had no contribution to make in the matter. The parties had to swallow the hard pills. And more so when Nigeria was divided into three regions- Eastern, Western, and Northern regions- the British in her characteristic manner gave a greater percentage of the land to the North so that the Northern region had a about 55%. In the light of this situation, the seed of political crisis was sowed and that was the starting point of political problem in Nigerian state. Had the amalgamation not taken place the situation must had been very different today and the story would have been a different history. In sum, Nigeria was created as British sphere of interest for business. Crisis of all sorts started raising their ugly heads from all sides.

Perhaps, what one may consider the value of the amalgamation is only in view of the population of the people and Nigerians can then proudly see themselves as the "Giant of Africa". A vigilant dog barks always. Can Nigeria really bark or is Nigeria a toothless bull dog? Your guess is as good as mine.

The place of the Nigerian Army and politicians in governance

It will not be far-fetched to say that Nigeria state found itself in the hands of both military government and civilian government right from the inception of amalgamation. British government was a force to be reckoned with. When the amalgamation took effect, the British government sealed off the South from the North. And between 1914 and 1960, that is a period of 46 years, the British allowed minimum contact between the North and the South because it was not in the British interest that the North be allowed to be pullulated by the educated South. That period of forty-six years of British rule can be said to be a period of military rule of a sort given fact that the British Government wielded excessive authority on their subjects. Of course, the British did not prepare the ground well for Independence because their interest was on commerce and the Bible. Hence, both the army and civilians were not well equipped for proper governance even before and after Independence in 1960.

In fact, the British Government in their usual manner saw to it that schools were to be few and the education was to be generally up to a standard only high enough to enable the recipients to keep records of accounting transactions in offices; and they made sure that there was an acute dearth of highly educated civil servants for administrative and political appointments. What was worse, the few Nigerians, with higher education were actively disliked by the majority of the whites who saw the educated class as threat to the security of the tenure of the whites. This attitude was what the Nigerian Army and civilian politicians inherited from British government. This is what, perhaps, explains the reasons for the crisis of governance in Nigerian state right from the onset till today.

I think that Chris Alli is correct when he says that "it is misnomer to talk about military intervention in Nigeria. What is pertinent is perhaps to refer to civil intervention in military governance since Independence" (Alli 2001:126). The point is that of now the Army is always in control of the Nation. The soldier changes from army uniform to civilian dress because it is the same person from one uniform to the other in Nigerian situation. The majority of Nigerian high ranking officers retire from military service into political arena almost immediately after their retirement. Of course, it is all in search of money and power.

In governance, the Nigerian Army and the civilian politicians share the same views more or less. And even in the mode of governance there is not much difference in the moral character and behaviour of the two groups of people in political development of Nigeria state. Perhaps, the little difference is that one governs by the constitution of the land while the other rules by Decrees. And it must be noted, however, that the military training differs greatly from that of the active politician and their leadership style is bound to differ from that of trained military personnel. Usually, the military leadership has his initial problems. Thus, according to A. K. Ocran:

> a military junta initially lacks a political platform. Even if a military leader should want to turn himself into a political leader this cannot

be easily done, at least in the initial stages, due to the absence of a political platform. It is also worthy of note that political leadership demands a set of values, qualities and characteristic different from those required in a military leadership (Ocran, 1977:98).

It is to be noted that it is not in the sphere of the military to rule. As a matter of fact the military are established for the specific tasks of national defence and preservation of law and order within the national boundaries. The military are by training and tradition separate from politics and are not actively taught the art of government. According to A. K. Ocran:

> soldiers should leave politics alone. When they try to run a country, in spite of their enthusiasm they run it badly because have they are, right from the beginning expected to assume the role policy-makers on a job which they have had no previous training. If they have to take- over, then they should be prepared to achieve their aims immediately and hand over as early as possible (Ocran: 94).

The politicians, on their own part, take interest in bringing soldiers into viable political parties for their personal protection with the result that the political parties become a mixed strew. Party manifestos are non-existence in most parties. And that is why politicians change from one party to another at will.

It is worthy of note that neither civilian government nor the military government has the ability to stop social evils in Nigerian state. There is corruption in the land. In fact, most armies that get involved directly and massively in running government become corrupt, but no one dares to say so for fear of unpleasant consequences. It is a known fact that the standard of morality of the military in any given country cannot be above that of the general standard of morality in the society as a whole. In fact, there is fire on the "mountain" of Nigerian state.

The Moral Decadence in Nigerian state

There is no gainsaying that the moral attitude of both the military and the civilian leadership before and after Independence has been "characterized by self-deception and hypocrisy". It is a truism to say that we lack responsible and exemplary leadership from birth of Nigerian state to the present moment. In fact, the greatest problem that brings the so called the "Giant of Africa" on her knees is corrupt leadership. According to C. Achebe:

> the seminal absence of intellectual rigor in the political thought of our founding fathers - a tendency to pious materialistic woolliness and self-centred pedestrianism, in short, political leadership in Nigeria state is nothing more than a means for immediate gain, instant wealth and fame, hence this material success has made Nigeria a favourable and fertile land for germination and growth of corruption (Achebe, 1983:1)

Come to think of it in Nigeria today, as I said elsewhere "many a time one hears Nigerians say: "We are in Nigeria, let us do it in the Nigeria way." There is a catalogue of such expression and I don't intend to enumerate all of them. What is important to note is that such expressions, if well understood, indicate that our moral values are in their lowest ebb; that in our national ethics, the end justifies the means (Eboh, 1980:10)

It is a known fact today that in Nigerian society both private and public sector are morally bankrupt. Very few people ever ask what will be good for their neighbours. The majority of Nigerian citizens are ready to go any place, and length and to use any means at the disposal whether fair or not to acquire whatever they want. According to Olu Awotesu in the *Daily Times* of Nov. 5 asserts that

> Nigeria is indeed a sick country, sick and rotten all over. She is sick because we are not honest, we are not sincere. "The military" who came to save the situation, are no better. They appoint incompetent people as civil commissioners and top government functionaries. Double standard, cheating and sectionalism characterize our society (Olo, 1977:15).

It is evident, then that the cause of justice is perverted openly in order to protect a few. Take, for example, when highly placed citizen commits an offence, all he needs to do is to beckon to his old schoolmates, secret society colleagues, ethnic relation or social club members to come to his rescue. And invariably, they come to his aid, of course neutralizing all the law enforcement agents. In other words justice and fair play mean nothing to the majority of Nigerians. A statement from a top government official during Wole Soyinka's interrogation, in his book, *The Man Die* confirms that justice is thrown into the dust bin in Nigerian state and hear what the official says in Wole Soyinka's book: "Sometimes Wole, we have to do things which…which we know are wrong. Really bad. But this is the set up…There are things I have seen here which make me…disbelieve in such a thing as justice" (Soyinka, 1978:56)

It is worthy of note that in Nigeria, for reasons which is inexplicable, most people irrespective of their education are materialistic in outlook, everyone wants money and property to the extent that many would not scruple to resort to any means, mostly foul, to acquire them. The general idea carried over from pre-independence days, that all money belong to government and therefore anyone can help himself to it, has not much helped the situation. It has led to wastefulness and theft of public money even by people who by virtue of their education know better. Civil and other government servants may be increased to meet expanding departments and indulge in large-scale bribery and corruption, for the sake of acquisition of personal property instead of protecting the government treasury and increasing administrative efficiency. Purely for the sake of satisfying political, family or other demands, there is mass promotion, often of inexperienced and unqualified persons to posts in the higher grades for which they are not suited by temperament, character or training. And such are the government officials who, for instance, rake off 10 per cent commission on every contract award. They use their positions to do all sorts of things like arranging government houses for friends and relatives, finding jobs for members for their family, getting cases off police stations and courts, arranging to establish shops for wives and girl-friends and so on or do favours to certain friends and relatives.

In short, materialism has become a stubborn reality in Nigerian state and it has taken strong grip on our society. Materialism as it is lived out in the society is the ideology that places the emphasis on the material rather than on the spiritual side of us. It is a refusal to face the fact of man's dual nature and the truth that our lives must be lived out as a tug-of-war and a delicate balancing, between the forces of body and soul, of animal and rational, of matter and spirit. It is an option for material values. Generally, we hardly theorize about it, or declare ourselves materialistic. We simply live it out. By implication we say with the Epicureans: "Let us eat and be merry today for tomorrow we die."

If you venture to ask a materialist: What is life? Surely, the answer that you will get is that life is eating and drinking, merry making, having enough of everything of this world. In short, for him, life is nothing but enough money to buy good food and drinks, a good and well-furnished house, a good and "one in-town" car, a good network of human connections to enable one to get anything one wants. In sum, for a thorough-going practical materialist, life is wealth and wealth is life.

Besides his excessive desire for wealth, he is also very anxious about power and authority. For him, what is important in life is that you are in control; you are in-charge; you are the manager or the director. Think of people who they and their children's children can never exhaust, yet their preoccupation in life is to "rule" in whatever circle they find themselves and when they are given the opportunity to rule any group of people they would like to remain in authority for "eternity" because for them life without authority is not worth living. For them, it is better to live a day like a lion as a ruler than to rule a hundred years like a lamb as subject.

Furthermore, for a materialist, Life is a game, "*haa-haa-wuu-wuu*", a gamble, scratch my back and I scratch your back your back. Life is "give and take". Life is getting anything you want through any means, fair or foul. Life is "fastness". Life, in sum, is "419" of various dimensions and magnitude.

Of the *fifty-seven* years of Nigerian Independence, the military government took the lion share of *forty* years and civilian government got only *seventeen* years. Neither the moral tone of the military government nor that of the civilian government is anything to write home about. It is one coin of the same sides. No side of the coin is better than the other.

In short, the moral tone of the leadership of Nigerian state is akin to Friedrich Nietzsche's Master- Slave morality and Nietzsche's proclamation of the death of God. Our leaders are simply die- hearts whose hearts desires is nothing else but power and wealth and they fear neither god nor man. They consider themselves as the measure of everything. And it can be said that their ideology stems from godless materialism and naked power which aims at life detached from morality

I sum it up the morality of our leaders to what I call the "morality of the market" (Eboh, 2015: 237). What is "the morality of the market"? It is a morality of no morality. It is a morality akin to Machiavelli's principle that "the end justifies the means. It is a morality of getting to one's end at all cost without looking to the right or left. It is morality of getting to where one wants to be without resource to any moral principle of right or wrong, good or evil. It is like what happens in the open markets where prices are not fixed and people buy whatever they want at whatever cost

Since their morality is neither religious nor social, individual opinion becomes a reference point and so standards become relative according to individual opinions. Good and evil is no longer absolute but become accommodated to individual needs and estimates. An individual becomes his or her own authority. Indeed, this is what the morality of the market is about.

In short, it is a known fact that our leaders are governed by no known moral principles or any known religious belief. The only morality they have is their heart desire. And their heart desire is that they must be in- charge of society at all costs with the sole purpose of satisfying their personal selfish interest and that of their group to the total neglect of the common good of society. And in order to achieve their purpose which, in most cases, is power and wealth, they constitute themselves into a powerful bloc capable of warding off any resistance from their subjects. This is why Nigeria can be considered as a nation at a cross-road.

The way out for the Nigerian state

As we can see from the moral tone of the Nigerian state above, it is obvious that we are at a point of moral shipwreck. And to avoid the moral "boat" from sinking completely the leadership crisis in Nigeria should be re-activated based on moral virtue of Aristotle. In fact, moral virtue is required of every citizen in a state, and more importantly in a higher degree from the leader who governs the state be he an army or a civilian. However, Achebe is optimistic:

> that Nigerian situation can be changed however difficult it may seem. But for this change to be realizable, the political leaders of the state must take the lead. They must change their ways, their leadership concept and aim, their attitude to politics. But all these require moral virtue which will definitely give rise to moral leadership (Achebe: 1)

The possibility of making progress in the leadership style in Nigerian state lies in leaders possessing moral virtues. The virtue of courage is required for a leader to stand his ground in what is good, right, and just. According to C.M. Ekwutosi:

> courage consists in the readiness to expose oneself to dangers...for the sake of some higher good, to suffer inconvenience, and not to shrink from death. Upholding political morality in a corrupt political atmosphere requires courage for the sake of good. A moral politician who possesses the virtue of courage does not mind whatever evil may befall him when he is doing what is right (Ekwutosi, 2006:121).

This is a kind of leadership that Nigerians need in this moment of political instability.

Over and above the virtue of courage a good leader must imbibe the moral virtue of temperance and justice. Temperance as D. Sullivan puts it is "the virtue that regulates the concupiscible appetite" (Sullivan, 1992: 207). Thus, it has to do with pleasure of the senses such as food drinks etc. A temperate man for Aristotle "craves for the things he ought, as he ought, and when he ought" (Aristotle, 2016: 127). According to him, "temperance requires living according to the direction of the rational principles, so that one will desire things necessary as one should and when necessary." (Aristotle, 943)

As we all know inordinate craving is the ill that has been befalling our political leaders. This often leads them into looting from the nation's treasury, money laundering and other related practices including to rigging in an election and lobbying to remain in power. Subsequently, this self-indulgence leads them into scandalous living for pleasure, consumerism, and ostentation. They also corrupt minds of their subjects, particularly the youths who after them will be leaders. And inevitably they grow up to continue in the same way.

Our leaders should shun these sharp, bad, practices and pay much heed to good habits of virtue of temperance. These virtues will enhance their integrity and honesty. And their subjects will accord them much respect.

Furthermore, the virtue of justice is very much needed in the Nigerian leaders. The virtue of justice is sine qua non for any leader worthy of his name. Justice for Aristotle is the greatest of all virtues, because with it one is not only exercises virtue towards himself, but also towards others. Thus, moral virtue of justice disposes one to do what is just, and also wish for what is just.

It is very notable that Nigeria is presently in a state of social injustice which is due to tribal difference and favouritism. In Nigeria, for example, job is mostly not granted on competence, but based on ethnic affiliation, often to the credit of mediocrity. If, for example, a president is elected into office, he fills the major positions of authority in government with his kinsmen and friends. Some election contestants earmark places where they got higher number of votes and then continue to favour them as is the case in the present regime. Hence, those who voted against the contestants are punished directly or indirectly. Other instances of injustice abound. Moreover pressure may also come from friends and family members who would seek favours from their "representative".

It is obvious, from the present situation of Nigeria that peace does not actually reign, because justice is lacking. Justice is alien to tribalism or any form of favouritism. This is why the circle of injustice continues to widen, giving rise to violence among the three tribes of Nigeria. But, it is not impossible to make things right. The problem can be solved by no other people than the leaders of the country. Hence, there is need for exemplary leaders who possess the virtue of justice. A moral leader finds the way, points the way and leads people through the way.

Humility is yet another moral virtue which a leader should possess. A humble person according to Aristotle though worthy of great things like honour, thinks himself worthy of little. Pride is a vice common among the ruling elite of Nigeria. They live in a world of self-glorification and as well involve in catapulting the country's image to the skies in selfish vaulting ambition with phrases like "the Giant of Africa" and so on, thinking that everything is right with hypocritical leadership. Thus, they engage themselves in showiness, callousness, vulgarity and dishonesty. Little wonder did C. Achebe say that "Nigerians are what they are only because their leaders are not what they should be" (Achebe: 111). Political leaders are therefore called to the moral virtue of humility in service.

Moral sphere of the National development

Morality and National development are tied together. They are two sides of the same coin in the development of a nation. As a matter of fact there are two main views of a nation's development. The two aspects of development of a nation must be fully developed for a nation to be considered as a developed nation.

The two main aspects of the development of a nation are material and non-material. The material concept of development emphasizes the development of such items as roads, bridges, hospitals, schools, electricity, telephones, water supply etc. Whenever adherents of this material concept of development speak, the attention is on those aspects of development that highlight the provision of improvement of needs of man. They mean the provision of food, shelter, clothing and general improvement of man's environment. This can be called economic development and Nigeria needs it now perhaps more than ever before. This, however, is not the only meaning of development. Another aspect of development is that of the mind or non-material development (Asiegbu, 1998:28).

The non-material concept of development emphasizes the creative power of the citizens and the need to enhance it. National development in this understanding becomes the liberation of the mind from prejudices, fear and superstition. More positively, it is the realizing of the creative potential of the citizen through ability to invent and contribute to knowledge. And some element of philosophy is needed for the development of the mind.

As we are aware, the main function of philosophy is to broaden man's vision of the world, life and its problems. And I agree with Dewey who assigned a social function to philosophy. Philosophy becomes a "vision" whose function to free man's mind from bias and prejudice and to enlarge their perception of the world about them. It is the area of shaping our mental attitude that, I think, philosophy can help us (Dewey, 1957:21). According to Russell, "the man who has no tincture of philosophy goes through life imprisoned in the prejudice derived from common sense, from the habitual belief of his age or his nation, and from conviction which have grown up in his mind without the co-operation or consent of his deliberate reason"(Russell, 1976: 91).

It is my firm conviction that most Nigerians go through life like blind men and they stagger along the road of life like drunken men. Their 'vision" of world, life and its problems is so narrow that national development and progress becomes practically impossible under such a situation. It is then imperative that we should, call down philosophy, with Socrates, from heaven to increase the dimension and clarity of the "vision" of the citizens of Nigeria on the world, life and its problems. The more our minds are developed the clearer our "vision" becomes and the more as individuals, we can give a detached breadth and scope to the conception of ends; the more, as individuals, we can give just measure of ourselves in relation to our society; the more, as individuals we become serene in our tortured and uncertain world.

What is at stake in the Nigerian situation is the indispensable need for self-situation and self-possession and self- denial- a mentality that we have acquired from our colonial masters. All efforts, therefore, should be geared towards self-fulfilment and self-realization for all citizens. Every citizen has a duty to contribute something to the growth of the society. Every citizen should give back something to society. No nation can ever be developed without embracing these two areas of development.

A developed nation places high premium on the meaning of human life and actions that enhance human life. Many great nations and civilizations of the world are known to have developed a high sense of morality. Conversely those nations with low sense of morality can rarely be described as developed in the true sense of the word. It is obvious that since the morality of materialism can be the morality of "everything goes" then "nothing goes" (Eboh, 1994:20). The moral tone of such a state will be at a standstill. This is, perhaps, why Omoregbe avers that "neither science nor technology can develop a country if its citizens are not morally developed. Development and morality go together. A moral nation is a great nation. (Omoregbe, 1990:197)

Conclusion: Whither "one Nigeria"

I decided to conclude this work with the title -"Wither one Nigeria"- because of the fact that Nigeria is seating on keg of gun powder. There are too many voices about "one Nigeria". People from low to high in the society talk about "one Nigeria" from two sides of their mouths and saying too many different things from the same mouth and what comes out of people's mouth are simply lies, deceit and hypocrisy.

My idea of "One Nigeria" can be likened to a palm kernel nut with two chambers inside one nut. The two chambers don't see each other; they don't talk to each other; they don't relate to each other as good neighbours. And the two nuts in the separate chambers are neither enemies nor friends. They are just there because they have to be there. One palm nut with two chambers is dormant. They are not going forward or backward. The nut is each chamber is maturing at its own pace. Each claims to be the owner of the one nut in which they inhabit. They are quarrelling always over the one palm kernel nut in which they find themselves. They are quarrelling endlessly in spite of the gap between two of them.

That is a typical Nigerian existential situation. The human relationship is dead in Nigerian state. Today for example, in Nigeria, there is no moral conscience, no principles, no ultimate rallying point, a body without a soul, where in the absence of an animating force leadership itself is impotent. The neglect of the spiritual has made us empty. The neglect of the spiritual has made indifferent to genuine beauty, peace and justice.

All that I am saying is that this is time for us as Nigerians to end the endless lies and deceit and decide whether we want to live together or not. And if we agree to live together, the basis of the union must be clearly spelt out. In doing this, two fundamental issues must be settled to smoothen and strengthen the union.

The two main factors that create crisis for "one Nigeria" are religion and resource control. These factors are the sources of crisis in "one Nigeria.

Firstly, the question of religious morality is taking a dangerous dimension in Nigerian state. It should no longer to be tolerated in modern time, multi-cultural, multi-ethnic and multi-religious state; any band of rampaging hoodlums can pounce on anybody or group: murder, main, rape, and destroy their properties in the name of religion, without the culprits being brought to book.

We all know that we were all born into one religion or the other. It is a fact of experience that none of us, including the religious bigots or their sponsors, can claim that they have ever seen God. If anybody disputes this fact he should be able to tell the whole world how God looks like. We cannot condone this kind of madness. It is nothing but the height of hypocrisy. Nigeria cannot live under such a siege for whatever reason. We must all tighten our belts to embrace religious tolerance for the peaceful co-existence in our "one Nigeria".

Secondly, resource control is another issue that requires urgent attention. Take for example, if I am able to harvest ten bags of rice from my one plot of land and somebody else from Lagos wishes to take over my ten bags of my rice because I have only two households and so I should keep only two bags of my rice while he takes eight bags of my rice because he has twenty households where is the justice?. If such a measure is to be taken in reality it does not make sense. It is certainly unfair, unjust and oppressive. I cannot be the person to cater for your large household to the detriment of mine. Justice demands that I cater for my household while you cater for yours.

The point that is being made here is that each state in Nigeria should be able to cater for its own citizens. Some states will be better off than some other states. Life will continue to go on all the same. And there will be fair play, justice and equity in the affairs of the nation.

In conclusion, the whole work is geared towards the role of morality in the development of the Nigerian state and my work is intended to add value to the excellent work of M. Chris Alli. Morality and nation building go hand in hand. Moral decay affects the entire Nigeria society. Hence, it can be said that we all like the sheep have gone astray.

In spite of all odds, there is still a way out. There is no perfect man on earth. The important fact to be noted is that the strongest among us is "fragile" or differently put, "even the angels eat beans" The best of mankind has something to put in order. We should not be afraid to look deeply into ourselves. These faults are part and parcel of human nature and environmental up-bringing. We should strive to "conquer" ourselves. In sum, every citizens of Nigeria should write and re-write his or her name and behaviour for the betterment of "one Nigeria".

References

Abubaka Tafawa Balewa (1952), speech in the Northern House of Assembly when he was the Prime minister of Nigeria

Achebe C. (1983), *The Trouble With Nigeria* (England: Heinemann Educational Books.)

Alli M C. (2001), *The Federal Republic of Nigerian Army: the siege of a nation*, (Lagos: Malthouse Press Ltd, 2001),

Anowai E. (2014) "Amalgamation of Nigeria: Unity or Conformity?" in L. Okika (ed) *The Nigeria Project: The Politics, The Challenges and Prospects* (Onitsha; A-Plus Technologies, 2014)

Aristotle (2001), *Basic Works of Aristotle* R.Mckeen (ed) (New York: Random House, 2001),p.1127

Asiegbu, LC, (1998), *Moral Philosophy and National Development* (Nsukka: Afro-Orbis Publications

Awotesu Olo (1977,) *Daily Times*, Lagos, Nov.5 1977

Chief Obafemi Awolowo, the then Leader of Western region

Dewey, J. (1997), *Reconstruction in Philosophy*, Boston: Beacon Press, 1957),

Eboh B,O. (1980), *Philosophy in the Growth of Nigeria*, (Onitsha: Veritas Press C)

Eboh B.O. (1990), *Living beyond Materialism*,(Enugu: SNAAP Press Nig Ltd, 1994)

Eboh B.O.(2015) "Rethinking Africa's Development crisis" in Igbafe, M.L and Agidigbi B.O (ed) *Explorations in African Philosophy: Essays in Honour of Anthony* (Ibadan: Bwright Integrated Publishers Ltd,)

Ekwutosi C.M. (2002) *Basic Issues in Ethics* (Nimo: Rex Charles & Patrick Ltd)

Ocran A.K. (1997 7), *Politics of the sword* (London: Rex Collings Ltd),

Omoregbe J.(1990), *Knowing Philosophy*, (Lagos: Joja Educational Research and Publishers Ltd,)

Russell B. (1994), *The Problem of Philosophy*, (London: Oxford University Press)

Sullivan D.J. (1992), *An Introduction to Philosophy* (Illinois; Tan Books Publishers)

Wole Soyinka, (1978), *The Man Died*, (England: Penguin books).

M. Chris Alli and the Peril of Religious Exclusivism: Religious Pluralism as a Panacea

Andrew F. Uduigwomen & Christopher A. Udofia

Introduction

M. Alli in his colossal and illuminating magnum opus, *The Federal Republic of Nigeria Army: the Siege of a Nation* (125), postulates Secularism as one of the core values of Nigeria. Alli bemoans the situation where, in spite of the value of secularism, some religious fundamentalists make absolute exclusivist theological claims whose imports invalidate the authenticity and legitimacy of other religions. Religious exclusivism in whatever disguise breeds inter-religious contempt and extremism which annul the possibility of constructive dialogue and predispose countries to the vulnerability of disintegration along religious lines. This piece identifies the panacea for religious exclusivism in the doctrine of religious pluralism practiced within the framework of the philosophical criteria of epistemological pluralism, human beneficence and social irenicism. The work concludes that the imbibement of religious pluralism and the concomitant philosophical criteria will avail Nigeria and the human society the needed therapy against the evils of religious exclusivism.

Unfathomably intertwined in the umbilicus of the culture of all people is the phenomenon of religion. Just like everyone is a cultural neighbour to everyone so is everybody, by extension, a member of one of the plethora of religions through which the human being fulfils his/her being as a *homo religiosus*. The reality of multiplicity of religions is a fact that cannot be speculated away. The forces of globalization have terminated and oblivionated the barriers that separated religions into disparate geographical and demographical collections. The contemporary human society is a society where all religions interface either through the social sphere, educationally, politically or via the multi-media. Cognizing this phenomenon of the profuse spread of multiple religions in the world, today, Jose' M. Vigil remarks that:

> Now we do not have to travel or leave our own environment to encounter people who behave differently than we do. In fact, many families today have members (especially younger members, whether blood relatives or in-laws) who practice a religion other than what was the "traditional" religion of the family (The Theology of Pluralism 28).

There was a time in the European history that Christianity enjoyed monopoly as the dominant religion. Such a state of affairs has become an antique of history and has given way to a contemporary state of fierce competition for authority among religions. The urgency of multiplicity of religions has heightened the need to fashion out a paradigm for dialogue and mutually respectful encounter among religions. This research sets out to provide such a model by proposing the practice of *religious pluralism* as a panacea for the problem of extremism among religions.

The Debate on Religious Pluralism

Pluralism is a polysemantic concept that has been employed by many thinkers to articulate and elaborate a spectra of issues and ideologies at the locus of which lies the idea of diversity. The remote history of religious pluralism is traceable to the emergence of political liberalism in the eighteenth century when Europe was advancing ideas that would proffer the needed panacea to sectarian violence, religious wars and religious intolerance. Since then, scholarly perspectives on religious approaches to diversity in religion are enunciated around the labels of Exclusivism, Inclusivism and Pluralism.

Exclusivism: The most preponderant theory that different religions uphold in their conception and appraisal of other religions is that of exclusivism. Exclusivism in religion conveys the import of epistemological absolutism whereby adherents of a particular religion aver that their religion has monopoly of truth and as such, is the sole way to salvation. In a riposte to the tenet of religious exclusivism, M. Chris Alli unveils the embedded contradiction in the exclusivist article by thrusting thus:

> One ponders the fate of billions of humanity if, no matter the state of our souls and the moral quality of our lives on earth, as individuals or collective followers of either Islam or Christianity or animists or atheists or Hindus, etc., which religion would qualify to enter the kingdom of God or Allah in the life beyond. If only one of these is the chosen religion of God, what would happen to billions of humanity who do not belong to the one so identified? Could God really allow the consumption in hell of billions of Christians or Moslems for the simple reason that they are all so identified? (*The Federal Republic of Nigerian Army: the Siege of a Nation* 125).

Most Muslims who advocate Islamic exclusivism make copious reference to some assertions in the Quran as divine justifications for religious exclusivism. Such assertions like: "Whosoever follows any other religion than Islam, it shall not be accepted of him and in the hereafter he will be among the losers" (3:85), "God's curse be upon infidels! Evil is that for which they have bartered away their souls. To deny God's own revelation, grudging that He should reveal His bounty to whom He chooses from his servants! They have incurred God's most inexorable wrath" (Quran 2:89 - 2:90), "Those that deny our revelations we will burn in fire" (Quran 4:56).

Religious exclusivism is not consigned to Islam alone. Biblical portions abound that are adduced by Christian extremists to defend religious exclusivism. In John 14:6 Jesus proclaims "I am the way, the truth and the life: no man cometh unto the father, but by me." The Chief Apostle, Peter corroborates Jesus' absolutist claim by asserting that there is no other name through which men may be saved except the name of Jesus (Act 4:10 - 12). This Biblical position conveying the sole authority on truth and salvation on Jesus has been accepted as an authoritative teaching and doctrine of the church and it is encapsulated in the popular Catholic dictum, "*extra ecclesiam nulla salus*" (outside the Church there is no salvation). The Catholic Church, being a leading Christian organization, reinforces the aforementioned Biblical tenets in her 1442 Council of Florence, where she categorically stated thus:

> The most Holy Roman Church firmly believes, professes and preaches that no one remaining outside the Catholic Church not only pagans but also Jews, heretics and schismatics could participate in eternal life. They would go to the eternal fire unless they become part of the Church prior to their death. No one, however great their almsgiving, even by shedding their blood for the name of Christ, can be saved unless they abide in the bosom and unity of the Catholic Church (Quoted in Hick and Hebblethwalte, 1980, p. 178).

This ecclesiocentric exclusivism of the Catholic Christian religion reigned supreme for centuries (about 500 years) as an infallible declaration and constituted the major rationale for belligerent evangelization and crusades toward non-Catholics and non-Christians who were viewed as a people in fire, as such any means of rescue and dreadful tactic; be it violent, degrading or in-human, were mobilized to bring people to the singular 'Name' for salvation.

Though the Catholic Church has departed and mitigated her stance on the "extra ecclesiam..." doctrine, she is yet to publicly repudiate the idea of absolutist theological exclusivism enshrined in the infallible Florentine proclamation.

The major philosophical problem that is associated with religious exclusivism is the problem of mutually contradicting monopolization of truth as attested to by the tenets of the various religions. For instance M. Chris Ali argues:

> ...large followers propelled by social, political and cultural circumstances prevailing in their times and areas of abode. These religious and ethnic diversities regulates inter-personal relationships and values. Consequently, in the Army, you have to be a Muslim to serve as aid-de-camp or military assistant to a Muslim officer. This is the pattern among most Christian officers (Alli: 23).

The logical implication of this opposing relationship among religions is that affirmation of the veracity of one religion completely cancels out or falsifies the veracity of any other religion. The problem of truth is a perennial philosophical conundrum that cuts across all the disciplines. There is hardly any unanimity among philosophers on the universally valid criterion of truth. Thus the question, what is truth? is an ultimate inquiry and invokes caution and humility from all stakeholders no matter how vast our knowledge expanse may be. This is so because human knowledge is as limited and finite as man.

Though the various religions recourse to different revelations, tenets, scriptures and divine personae as justifications for the truth of their religions, the lack of univocal accord regarding the criterion for justifying the truth of the different religions is a pointer to the fundamental inevitability of pluralism of truth.

The issue of truth and authenticity will be discussed later in this work, but it has to be stated at this juncture, that the averment of religious exclusivism that only one religion is true is a disposition that has been identified as the major underlying raison d'etre behind all intra cum inter-religious belligerence. Humanity always bears the toll and the devastation resulting from such clashes as years of human toil and civilization are reversed almost irretrievably.

> Today, another religion has interjected itself into the Nigerian socio-dictionary. They call it fundamentalism. It is amorphous, self-regenerating and all pervasive; sometimes, even deity has to be qualified by it, as well as after life. This new and strange phenomenon has taken a stranglehold on the lifeline of all Nigerian and components tribes. It frequently demarcates our individual social status, privileges and access to public good. Often, it finds expression in world-wide terrorism, aviation provocation (Alli: 5).

It has to be stated categorically that religion ought to be at the service of humanity, thus, every tenet of religion that negates this essence of religion is nugatory and repugnant and as such should be doggedly discountenanced.

Inclusivism: The non-pluralist parochial absolutist mind-set of monopoly over truth and salvation has been severely criticized as an imperialist mechanism and subtle instrument for violent extermination. Inclusivism was proposed to compensate for the ills of Exclusivism. Proponents of Inclusivism seem to project the thesis which avers that all religions have a share in the truth of the one religion.

A leading advocate of inclusivism is Karl Rahner, the Catholic theologian who developed the theory of "anonymous Christians." Rahner ("Christianity and Non-Christian Religions" 22 - 38) develops the thesis of inclusivism by arguing that God intended salvation for all men through Christianity and that the revelation of God to men is a historical process which must not necessarily occur to people of different places, creed and culture in a chronologically simultaneous manner. This implies that people of other religions implicitly share in God's intended act of revelation of Himself to all humanity through Christianity. Therefore, the non-Christian religions which aid the realization of a salvific life are to that extent legitimate religions and a true follower of such a legitimate religion cannot just be addressed as a non-Christian but an 'anonymous Christian'.

Rahner's inclusive axiom was of immense influence to Christianity. His concept of 'anonymous Christian' was instrumental to the volte-face of the Catholic Church in the second Vatican Council (1962 -1964) about non- Christian religions. In that council, the Church pronounced, against her former exclusivist posture, that:

> The Catholic Church rejects nothing which is true and holy in these religions. She has a sincere respect for those ways of acting and living, those moral and doctrinal teachings which may differ in many respects from what she holds and teaches…She therefore urges her sons, using prudence and charity to join members of other religions in discussions and collaboration. (40)

The cited assertion passes as a qualitative change of position by the Catholic Church which is universally perceived as a traditional institution entrenched in conservatism, dogmatism and near unreformable doctrines. The quantum leap brought about by the second Vatican greatly improved inter-religious dialogue and fired ecumenism beyond the mere intra-religious stratum to the inter-religious realm. This change in position, above all, encouraged a revolutionary change in consciousness and became the fertile ground for launching discourses on a new and radical idea on diversity. This radical idea was religious pluralism which is the last school of thought that this essay will expose.

The exclusivist Islamic position which is discussed above is however said to be mitigated in other portions of the Quran. Some advocates of inclusivism in Islam maintain that the exclusivist position is held by Muslim extremists and they exaggerated it so as to suit their whims and caprices. Ayatollah Murtadha Mutahhari (*Islam and Religious Pluralism* 35-41) argues that there are three schools of thought on the question of whether non-Muslims who have done good deeds are condemned to eternal damnation in hell.

The first is the school of Intellectuals. The intellectuals are of the opinion that God does not discriminate among human beings as such, good deeds done by any human being in spite of religious affiliation ought to be rewarded by a just God. The advocates of this position refer to such portions of the Quran which say: "Truly the believers and the Jews and the Serbians and the Christians - whosoever believeth in God and the last Day and doeth deeds of piety - no fear shall come upon them neither shall they grieve" (5:69).

The Serbians in that quoted portion are not clearly delineated in the Quran, so, some scholars view them as those who do not have a specific religion but believe in God. This group asserts the primacy of good works as the basis for salvation. In opposition to the intellectualists, is the rigid, pious group. They argue that the position of the intellectualist implies that there is no difference between Muslims and non-Muslims. If such a difference is obliterated, then the essence of being a Muslim is extinguished. The group asserts that the difference and essence of being a Muslim can be sustained only if the good deeds of Muslims are accepted to the exclusion of non-Muslims or for the evils committed by Muslims not to be punished in exclusion of non-Muslims. In substantiating their argument, the group refers to the fourteenth chapter of the Quran which states that the deeds of non-Muslims are like ashes blown away by the wind. This group holds the primacy of belief and faith as the bases for salvation. Mutahhari (35) observes that beyond the logics of the intellectualists and that of the rigid pious group, there is a third school of thought which he calls the third logic and it encapsulates the particular philosophy of the Quran on the subject matter of Muslims and non-Muslims. He argues that some people become Muslims as a result of circumstances of birth, geographical location or through research and study for the truth. If someone diligently searches for God through research and the truth is concealed from such a person without the person being at fault, God will not punish such a person. He cited the case of Descartes who embarked on a rational search and proof of God but ended up with Christianity as his religion. He observes that though Descartes opted for Christianity because it was the official religion of his country, Descartes was not opposed to the possibility of existence of another religion better than Christianity. Such people who have no conflict with the truth cannot be called unbelievers from the Muslim's perspective but 'dispositional Muslims'. Thus with this argument, the position of rigid pious group on the faith or belief based dichotomy between Muslims and non-Muslims is annulled. But "the use of religion as a political instrument had been introduced into the geographical space known as Nigeria as far back as the assault on indigenous belief systems began, long before the colonialists handed over the state to a new set of neo-colonialists in 1960." (Alli: 125)

Regarding the good deed argument, he distinguishes between society-related goodness and actor-related goodness. The former is made up of actions which are beneficial to the society. Most of the outward acts of goodness could be done with negative intentions and the society only applauds the outward beneficial outcome of the deed. For this first and social dimension, the goodness or evilness of an action depends on the external outcome of the action. Actor-related goodness refers to act performed by a person which are borne out of good intentions and motives. This is the spiritual second dimension of goodness or evilness of an action.

The author avers that both the social and spiritual dimensions must be satisfied for an action to be termed good or otherwise. This reasoning therefore invalidates the view of the intellectualist that good deed is equal for all people. The submission of Ayatullah here is that the outwardly oriented good deeds of people that are not activated by a corresponding good intention or motive would be repudiated as worthless by God.

Pluralism: Our dimension of pluralism in this context is limited to religious pluralism. The core advocate of this position in the scholarly world is the philosopher of religion, John Hick. He views religious pluralism as a belief which abhors the monopoly of any religion over truth and the salvific process ("Religious Pluralism and Islam" www.johnhick.org.uk.). He sets out to occasion a "Copernican revolution" in the universe of faiths whereby religious exclusivism, which he equated with geocentrism, is viewed as a prototype which has a singular religion at the centre with all other religions revolving around it is superseded by religious pluralism, which he equated with heliocentrism, which is the prototype which has God at the centre with all the religions revolving around it as planets. Hick ("The Theological Challenge of Religious Pluralism" 156 - 171) posits two principles as the premises for his conception of religious pluralism. The first is at realm with Kant's Copernican revolution which asserts that the process of knowledge acquisition is not a passive process whereby the world imposes itself on our knowing mind but an active process whereby the mind processes information and constructs meaning about the world in consonance with our human system of perception. The second principle avers that there is a distinction between what things are in themselves, Noumena and what appears to us through our cognitive medium, the Phenomena. He reasons that our awareness of the Ultimate, which people call various names is differently conceived, experienced and responded to within the different religions of the world. However, the noumenal Real, transcends the realm of conceptual experience, therefore we cannot know it as it is in itself but only as it is conceptualized through the knowledge frameworks of the various religions. He further elaborates this position by observing that "God in God's ultimate eternal self-existent being is ineffable or as I would rather say, transcategorial, beyond the scope of our human conceptual system" ("Religious Pluralism and Islam" www.johnhick.org.uk.).

In essence, religious pluralism is a school of thought that calls for universal ecumenism of religions as a universe of faiths that are equally valid and legitimate media of knowing the Supreme Being. It denounces the arrogation of absolute authority by one religion against other religions and holds that no religion possesses monopoly of knowledge of the ultimate nor does any religion enjoy and grant exclusive access to salvation. Yet

> in 1986 the Federal Government secretly sent a powerful delegation led by a cabinet Minister to a meeting of Islamic states under the

umbrella of Organization of Islamic Conference (OIC) at which Nigeria's Flag was flown presumably as an observer. The hue and cry that followed this led to the precipitate retirement of the number two citizen and Chief of Staff, the bright, swash-buckling Commodore Ebitu Ukiwe of the Nigerian Navy. (Alli: 126)

Religious exclusivism and humungous crimes against humanity

The horrific experience humanity has had as a result of religious exclusivism has left an indelible scar on the psyche of human beings. The opinion that one religion is superior to others because it possesses sole epistemic and salvific authority accords the adherents of the religion in question the impetus to violently prosecute the dogma and defend the tenets of the particular religion to the point of embarking on crusades for the forceful conversion or extermination of those who refuse to align with the tenets of their religion. The expression of this attitude is identified through different nomenclatures, ranging from religious extremism, fundamentalism, fanaticism, radicalism and lately, religious terrorism.

History is replete with horrendous cases of religious extremism that culminated in the perpetuation of massive crimes against humanity fuelled by extreme prosecution of religious belief. Most religious leaders are said to have suffered prosecution and death as a result of professing a belief that is not homogenous to the prevalent belief system. Jesus was executed because his teachings were not at realm with the traditional Jewish religion. The leader of Islam, Mohammed is said to have been driven out from many countries due to the fact of upholding an opposing religious belief. The Christian belief that the Jews committed deicide propelled the persecution of the Jews in the medieval time and became a major rationale for anti-Semitism which resulted in the Nazi Holocaust of the 1940s. During the medieval time the same religious extremism led to the nefarious activity of burning at stake of people who were believed to be heretics, dissenters or worshippers of Satan. The European religious wars of sixteenth and seventeenth centuries were informed by the attempt of different Christian groups namely, Catholicism, Lutheranism and Calvinism to exert supremacy over one another. The death toll from this war is pitched between 5.5 million and 18.5 million ("What were the Religious Wars/ Wars of Religion?" www.cbn.com). In a graphic analysis, the document authored by The Truth reveals that religious violence prosecuted by Muslims in history has led to the killing of 51 million Christians, 80 million Hindus, 10 million Buddhists, and about 120-125 million Africans (Islam: Religion of Peace or War?). Racism, imperialism and other forms of discrimination are carried out with religious legitimation. The racial imperialist invasion and enslavement in Africa were conducted on the basis that the religion and race of the colonial masters were superior to those of the natives. The caste system in India is premised on the doctrine of divine institution while the oppressive discrimination against women in most religious groups is often defended as a divine ordinance. Our country Nigeria has remained perpetually under the travails of religious extremists. Since the onset of democracy in Nigeria in 1999 to this present time (2017), Nigeria has been under the asphyxiating violent grip of the Boko Haram Islamic terrorist sect who capriciously maintains that Nigeria must become an Islamic theocentric state or goes into extinction. The carnages, pillages and human kidnappings committed by this group have comatosed all known pillars of belligerence by their sheer unquantifiable magnitude and have engaged the country on a retrogressive course of recoil to the despicable Hobbesian state.

Religious extremism as a bane to national integration and security

Our country, Nigeria has been described in most quarters as the most religious country in the world (Blueprinting.com 2012). This tag speaks volumes about our religious diversity. Our existence as a nation of multiple religions ought to constitute a formidable platform to inculcate religious tolerance. The paradox, however, is that our religious multiplicity breeds inter-religious rancour and intolerance that have left the country bleeding from the un-healing sores of fanaticism. Fanaticism has diffused into the consciousness of Nigerians to create a condition of antagonistic polarity which is a threat to the cohesive socio-political existence of Nigeria. Since the major political blocks of the North, West, South and East in Nigeria are carved along religious lines with a demography which shows Muslims as the majority in the North and West while Christians constitute the majority in the South and East, this has resulted in a state of violent fissility between the Muslim and Christian political zones.

This rivalrous state that characterizes the major political demographics as well as most of the conflicts we have experienced in Nigeria can be clinically traced to the quest for supremacy among the two major religions in Nigeria. The sentiment of religious hegemony is so prevalent to the extent that national consciousness which is an imperative for existence as a nation has been eroded. In Nigeria, sensitive political decisions which ought to be taken from the premise of national unity are either vigorously projected and upheld or dangerously hunted and murdered on the basis of consistency or inconsistency with some religious tenets and expediency.

It is pertinent that we remind ourselves that section 38(1) of the 1999 Constitution of Nigeria dictates that "Every person shall be entitled to freedom of thought, conscience and religion including freedom to change his religion or belief and freedom either alone or in community with others, and in public or in private to manifest and propagate his religion or belief in worship, teaching, practice and observance". This constitutional provision envisions our existence as a pluri-religious entity and does not in any way imply a mono-religious culture. It is therefore in this light that every attempt to register Nigeria as a member of any religious organization is tantamount to a breach of the constitutional provision in section 10 which solemnly affirms that "The Government of the Federation or the State shall not adopt any religion as State Religion". This constitutional provision clearly prohibits any attempt by the federation or the individuating units to project, protect and propagate any religion as a state-sponsored religion. It is, therefore, an assault on the grundnorm and sense of nationality of the people for any group or sect in Nigeria to be calling for the forceful imposition of a particular religion on Nigeria.

All public or clandestine attempts to Christianize, Islamize or adopt a particular religion as the state religion in Nigeria is a threat to national integration and security which drags Nigeria to the brink of anarchy. The widely speculated claim of the possible disintegration of Nigeria is not borne out of the decoding of a complex scientific thesis but predicated on the logical inference of the bastardizing atrocities committed by the various religious fanatics who insist that it is either Nigeria exists as a mono-religious nation or it does not exist at all. How can Nigeria be rescued from the brink of bastardization and disintegration occasioned by religious exclusivism? The possible panacea for this dilemma shall be the crux of the next phase of the discourse.

Religious pluralism as the panacea for religious extremism

The major attraction of religious pluralism is that it promotes tolerance among religions. The attitude of tolerance which is required by religious pluralism can be cultivated by the inculcation of some core philosophical principles as the truth and authenticity criteria for the validation and harmonious plural existence of religions in Nigeria. These criteria include:

i. **The Criterion of Epistemological Pluralism:** The leading cause of rivalry among the different religious bodies has been the claim of monopoly over truth by different religions. Epistemological pluralism contributes some cardinal ingredients to interreligious dialogue. This criterion recognizes the fundamental multidimensionality and complexity of the absolute Truth and the fact of its manifestation in different ways to people of different religions. It manifests itself as the Allah to Islam, Adonai to the Jews, the Holy Trinity to Christians, Brahman,Tao, Vishnu to the different Eastern religions and the supreme deity of African traditional religion known by different names, etc. The different religions should be viewed as the different apertures for knowing the absolute and none should arrogate to itself or be conferred with the imperial title of absolute dominance over other religions nor should any religion be viewed as possessing an exclusive epistemological license to the Absolute.

ii. **The Ethical Criterion of Human Beneficence:** Religion exists as a medium for the fulfilment and realization of the nature of man as a *homo religiosus* who possesses an inherent transcendent element that yearns for the Absolute. So religion is a vital appurtenance in the strife of man to achieve the total vortex of goodness necessary for completion of humanity. This ethical criterion for religion can be couched in two ways:

i) *The Positive Rubric.* This rubric avers that the ennobling virtues that enhance the betterment of human existence should be maximized by the various religions. The rule of this rubric states that the level to which the moral condition of humanity is improved due to religion should be the moral parametric gauge for determining the goodness and truthfulness of a religion.

ii) *The Negative Rubric.* This rubric embodies the rule which denounces as bad and false any religion which minimizes or impedes the realization of the totality of the ennobling human values. Every religion that diminishes humanity, disrespects human rights, extenuates charity, denigrates freedom and polarizes humanity is to the extent of such inconsistency with the positive human moral orientation a bad and false religion that ought to evoke immediate rebuke and disapproval.

Truth and goodness are intricately intertwined and they transcend religious confinement and affiliation. It is in this respect that the determination of the truth and goodness of any religion cannot be conducted based on the limited particular criteria enshrined in each religion but can only be achieved through an appeal to the discipline of philosophy which provides the fundamental universal framework for the cognition of such transcendent values. A true Muslim or Hindu is a good Muslim or Hindu and their goodness will be as true as the goodness of an atheist or that of a Christian. Truth and goodness are universal categories that cannot be defined exclusively using the nomenclature of any particular culture, creed and race.

Though every religion contains within themselves some particular criteria for truth and goodness, adherents of all religions should realize that none of the particular criteria can be whimsically imposed on other religions. Such approach will result in inter-religious clash and a situation whereby every religion will want to impose its whims and caprices on others. This will reinforce extremism and defeat the gains accruable from inter-religions dialogue. Positive inter-religious encounter can be achieved not by direct exclusive invocation of the truth and goodness criteria embedded in the Christian Bible, the Muslim Quran, the Hindu Gita, the Buddhist Sutras or the traditions of other aboriginal religions but by reference to the transcendent and universal criteria of truth and goodness churned out by the canons of reasonability which does not bear any idiosyncratic trademark.

iii. **The Criterion of Social Irenicism:** Religion should be both a ladder to the divine and a conciliatory bridge among humanity. In its vertical orientation, religion derives the spiritual impetus necessary for the fulfilment of its horizontal orientation of serving as an instrument of peace among men. It should denounce aggression and belligerence and provide succour and solace to the wounded and desolate. The irenic vocation of religion should not be limited by creed, race or nation but should be a universal non-belligerence criterion for all true religions. Enshrined in this criterion is the demand that no religion should exhibit aggression but should instead be the rallying force for galvanizing humanity and the paradigm for reconciliation in the time of distress.

Conclusion

The Nigerian government, in 1997, committed a prohibitive and inflammatory act of registering the country as a member of the Organisation of Islamic Countries (OIC) (Alli 126). This act was a flagrant negation of the purported secularity of Nigeria and an affront on the sensibility of Nigerians as a multi-religious people. This prompted every reasonable Nigerian in the ilk of Alli to query: "should any government worth its salt promote a sectional religion clandestinely in a secular state for the benefit of a region?"(Alli 126). In this work, religious exclusivism is identified as the singular causal force that can impel a country to take such an ominous move. Essentially, the work located religious pluralism as a panacea for religious exclusivism and stipulated three cardinal philosophical principles, namely, epistemological pluralism, human beneficence and social irenicism as the truth and authenticity criteria for the validation and peaceful mutual coexistence of all religions in Nigeria.

References

Alli, Chris M. (2001), *The Federal Republic of Nigeria Army: The Siege of a Nation.* Lagos: Malthouse

Blueprinting.com(2012), Politics of Insecurity and Religious Crises. http://blueprint.com/politics-of-InsecuritY-and-Religious-Crises-2,

Hick, John "Religious Pluralism and Islam". www.johnhick.org.uk.

Mutahhari, Ayatollah Murtadha (2006), *Islam and Religious Pluralism*.UK: World Federation of Khoja Shia-Asheri Muslim Communities.

Rahner, Karl (2001),"Christianity and the Non-Christian Religions". *Christianity and other Religions.* John Hick and Brian Hebblethwaite Eds. Oxford: One world.

The Truth Islam: Religion of Peace or War? www.cbn.com, 2014.

Vatican 11 (2001) , "Declaration on the Relation of the Church to Non-Christian Religions," *Christianity and other Religions.* John Hick and Brian Hebblethwaite Eds. Oxford: One world.

Vigil, Jose (2008),*The Theology of Religious Pluralism.* Zurich: LIT VERLAG,

"What were the Religious Wars/Wars of religion?" www.gotquestion.org.

Federalism and Philosophy of Development

Chapter 9

Mohammed Chris Alli, Militocracy and the Crisis of Leadership in a Plural State

-Chidozie Okoro

Introduction

The problematic of leadership in contemporary Africa is so hydra-headed and seems insurmountable all because of the stubborn adherence to colonial structures that are meant to divide Africans further. Worst still, the refusal to return to the pre-colonial pluralistic structure of Africans has rather made the situation more alarming. Nationalism in Europe and Asia has been mostly ethnically based and this largely explains why these other parts of the world have been very authentic in the reformation and transformation of their various societies to the global pedestal of humanism. In contrast, nationalism is contemporary Africa has consistently followed the determined path of colonial structuring. This will definitely not allow for liberation and emancipation in the true sense for the simple reason that freedom cannot be garnered upon a foreign structure. This, basically, explains why the project of decolonization completely failed. It is against this background that militocracy or military rule in Africa is considered an aberration in the sense that it defiantly continuous to truncate the genuine effort of evolving a strong indigenous ideological foundation for the emancipation of Africa. It is also in the forgoing light and in agreement with Mohammed Chris Alli that militocracy is considered to be a siege on the new nation states of Africa.

Military governments having no democratic pretensions, no matter how benevolent, manage security, while democratically elected governments manage freedom. Military governments by their nature are abnormal, they are also transitory and even temporary (Alli, 2001:150).

> The average Nigerian leader spends 80 per cent of his energies on regime survival and the politics of crisis management. It is therefore for these reasons that national self-examination and assessment become compelling and inevitable...The alternative is a bloody revolution, both of a class and of classic nature, or a tribal insurgency, or a surging of nationalism by constrained smaller tribes of the nature of Eritrea, the Kurds and Ijaws. History is against Nigeria's current path to greatness and glory for now, it inhibits our energies and frustrates our resolve as constituents of a united entity (p. 220).

The above quotations summarize the story of Nigeria as captured by Mohammed Chris Alli in his masterpiece, *The Federal Republic of Nigerian Army: The Siege of a Nation*, which can be described as an eclectic perusal of the problematic of structure and leadership of a plural polity. In one fell swoop, the book makes comprehensive and holistic representations of Nigeria from perspectives that are historical, cultural, political, ideological, economical, psychological, psycho-analytical and philosophical. Most vividly, the process by which the Nigerian polity evolved is vehemently questioned, just as the author loudly wonders if indeed Nigeria qualifies to be called a body politic. Of all the emergent new states created by the colonialists, Nigeria presents the most nauseating and complex structure, making governance intricate and cumbersome. Little wonder the author aptly describes Nigeria as a "fatalistic polity" (p. 137).

Balkanization, through the scramble for and partition of Africa, made Nigeria an ensemble of over 250 ethnicities. And since colonization could not endow these ethnicities with a common heritage, the Nigerian space became an arena for stampede among the triumvirate of Igbo, Hausa and Yoruba. With the antecedents of the coup and counter coup of 1966, the Civil War afforded the northern predators the opportunity to firmly grab Nigeria, thereby reducing leadership in the country to the triumvirate of Hausa, Fulani and Kanuri (all of northern extraction); who use the military as an instrument of subjugation to ensure the continuous grip on power (see p. 133 and chapter 11). Eventually, military dominance of Nigerian politics transformed the country from a democracy into militocracy.

Militocracy has been variously defined as militarism, military rule or kakistocracy. It is a junta government or government of the military cabal or military clique. It is a government solely imposed by the military for the military and by the military. It is a government of military dictatorship wherein political power resides with the military. It is similar but not identical to stratocracy, which is the same as a state governed directly by the military. Its basic feature is that it operates by garrisons. In other words, a garrisoned state is a militarized state, which M. C. Alli technically renders as "polity militarization" (p. 162). Overtime, militocracy has left Nigeria "totally militarized' just as 'the military has become dangerously politicized" (p. 199). What more, democracy in Nigeria has been hijacked by the "militricians" (p. 194) of dominantly northern extraction. Retired military officers are not only the custodians of Nigeria's democracy, they in fact, have transformed themselves into civilian leaders.

But the military have their own reason for wading into Nigeria's politics. One of such reasons is contained in the speech delivered in October 1999 at Harvard University by General Obasanjo who, according to M.C. Alli, confirmed that:

> Military incursion into African politics in the sixties and the seventies were generally greeted with degrees of euphoria. The ordinary African felt a sense of security with the uniform, so to speak. And political thinkers, in disregard of their liberal philosophical roots in democratic theory, hailed the unelected military rulers of the postcolonial state by ascribing to them several virtues. According to the literature of the day, unlike the politicians who were prone to corruption, the military by training, comprised an officer class of honest gentlemen. Whereas the politicians were parochial, the military had broader orientation towards the nationalist interest. The politicians were also burdened with the alleged subjectivism and irrationalities of traditional cultural heritage, whereas the military, by virtue of their profession, were imbued with technical rationality, as well as efficiency. These professional attributes were regarded as eminently functional for development and political stability (p. 179).

If we contrast the foregoing quotation with the opening citations made above, it would seem that the Nigerian state started on a faulty note. Put differently, if society is comparable to a tree and we go ahead to make analysis of the Nigerian tree, it will not be wrong to conclude that the Nigerian tree, from the beginning, suffered abnormal growth in the sense that it had its branches to the ground and its roots pointing skywards. This obvious abnormality in growth could well explain why the Nigerian polity has continually being in disarray and impermeable to serene and cohesive governance. So, to the fundamental questions: Are security and freedom necessarily dichotomized and irreconcilable? And are the military professionally trained to govern? These fundamental questions need to be philosophically dissected in order to put things into proper perspective.

Emergence and Essence of Society

How did society evolve and what is the essence of its evolution? From Plato to the philosophers of social contractarianism, various reasons have been adduced for the emergence and essence of the society. For instance, in The Republic, Plato advanced economic factor as that which necessitated the emergence of the state and also determines its essence:

> ...a state comes into existence because no individual is self-sufficing; we all have many needs. So, having all these needs, we call in one another's help to satisfy our various requirements; and when we have collected a number of helpers and associates to live together in one place, we call that settlement a state...Apparently, the state owes its existence to our needs, the first and greatest need being the provision of food to keep us alive. Next we shall want a house; and thirdly, such things as clothing (1966: 54-55; Part II, Chapter VI).

For Plato then, the bare necessities of life catalysed humans to engender society into being. The fact that these bare necessities of life are economic throws up a greater challenge of coordination and cooperation which makes societal engineering inevitable. In essence, the coordination and organization of economic activities equals the coordination and organization of the society, which happens to be the goal of politics. Politics is about governance, governance has to do with the ability and capacity to coordinate and organize societal affairs which in turn entails leadership, making governance and leadership coordinates. To be a leader one must possess virtuous qualities such as courage, temperance, prudence, liberality, candour, etc., all of which combine to define steady character. For this reason, Plato and most political philosophers make ethics the foundation of politics.

Consequently, the essence of society as it relates to politics is to ensure that justice is obtainable. In other words, the end of politics is to institute justice in the state and justice in turn consists in ensuring fairness, equity and balance in the polity. It is in this sense that Plato renders justice as the act of giving to everyone his/her own due (p. 8; Part I, Chapter II). It is the judicious management of societal resources that result into wealth creation or what Plato classifies as "the luxurious state" (Part II, Chapter VII). He then made analogy of justice in the soul (i.e. the human personality) and justice in the state. The human personality comprises the head (i.e. reason), the heart (i.e. the spirited part of man) and the stomach (i.e. the lower appetites) which correspond to the Philosopher King, the Soldiers or Auxiliary and the Artisans in the society respectively. Justice in the soul is obtained when reason governs, directs and coordinates the affairs of the appetites. In the society, the philosopher king as the guardian, should govern, not the soldier or the artisan.

The soldier and the artisan are people of untamed emotions who have not attained maturity or harmony of the soul and are incapable of instituting justice in the polity. This, perhaps, explains why Plato advised that people of the heart and the stomach should be distanced from governance, it also explains why he insisted that kings must be philosophers or that philosophers must become kings. He also developed a rigorous education system for leadership which include the study of drama, music, poetry, physical training, mathematics, arithmetic, geometry, solid geometry, astronomy, harmonics and dialectics; supposed arts and sciences that train the soul to attain justice and replicate same in the society (see Part II, Chapter IX and Part III, Chapter XXVI).

Philosophers after Plato do not disagree with him that justice is the highest point of political organization, the manner of what constitutes justice and how justice could be obtained are the things in contention. Whereas Plato conceived moral goodness to be the highest point of justice, Aristotle in his *Nichomachean Ethics* conceived it in the pursuit of happiness (i.e. the theory of eudaemonism), Epicurus saw it in the pursuit of pleasure (i.e. the theory of hedonism), Jeremy Bentham saw it in the theory of utilitarianism, which is further anchored on the hedonic calculus of the – greatest happiness for the greatest number.

Philosophers of the contractarianism theory took the discourse to other heights. For Thomas Hobbes as it is for Immanuel Kant, the evolution of the society meant the taming of bestial and brutish nature of humans. In the understanding of Hobbes, before the evolution of society, humans lived in the state of nature whereby life was brutish, nasty and short, disallowing commerce, economy and industry, thereby necessitating the evolution of the society and the investment of absolute power in the Leviathan, whose duty it is to institute civil order. This act of humanizing the bestial and brutish nature of humans, making the unsociable social, culturing the uncultured, enlightening the unenlightened and civilizing the uncivilized; Kant describes as the – unsocial sociability. Thus, for Kant "man is destined by reason to live in the society with fellow men and in it cultivate himself, to civilize himself, and to make himself moral through the arts and the sciences" (1974: xxi). Rousseau and Locke on the other hand, uphold the view that man is by nature innocent, but that society, through its complexity, corrupts man to be evil. Hence, the essence of civil rule is to reform society so that the best of man can blossom.

Ultimately, the political organization of society for economic prosperity is made most possible by justice, while justice in the society in turn promote security and freedom for the purpose of peace and stability.

Security and Freedom in the Society

From the perspectives of Plato, Hobbes and Kant, the ultimate reason for the evolution of society is to guarantee security and freedom to her inhabitants. This is further substantiated by the following Igbo proverbs: *igwe bu ike* – togetherness is strength; *ibuanyidanda* – with solidarity, no burden is insurmountable for members of the society; *mbikota bu ndu, mbisasi bu onwun* – cooperating and coexisting together is security, lack of cooperation and coexistence is insecurity and death.

There is need for security both within and outside the polity. Security within the state or intra-security deals with the limits of freedom of the members of the society with regards to their rights and duties, while security outside the state or inter-security refers to how states relate with each other as it concerns the limits of freedom, of the rights and the duties of every polity and her members in interdependence with other polities at the regional, continental and international levels. There is also security against the vagaries of the forces of nature as well as the responsibilities we bear towards nature itself. In other words, since society is people oriented, it follows that the only way to keep society safe and secure is by ensuring that every member has a sense of belongingness, because, it is when people feel obligated to society that they gather the will and the courage to fervently protect it. A secured state is one in which her members have a sense of patriotism and there is no patriotism when the citizens have no free access to the good things of life. This is where justice, along with other factors such as acceptance, legitimacy and stability, become the coordinating points between security and freedom.

In contemporary times, John Rawls and Robert Nozick, discuss the issues of security and freedom in a democracy. In several of his works (*A Theory of Justice, Political Liberalism and Justice as Fairness: A Restatement*) Rawls developed the theory of political liberalism. He distinguished a liberal state from decent, outlaw and burdened states. A liberal state is a people oriented state based on the principle of reasonable pluralism and with the following ideals:

- protecting its political independence, its territory, and the security of its citizens;
- maintaining its political and social institutions and its civic culture;
- securing its proper self-respect as a people, which rests on its citizens' awareness of its history and cultural accomplishments (*Stanford Encyclopaedia of Philosophy*, 2017: online).

A decent people or state is one whose affairs are organized based on a comprehensive dominant doctrine of either religion or culture, not on the principles of political liberalism and reasonable pluralism. Though the activities of such states or peoples may be well structured, but minority groups such as women and non-natives, may be excluded from certain rights. Outlaw states are non-complaint to the fundamental rights of people and the common ethic and rule of justice of the international community, while burdened states lack the resources to accomplish standards required of an egalitarian society.

Security and freedom in the liberal state is attained based on the principle of – justice as fairness, which captures the ideal sense of justice within the liberal state. Rawls further distinguishes two guiding ideas of justice as fairness from two principles of justice as fairness. The two guiding principles of justice as fairness comprise the negative and positive theses. The negative thesis states that factors such as circumstance of birth, gender, ethnicity and race are purely accidental and should not be allowed to deny any member of the society his or her fundamental rights; to do so would mean to demean or dehumanize such individual or individuals. From this derives the positive distributary thesis wherein Rawls espoused the idea of – equality-based reciprocity, which states that: all social goods are to be distributed equally, unless an unequal distribution would be to everyone's advantage. This is further regulated by the two principles of justice as fairness as follows:

First Principle: Each person has the same indefeasible claim to a fully adequate scheme of equal basic liberties, which scheme is compatible with the same scheme of liberties for all;

Second Principle: Social and economic inequalities are to satisfy two conditions:
1. They are to be attached to offices and positions open to all under conditions of fair equality of opportunity;
2. They are to be to the greatest benefit of the least-advantaged members of society (the difference principle). (Rawls, 2001: 42–43).

Consequently, as it pertains to security and freedom in the polity, the hallmark of justice as fairness for Rawls is that fairness requires that in "public political life, nothing need be hidden…there is no need for the illusions and delusions of ideology for society to work properly and for citizens to accept it willingly." (2005: 68–69).

Still on the matter of security and freedom in the society, whereas Rawls leans more towards Plato and rejects Bentham's utilitarianism, Robert Nozick leans more towards John Locke and Immanuel Kant. Following Locke's argument that government exists to protect the lives and property of the people and Kant's second categorical imperative to treat humans as kingdoms of ends, not as means only, Nozick, in Anarchy, State and Utopia, developed the theory of minimal state based on the principle of justice as entitlement. The doctrine of libertarianism by Nozick, as opposed to Rawls liberalism, seeks for minimal participation of the state in the lives of individuals and groups that make up a polity. It is in this sense that Nozick speaks of the people as self-owners whose individual rights are guaranteed by the degree of state interference. Should the state equitably and satisfactorily guarantee everyone's rights that would amount to utopia and should the state allow individuals as self-owners the freedom to attain their rights on self-term that would amount to anarchy; thereby making the role of the state to be regulatory through reasonable coercion. This account of Nozick may be described as a compelling defence of the state, particularly, free-market libertarianism. It is in this sense that Nozick submits that "the need for security justifies only a minimal or 'night-watchman' state, since it cannot be demonstrated that citizens will attain any more security through extensive governmental intervention" (1974: 25-27). To be pungent, security and freedom are inseparable Siamese Twins in matters of state organization.

M.C. Alli and the question of the emergence of the Nigerian State

In chapter 7 of the book, *The Federal Republic of Nigerian Army: The Siege of a Nation*, M.C. Alli clearly shows that the Nigerian state is not one that was evolved by Nigerians, but was rather put together by the British colonial masters for their own convenience. "The colonial office', says M. C. Alli, "realizing the financial burden of sustaining the administration of the North, decided to bring the Northern and Southern Protectorates and Lagos Colony together under a single unitary administration in order to laden the Southern economy with the administrative cost of running the North" (2001: 92). Nigeria is therefore a "colonial amalgam" otherwise known as "new state" (see Ogundowole, 2006: title page & 2011: 145), it is not a social contract of the peoples and cultures that comprise the Nigerian polity.

Given that the state by every status is a deliberate and conscious creation of the people, by which they decide all by themselves what ideals, values and legal system that should uphold the polity, the question then arises if Nigeria can indeed be called a state in the real sense of the word? An imposition is never a creation of the people and would as such not augur well for the people; instead, the compressed strange bed fellows will perpetually struggle to stampede each other out. Worst still, the transposition of the colonial order meant the transvaluation of values from the traditional notion and structure of governance to the transposed principles and structure of governance, hence, the uprooting of the African superstructure for a foreign one.

From the 1953 Constitutional Conference, regional autonomy and self-government began to be gradually installed, which eventually culminated in the Lyttleton Constitution of 1954 that ushered in federalism as Nigeria's governmental system. In M. C. Alli's view:

> These constitutional landmarks formed the building blocks for articulating and promoting a participatory system of government in which all the component parts and nationalities constituting the Nigerian union should have found self-expression and sense of belonging (2001: 89).

Lamentably:

> Structurally, these arrangement contained seeds of instability and inequality that were to create fears amongst the underdogs and place the portals of power at the steps of the three main tribes (Hausa/Fulani, Igbo, Yoruba triumvirate) within the geographical north, east and west (Ibid.).

Britain as a plural society fashioned a governmental system that grants self-autonomy to all her ethnic nationalities thereby allowing each of them (England, Scotland, Wales and Northern Ireland) the opportunity to develop along the line of her culture. Therefore, Britain knew how strategic and structurally important culture is to the sustainable development of peoples and nations. Yet, the same Britain went ahead to superimpose a hybridized and most complicated social and political structure that is intricate and difficult to sustain, thereby hampering genuine development. Nationalism in Europe had always either been ethnically based or brought about the unification of ethnic nationalities. This is the case with the Italian and Prussian unification in the nineteenth century Europe. In the twentieth century, the dreaded Soviet Union got defunct; the same fate bedevilled the huge Balkan states of Yugoslavia and Czechoslovakia; all of which have splintered into ethnic nationality states. Most recently, Russia is entangled in the battle of unifying all Russian speaking people to the Russian Federation. The reverse is the case in Africa where African leaders vehemently fight to obliterate any opposition that will dear challenge the imposed colonial order, notwithstanding the fact that the superimposed structure is antithetical to the traditional societal structure of Africans.

In traditional Africa, society was seen as an organic whole animated and motivated by spirit or life-force. Colonialism brought a new notion of society that is structured on matter. This materialist doctrine of society sees the "state as man-made and therefore partly an artificial coordinating structure superimposed on a pre-existing natural community or nation" (Anyanwu, 1981: 297). The homogeneity of traditional societies was balkanized and brutally splintered. Fred G. Burke put this point succinctly thus:

> We need add little about the manner in which African boundaries arbitrarily separate cultures, languages and natural regions. The artificial delineation of what have since become sovereign states, when added to the small scale of indigenous traditional African cultures and societies has reversed the orthodox process of nationalism whereby linguistic and cultural communities seek to win independent state status (1964: 86).

Because the federal system imposed on Nigeria blatantly fails to acknowledge the multi-plural nature of the country, ethnic nationality agitations for self-autonomy will continually be rife. Not when Nigeria's federalism privileges 'majority will' over and above the African communalistic notion of 'general will' based on the principle of holistic pluralism. In the view of M.C. Alli, this accounts for the reason why:

> Each of the arbitrary regional groupings was engulfed subsequently in a deadly struggle to enforce their respective hegemonies within their respective regional enclaves. This struggle has been extended to the centre in the effort to promote relative but respective advantages. The principle of representation anchors political power and central control in the notion of game of numbers by which the party with the highest votes cornered the plums of office at the centre. By every means imaginable, each strove to maintain a favourable tilt and dominance, not only at the centre but also within the regions. This condition explains the restiveness and sense of loss that has characterized Nigeria's political equations and continuing mutual fears, cries and instability (Alli, 2001: 89).

Before the colonization of Africa, the states and nations of Africa were not only fully autonomous, but in charge of their resources both renewable and non-renewable. Colonialism completely denied Africans both political autonomy and access to the resources of their lands. The emergence of the newly independent states of Africa was supposed to restore back to Africans the autonomy and the resources that they lost (the instrument for achieving this being the constitution), but this never happened. Rather, internal colonization replaced external colonization. In the case of Nigeria, the constitution became a means for enthroning ethnic superiority and military dictatorship, the instrument through which unitary federalism was foisted on Nigeria. Thus:

> While constitution-making since independence in 1960 has been marked by seemingly wide consultations, the products without exception, have been doctored and altered by successive military dictators, often, in the process, burying the hopes and aspirations of some weak national interest groups or fundamental state issues...successive constitutions have lacked civil and sovereign authority. Military governments who derive their legitimacy from their blazing tanks and rifles impose them on the nation, as it were. These constitutions have been deficient in conception, lacking in wide national participation and appeal. Being therefore unrepresentative of the people, they have without expression, been without peoples'

general acclaim, protection and participation (90 – 91).

Worst still: "No constitution has been a subject of plebiscite since independence and so long as constitutions have the approval of the big three, all manner of rationalizations will be adduced to justify the outcome" (p. 91). And to maintain the forced unity of Nigeria, fundamental issues that are germane to the stability and sustainable development of the state are declared as "no-go areas" (Ibid.). This makes Nigeria a nation built on the imbalance of "triangular factors' and 'triangle of fears" (pp. 92 & 94), whereby, out of over 250 ethnic groups that make up the state of Nigeria, only three dictate national affairs and out of these three of Hausa/Fulani, Igbo and Yoruba, one (the Hausa/Fulani) plays the dominant role, thereby creating a lope-sided structure of governance and leadership. This obvious imbalance makes Nigeria most delicate and unstable in the sense that the nation's unity is based on the oil resource of Niger Delta; a fundamental factor which M.C. Alli strikingly captures thus: "But for the Niger Delta oil resource, Nigeria as we know it today would have disintegrated since independence. What may be on the ground would be a multitude of nation states on the River Niger/Benue areas of West Africa" (p. 93). This delicate unity is forcefully kept together by the North predicated on four strategic leverages, namely:
i. geography,
ii. the Ahmadu Bello's 'north for the north' or northernization, language which eases intra-regional communication,
iii. religion which provides political connection and rally, and
iv. the military as a fall-back position should these demographic advantages be neutralized – with the latter explaining the sophisticated design of a military high command that is exclusive and responsive to northern interest (p. 95).

The blatant lack of ideology coupled with the northernization of the military has not only put the nation in disarray, but has clandestinely turned the nation into a military pariah state whereby the common will of the citizenry is stifled for the interest of the cabal. This leaves a serious question mark on the essence of the Nigerian state.

M.C. Alli and the question of the essence of the Nigerian State

By essence is meant the fundamental features, the basic attributes, nature, characteristics or intrinsic qualities that make a thing what it is. To speak of the essence of a thing is to inquire into the meaning or the value of that thing. The theory of meaning or value properly so-called is known as axiology. Axiology is the philosophical theory of value, embracing ethics and aesthetics mainly, and extending to other human endeavours that are technical, prudential, hedonic, political, economic, financial, scientific, and technological. Generally, value orientation in life helps to determine focus, direction, goal and purpose of an individual, project, organization or society. This makes the probe into the essence of the Nigerian state very cogent.

On a social/political premise, essence refers to the value orientation or core values of a society that are usually encoded in national ideology. In other words, the essence of any society is defined by her ideological orientation realised as social consciousness. Ideology as a form of social consciousness became prominent in the philosophy of Karl Marx. In the preface to his work entitled: *A Contribution to the Critique of Political Economy*, first published in 1895, Marx stated thus:

> In the social production of their life, men enter into definite relations that are indispensable and independent of their will; these relations of production correspond to a definite stage of development of their material forces of production. The sum total of these relations of production constitutes the economic structure of society — the real foundation, on which raises a legal and political superstructure and to which correspond definite forms of social consciousness. The mode of production of material life determines the social, political and intellectual life process in general. It is not the consciousness of men that determines their being, but, on the contrary, their social being that determines their consciousness (culled from Google).

Ideology as social consciousness is the place where theory and action combine through policy for the establishment of political stability and the attainment of economic prosperity. It is based on the foregoing that Nkrumah states that "practice without thought is blind; thought without practice is empty" (1978: 79). Robert Putman on his part defines ideology as "a life guiding system of beliefs, values and goals affecting political style and action" (cited by Thomson, 2007: 31). Ideology is the practical and pragmatic way by which the entire principles of philosophy are made relevant to the task of economic development. It usually encompasses the entire range of systems of ideas and theories of beliefs present in an era or in a society (Plamenatz, 1970: pp. 24, 74 & 131). Hence, any profound ideology should clearly spell out a consistent and comprehensive theory about society, man, mind, cognition and so on, which serve as anchor for programmes that are economic, political, social, educational, cultural, legal and so on. On matters of economic development, ideology should identify the problems confronting a particular society and proffer solutions; it should identify the resources of the state, human and material, and what the state lacks; it should specify how a state can go about to surmount her economic limitations and at the same time proceed on the effective management of her resources for the good of all; it should also specify that the task of economic development is one that requires strict professionalism for the enthronement of discipline and excellence since only this can ensure adherence to the blue print or plan for economic development in order to ensure that waste is avoided and that labour is well articulated and rewarded. This is the point where policy matters most.

Policy is a deliberate plan of action to guide decisions and achieve rational outcome(s) which may apply to government, private sector and other groups. Ideology and policy are interwoven in the sense that while ideology provides the sight or light for policy and planning, policy on the other hand is the very instrument for bringing ideology into fruition. The accomplishment of national and economic development through ideology and policy is however, not possible without a think tank who through strict supervision ensures that the goals of ideology and the action plan of policy are well articulated and implemented for the good of all. The watchwords here are discipline or the iron determination to succeed, professionalism backed with sound educational system, the liberal attitude that allows for freedom of thought, fosters competitive spirit and prevents group thinking which encourages sloganeering and unnecessary bureaucracy, and the moral uprightness to remain above board at all times.

Considering the role ideology plays in ensuring social cohesion, political stability and economic prosperity, Kwame Nkrumah propounds the view that ideology like morality should unite the actions of millions towards specific and definite goals and to achieve this, the ideology of a society needs to employ a number of instruments.

The ideology of a society displays itself in political theory, social theory, moral theory, (and economic theory), and uses these as instruments. It establishes a particular range of political, social, moral, (and economic) behaviour, such that unless behaviour of this sort fall within the established range, it would be incompatible with the ideology (Nkrumah, 1978: 59).

Therefore, the role of ideology in ensuring national cohesion and economic development in a polity is holistic. This makes ideology the fundamental drive behind nationalism and the nationalistic mobilization of the populace towards social transformation and economic prosperity.

From the first republic to date, there has been a plethora of ideologies in Nigeria among which are Nnamdi Azikiwe's Neo-Welfarism, Obafemi Awolowo's Democratic Socialism, Chuba Okadigbo's Populism, Amiko Atimomo's Jindadi Jamaa, E.K. Ogundowole's Self-Reliancism and Aminu Kano's *Talakawa* ideology. Unfortunately, all of these have been supplanted by a new wave of ideologue called militocracy or kakistocracy which thrives on the principle of 'militrickism' (my coinage). Since the military took over governance in 1966, Nigeria has been bereft of a profound ideology for directing the affairs of the state. Instead, what obtains are some "core values of the Nigerian state" (Alli, 101) which are federalism, revenue allocation, federal character/quota system, citizenship, secularism, rule of law and democracy (see pp. 104 - 134). Ordinarily, these core values are germane to the healthy existence of the Nigerian state, except that they lack ideological anchor and coordination. This apart, militricians, as the custodians of militocracy, with their penchant for militrickism have inadvertently crashed all the core values of the Nigerian state. Needless to say, militrickism is the chief blemish that aggravated other problems in the Nigerian state namely squandermaniaism, pre-bendalism, patrimonialism and neo-patrimonialism, all of which have not only combined to assign Nigeria to the bottom ladder of sheer consumerism, but have also hampered stability and economic development.

In the view of M. Chris Alli therefore, between the compradors and the conquistadors, governance in Nigeria has been reduced to sheer patronage all because: "We are being governed by ordinary men and women who have turned us against ourselves and against the nation, and ordinary men and women regrettably do not build great nations" (p. 102). Militarism has enthroned upon Nigeria and Nigerians government of the cronies and the cabal, or what Fela Anikulapo Kuti calls *padi-padi* government. Visionless, inept and corrupt, they have turned the Nigerian Project upside down. For instance, "the concept of unity in diversity has become unity in bondage or neo-colonialism (i.e. short of internal colonization)', just as 'the concept of equitably shared wealth has become captured wealth'" (p. 103) for supposed looters. Thus, with large scale "debauchery and mindless authoritarianism" (see p. 105) the federated units that made up Nigeria from inception, were (on the excuse of arresting the nation from disintegration) by fiat, lacerated into states that are dependent on the centre for survival, thereby turning Nigeria into a centralized garrison state. This grave anomaly has never augured well for Nigerians as:

The federal government has become a regular and monthly paymaster, and the states, its waste pipes, accounting to no one in particular, not even to its subjects or itself. Many otherwise vibrant and enterprising nationalities have been reduced to beggarly, unproductive natives living off the central government. Commodity and raw material produce for which Nigeria had been famous have been neglected and ignored. What is in place is a skewed federal revenue allocation formula that emphasizes land mass, need, population and other weird factors, rather than derivation, for sharing the national cake. It is a perfidious arrangement that reflects the greatest injustice in the national system (pp. 106-107).

The replacement of true federalism with unitary federalism was made possible by the combined efforts of the military, and their political and elite cohorts. This, eventually, created a lope-sided revenue sharing formula that has completely supplanted derivation policy for distribution which operates on the principle of discrimination. Coupled with this is the tension and stampede among the triumvirate or the big three (Hausa/Fulani, Yoruba and Igbo), who in plotting to out-manoeuvre each another, reduce the minority ethnic groups to crump eaters. On this matter, M.C. Alli reports Gamaliel Onosode's view on the sharing formula thus: "the history of revenue allocation between 1951 and 1979 provides strange revelations about policies by various governments that have continued to under-develop the oil-rich Niger Delta" (p. 114). Besides, it was in the bid to frustrate the Biafran secession during the Civil War that "the duo of General Yakubu Gowon/Chief Obafemi Awolowo appropriated all resources in the territory called Nigeria to the central government" (p. 117). From this moment onward, distribution by discrimination became the order for revenue allocation in Nigeria, whereby encroachment and conscription of the minorities' resources by the big three became rife. This, logically, makes Nigeria a nation in limbo, bound together by force; in the process, justice, equity and fairness are distanced from the Nigerian polity. As M.C. Alli bluntly puts it:

> The truth of the matter is that the entity called Nigeria was conceived, constructed, cemented and held together by force, threat of force, deceit and subterfuge to the ultimate benefit of the Hausa/Fulani, the Yoruba and Ndigbo, in that arithmetical progression (Ibid.). These three "contribute nothing tangible but sheer insensitive politics and confusion to the polity in their self-consuming, nationally debilitating, no-holds-barred, barefaced greed for regional and tribal hegemony and ascendancy" (p.115). It is in the bid to maintain this sectorial and hegemonic advantage that the "Federal Character/Quota System" (p. 119) was created. But the bare facts on ground amply and continuously demonstrate that Nigeria is ill-structured and yet to evolve as a true polity; whose forced unity is perpetually threatened by its uncoordinated heterogeneity as witnessed in the sharp divide between citizenship and indigeneship (see p. 122). In the process the secularist posture of the nation has been severely truncated by religious sentiments, which is another cankerworm that has bedevilled Nigeria. These combined factors, coupled with the militarization of the Nigerian psyche and the politicization of the military, further traumatizes the nation: with the brutal rape of the "rule of law" (p. 127), justice and liberty will be consigned to the dust bin. In the first place, a garrison is not the same as a civil society because the rules

that play therein are not exactly the same. So, garrison commanders do not necessarily make good leaders.

M.C. Alli is forthright on this very matter.

The reality of military law is that by practice (in the Nigerian military), it is conducted to impose discipline and command unqualified obedience, obey before complaint. With the civil population, it does not work that way. The whole system and the structural exclusivity of military law and attitude cannot be transferred to the civil condition (p. 129).

Because we have allowed this to fructify and foster, we as a people have guillotined justice system in our society and have "therefore shifted the justice system from the courts to the temporary halls of military justice management" (Ibid.). Alarmed, the people as the downtrodden wail about the judiciary and the justice system in the country, while the judiciary in turn lament their handcuffed and handicapped condition; our hands are tied, has become the clichĭ in the Nigerian judiciary arena. Thus, with the handcuffing of the judiciary and the press, both representing the last hope and voice of the populace, democracy was long dead in Nigeria. In the words of Fela Anikulapo Kuti, democracy in Nigeria has become the demonstration of craze or crazy demonstration. Campbell Shittu Momoh on his part declares the – funeral of democracy in Nigeria. In fact, democracy in Nigeria has merely manifested the following features.

i. Eliocracy which means "the rule of the elites over the people and the clever replacement of the people's positive power with the nebulous and abstract people's will" (1994: 41).

ii. Ochlocracy or mobocracy which portrays: "Democracy as ultimately the tyranny of the vociferous and noisy minority over the quiet, silent majority. Democracy is merely a system of politicking to plot or acquire and remain in power. It is not really a system of governance and so cannot be equated with either good or bad governance" (pp. 31 - 32).

In Momoh's view, democracy in Nigeria is not about the rule of law, it does not protect the rights of the people, it does not promote the wellbeing of the people; rather, it entrenches corruption, denies the people of their rights and erodes the basis for their economic and political empowerment.

Consequently, by essence, Nigeria is yet to evolve into a polity and the principal reason for this is that the factors responsible for the emergence of Nigeria which in turn determine the essence of putting the Nigerian state together blatantly violate the rules of social contract as outlined by philosophers worldwide. This disparaging factor is largely responsible for what M. C. Alli has christened "the Nigerian factor" (2001: Chapter 9), which clearly demonstrates the nonchalance, lack of patriotism and large scale corruption among Nigerians. To be succinct, the Nigerian factor is a clear indication that Nigeria is yet to evolve as a polity in the ideal sense of the word and if ever it has evolved as an ideal polity, the rot, decay and decadence in it attest to the blatant fact that Nigeria has become a failed state. Hash as this may sound, M.C. Alli thinks it is the obvious fact. He has this to say about the Nigerian factor:

> It is a euphemism for operating outside the laws or rules, or seeking to moderate them. It is a twister of norms and laws guiding officials and non-officials in the conduct of affairs. The full spectrum of national life: constitution, laws, cultures, religions, ethnicity and status provide its operational environments and parameters. Its greatest articulation lies in its propensity to dilute principles, discipline, law and order, rules and regulations...It is an escape valve and excuse for failures and incompetence, seeking for and hiding behind a scapegoat that will bear the burden of guilt (pp. 135 & 137).

Mohammed Chris Alli reasons aloud that on a general scale, "the Nigerian factor is a loose term, presumably, a warning that things are not what they appear to be" (p. 137). And insofar as this syndrome depicts a sense of "outright lawlessness" (Ibid.), it means that danger looms large for Nigeria; because, a complete state of lawlessness clearly paints the picture of a nation that operates on impunity and a total loss of direction. This state of anomy not only leaves a sour taste in the mouth, but calls to question the ability and capability of the Nigerian leadership, particularly the military, in piloting the affairs of the nation. We are thus back to the questions of security and freedom in the polity.

M.C. Alli and the question of security and freedom in a Plural Nigeria

A society is said to be plural in nature if it is multi-ethnic, multi-racial and multi-religious. Nigeria is multi-ethnic and multi-religious, while United States of America is multi-racial and multi-religious. It is therefore not surprising that John Rawls and Robert Nozick, two American philosophers, ponder on how best the institution of justice can be coordinated to galvanize security and freedom a plural polity. So, while Rawls speaks of liberalism and reasonable pluralism, Nozick speaks of libertarianism and the minimal state. And whereas Rawls theory is both state and people directed, Nozick's is more people-oriented. The African perspective agrees more with Rawls. For instance, as the Igbo African would say, society is both people and state oriented as one can hardly think of fish without water and vice versa. This is the fundamental reason why the broom is used in representing African communalism. It is impossible to think of broom without the broom sticks that comprise it and vice versa, neither does a broom stick make a bunch of broom. In that order, no individual can make a society just as society cannot be without the individuals. Hence, man and state are inseparable and complementary.

Security and freedom are crucial to the existence of civil society, if not, the society in question cannot be said to be a body politic or a state. For this reason and from antiquity to date, philosophers have theorized on the best form of government that would yield the best form of governance, just as they have also pondered on the best kind of ethical theory that would make the realization of optimal justice in the society possible. Plato and Aristotle favoured aristocracy or government of the wise, while the contemporary world favours democracy or people oriented government. On the question of the ethical theory for obtaining optimal justice in the society, Plato proposed the Ideal state governed by the ideal king, Aristotle propounded the theory of eudemonism, Jeremy Bentham espoused the doctrine of utilitarianism that operates on the principle of hedonic calculus (i.e. the greatest happiness for the greatest number), Immanuel Kant tinkered on deontological ethics which is further anchored on the categorical imperative, Nietzsche proposed the ethics of the noble and the ignoble, Confucius preferred the governance of the sage, while the existentialists propounded the doctrine of authenticity. But the finest of governmental theories and structures as well as ethical doctrines of justice will lie fallow without the right calibre of men and women. It is for this reason that philosophers all agree that security and freedom in the society could best be achieved with the enthronement of virtuous or morally upright individuals, also known as moral exemplars or political virtuosos.

Security and freedom were paramount in the communalistic setting of traditional African. But as earlier mentioned, the traditional order was torpedoed by the colonial order which foisted on Africans alien system of governance. Worst still, the manner of colonial administration in Nigeria was purely military, making Nigeria a garrison territory from inception. M.C. Alli makes the view of Ambassador B.A.T. Balewa on this issue accessible:

> As a military man he (Lugard) felt a lot more at ease with people of similar background in the development of his policies in Nigeria. This seems to explain his preference for ex-military officers to man key positions in his administration (Balewa, 1990; cited by Alli, 2001: 110).

The above statement of B.A.T. Balewa is reiterated by M.C. Alli thus:

> Nigeria has been ruled since 1900 by either a military government, a quasi-military government or by a command system that derives authority from the soldier's mind set for authority, unity of command and obedience ... By training, inclination, antecedent, attitude and aptitude, it will become indisputable that the military which has ruled Nigeria for 87 years of its (more than) 100, has created a psychological bastion against rational democratic ideals, awareness and practice as conceived by our founding fathers in 1960 for a federal democratic nation (2001: 110).

He further states that:

> It is empirically evident that the militarization of Nigeria and its manifestations were deeply implanted by Lord Lugard who centralized power and command in his duplex in an emerging settlement we now know as Kaduna. An exception would perhaps be during the short-lived intervention of the civilian governments of 1960 – 1966, 1979 -

1983 and from 1999 to date (the italicized are mine Ibid.).

Centralization has never and will never augur well for security and freedom in a plural state. This is where the United States, though multi-racial and multi-religious, is sharply different from Nigeria. Independent states came together to form a commonwealth known as the United States of America. Obviously, a united system is either federated or confederated and is quite different from a unitary system. Besides, each of the components of the United States is economically independent, creating much room for stability, legitimacy, acceptability and progress. In Rawls' and Nozick's parlance, this liberal and libertarian spirit allows for the flowering of justice, equity and fairness, which are the hob for security and freedom in the state. In other words, security and freedom in the state are not about jackboots and mortars; both are never about coercion and intimidation. Because, the primary reason for the evolution of society is to provide security for the people to freely transact their businesses in a serene environment. This wise, the role of government is to continually ensure a level playing field and a stable environment for the citizens of a polity to actualise their hopes and aspirations without rancour and bitterness.

We are therefore back to the admonition of Plato not to allow the auxiliary or soldiers and the artisans to become leaders. In his view, these calibre of persons lack the training and ability for cerebral decision making and policy implementation without recourse to unnecessary emotions. Needless to say, social and political philosophers seem to agree with Plato that civil leaders must in their rights be virtuosos. Virtuosos are men and women of steady character who have attained the Olympian status of beatific vision and have acquired virtuous attributes such as prudence, courage, liberality, temperance, frugality etc that are required self-mastery and dynamic leadership. In the view of M. C. Alli, soldiers should at best ensure that the protection, sanity and dignity of the constitution, they should never usurp the mantle of leadership because they lack the temperament for civil authority and long term effective administration that make security and freedom possible.

The soldier may be the instrument of rapid and short restoration as we have seen in Pakistan in later years, but they cannot and should not constitute themselves into the solution in a multi-national composition like Nigeria and similar environments. They not only lack the temper, they only behave like task forces, engrossed in short-term solution but adding nothing to established systems (p. 85).

M.C. Alli fervently believes that the military in a plural society or any society for that matter should restrict itself to the provisions of the Constitution.

The soldiers' role in the political environment and as defined in the constitution of the land should be respected. If soldiers must intervene in governance directly, then the Nigerian constitution ought to be altered and amended to accommodate the contingency for military intervention, any such political adventure is manifestly illegitimate and grossly illegal, no matter what the expedients may appear to be (Ibid.).

Consequently, coup plotters as interventionist gangs have no right whatsoever to disrupt the smooth flow of governance. And given the fact that these series of interventions set the nation several years backward and also cause serious harm or injury to the holistic psyche of the nation, M. C. Alli argues that there must be a constitutional way of punishing interventionist gangs after they must have adjudicated office. His scorn for coups is hash. "I have strong disdain for coups, they change nothing and they influence nothing fundamental." (p. 87). His averseness to coup plotters and military regimes in Africa are founded on the following reasons:

i. Military regimes in Africa disrupt the democratic process and by so doing jettison the rule of law
ii. Military regimes in Africa stifle the separation of power thereby allowing for much injustice in the land
iii. Military regimes in Africa create the impression that power and authority flows from the barrel of the gun, not from the people
iv. Military regimes in Africa create the impression the security of life and property lie in the dreaded military uniform re-enforced by jackboots and mortars
v. Military regimes in Africa are largely known for the abuse of human rights and for obstructing press freedom
vi. Military regimes in Africa and particularly Nigeria have a way of enthroning mediocrity and corruption by encouraging large scale sectarianism by way of tribalism and religious bigotry. Or "how do

you explain to a young mind of ten to twenty years of age that his/her opportunities in his/her country, not of his/her choice, but by birth are foreclosed no matter how superior his talents may be, because of quota system"? How do you explain to a young Nigerian mind that his/her opportunities are limited by the very fact of his/her tribal origin" (p. 86).

The submissions made and questions raised above further rest on the issues of security and freedom in the state to which thinkers as Jeremy Bentham and Baron Montesquieu had pondered upon in their books *The Theory of Legislation* and *The Spirit of the Laws* respectively. Bentham is of the view that the relationship between security and freedom further rotates on the intermingling between rights and duties in the society, which he considers to be onerous. Or how does the state grant me the right to property without simultaneously putting the burden on the other to obey such right and vice versa? The inter-relationship between right and duty simply oscillates. Montesquieu on his part feels that the best way to create balance in the society for the enthronement of justice and assurance of security and freedom, for the sake of stability and peace, is through the separation of powers, which in turn allows for checks and balances. In other words, security and freedom in the state, as Plato earlier stated and as reiterated by Montesquieu, are made possible when organs of the state and individuals play their roles within the prescribed limits.

M.C. Alli realizes the fact that freedom is more than an essential component of security, it in fact the basis for security, stability, unity and peace in the state:

> Once freedom of thought and opinion are abridged, the entire machinery of adjustment in a group will be jeopardized, it will be impossible to compare ideas and to come to rational judgement regarding group policies. It is not only ideas that may evaporate, national institution will be compromised...Dialogue and discussion bring about a sifting of ideas whereby the weaknesses of that 'which is' are determined (pp. 153 – 154).

By stifling freedom of thought and speech, military regimes blatantly demonstrate that they "either do not understand the implications of democracy or have no confidence in the ability of the people to exercise their constitutional roles" (p. 154). Hence, by impeding human freedom, the Nigerian military not only become vicious but as well visionless thereby constituting themselves as the very fountain of insecurity. Impliedly, security in the society is made possible when individuals and groups alike obey the limits of their freedom.

Freedom is metaphysical because it derives from the free flow of human consciousness, which in turn fires the zeal of the human will to excel. Consciousness in itself is like the concurrent continuous tide that does not ebb. It can then not be impeded. A conscious individual is a free person who remains resolute and undaunted by life's vicissitudes. It is in this sense that Fredrick Nietzsche speaks of the will to power. It is in this sense that Jean Paul Sartre asserts that man as a conscious being is condemned unto freedom and as condemned unto freedom, man is a diehard fanatic. It is also in this sense that Hegel, in his notion of historical freedom, states that a conscious and free individual is laden of ambitions and remains undeterred until his visions and missions are accomplished. Following this line of thought, M.C. Alli states thus: "Almighty God has created the mind free, all attempts to influence it by temporal punishment, or by civil incapacitation, tend only to beget habits of hypocrisy and meanness" (p. 155).

A hypocritical society comprise sick minds, sick minds in turn are the fountain of all the ills that bemoan the polity the height of which is unbridled corruption. Little wonder philosophers had always admonished that the most proficient way to tame human will/freedom and attain security in the society, is that leadership and governance should be tailored towards the establishment of profound institutions that moderate and regulate human activities in the polity, such that individuals and groups can equitably derive and contribute their little quotas to the growth and development of that polity without sinister conditions. M.C. Alli puts it this way:

> Put more succinctly, your exercise of your freedom, as they say, stops at the tip of my nose. No freedom is therefore total both from the state point of view and in relation to individual citizens. Conversely,

> government should not be free to act as it chooses and this is where the odium of the scandalous manipulation of the law and legal processes by the military is most evident – retroactive decrees, disregard for court rulings and the curtailment and under funding of the judiciary (p. 157).

In contemporary terms, free judiciary and free press are the determinants of a civil polity. As earlier stated, the judiciary is the last hope of the common man, the press is the voice of the common man, both are the regulating mean between the downtrodden, the elite and the government. Wherever the two are stampeded, what results is peace of the grave yard, which in turn creates a hyper level of deviancy and hypocrisy that heighten corruption, thereby leaving the polity insecure.

M.C. Alli and the challenge of leadership/governance in Nigeria: the way forward

The challenge of leadership and governance forms the central discourse on the common good, which thinkers worldwide had preoccupied themselves with over the years. How best could a plural Nigeria as a colonial amalgam or new state resolve the mammoth problems confronting her and possibly attain her Eldorado dreamland? What manner of governance could best resolve the numerous problems that hamper Nigeria's growth and development? The first question borders on process, while the second borders on structure. From M.C. Alli's masterpiece, *The Federal Military of Nigerian Army: the Siege of a Nation*, a number of philosophical orientations for tackling the problems of the process and the structure that would assist in ameliorating the Nigerian condition can be teased out.

Firstly, there are fundamental reasons for the restructuring of Nigeria which range from tribalism, unbridled nationalism, religious falangism, pseudo-Machiavellianism to "hierarchical authoritarianism" (p. 105) and mal-structuring that all combine to fuel corruption and mal-administration in the land. On the foregoing issue, M.C. Alli states the obvious fact thus: "It is universally evident that the Nigerian project, as conceived by our founding patriots, is now defective and is akin to a car immobilized by a knocked engine" (p. 98). Matters were made worst by the discarding of the 1963 constitution which led to the "destruction of federalism in Nigeria" (p. 105). On top of this came the Olusegun Obasanjo's 1979 infamous constitution that by its "Land Use Act and revenue formula" (Ibid.) completely uprooted any hope for true federalism. This created "inequity and unfair relationship between the various nationalities" (p. 111), making "tribal trust or distrust of other tribes an essential element of protection and survival" (p. 143). Protectionism, the blind impulse to survive and maintain the vantage position at all cost, manifests its ugly head in the elusive, cheating, conniving/compromising and dangerous spirit called 'the Nigerian factor', which has in turn crystalized into pseudo-Machiavellianism. How else should one describe the fallacious thinking that "the means fortifies the end or that the end justifies the means" (Ibid.). This, at best, is a warped kind of logic, irrational, illegal, foul, soulless and weird. With the enthronement of militocracy, corruption and kleptocracy have become permanent features of Nigeria such that:

> The dividing line between honesty and kleptocracy in Nigeria lies in the realm of opportunity. Those who had a chance and access to public treasury, do not grumble, those who did not have the opportunity to exercise quick fingers blame everyone else for corruption. This is the depth and culture of corruption in Nigeria. It is also more than the factor of money or thievery (p.53).

At all levels of governance, appointments are not made to spearhead growth and development, but to reward friends and placate godfathers, the fact that these set of leaders are inept does not make any difference. Hence, for M.C. Alli, the situation is hopeless because our: "Society extols appearances more than it does intellect, talent and skill. It eulogizes and acclaims the vampire-like cloak and dagger manoeuvring for power that has been entrenched in the Armed Forces and in the Nigerian psyche" (p. 69). It is such that Nigeria has become "a no-win environment in moral terms" (p.53). This grave and gloomy circumstance notwithstanding, M.C. Alli propagates the need for moral rearmament or moral rectitude based on the principle of discipline or self-mastery. As he states: "My attitude to the Nigerian condition is that office is relevant if it can promote change, force change, advance change in a society replete with injustice, fraud and inequity as they are today." (p. 70).

At this juncture, M.C. Alli challenges Nigerians to summon the courage and journey inwards, to the ground of all human activities wherein the solutions to all human problems lies. The self as the mind is the metaphysical foundation for all developmental endeavours. Wise nations seek after great minds and empower them as leaders. Mind is the light in man, it is the being in the human, once the mind or the being of man is side-lined, light cannot be beamed, illumination is dwindled, what remains is mere carcass, which represents rot, decay and death. M.C. Alli boldly affirms this: "I believe that the mind, and not passion or emotion should rule human ambition" (p. 84). This sounds more like Plato speaking. He goes on to say: "The lure of office and its grandeur, power and authority are transient. Their light and import lie only on the lips of humanity, when man is no more or when man/woman is bereft of these accoutrements" (Ibid.). Regrettably, the transient and the ephemeral not only becloud the gaze of Nigerians, but engage the totality of their attention. This penchant for crass materialism can never yield a great nation because all consumables are bound to dwindle and be exhausted with time. This is an inescapable law.

Away from the dark side of life is that path of humanism that solemnly promises constant glimmer of hope.

The great minds in history, in all fields of human endeavour who have captured human respect, affection and endearment are also those who have caused the least pain and anguish. They are also those who have broadened the vistas of human frontiers, those who stood by the light of truth, unfettered human expression, freedom, love, compassion and progress. The pursuit of these sublime ideals and goals are not without price, penalties and doubts (Ibid.).

Again, M.C. Alli is convinced that the pursuit of humanism is not possible without courage, that mark of the brave and the wise, which propels great minds (men and women of steel) to remain undaunted in their struggle to accomplish the greatest height for humanity. Such men and women are virtuous individuals who unwaveringly stand for truth, value and knowledge.

Man may be intimidated by force or threat of the use of force, by deprivation and degradation, but the human spirit coupling the mind is capable of, and is endowed with, an inestimable capacity to transcend over matter, right over wrong, truth over falsehood and light over darkness (p.85).

At this point M.C. Alli re-echoes the Socratic dictum about self-examination and self-mastery. "But as the maxim goes, if you believe in nothing, you will fall for anything. Indeed, a man who has nothing to die for is living a worthless life" (Ibid.). This submission of M.C. Alli immediately calls to mind the great debate in political philosophy about the inseparability of ethics from politics. Ethics has the goal of training the ideal humans, while politics is principally concerned with the quest for the ideal state. If the task of attaining the dream of the ideal state must necessarily be accomplished by ideal humans, it follows that ethics and politics are simply interwoven.

Convinced that that Nigeria needs urgent bail out from quagmire, M.C. Alli advanced revolution and pluralistic federalism as possible ways of ameliorating the problem on ground. In place of coups, he "believes in revolutionary action, particularly in environments that make peaceful change impossible" (p. 87), as the possible way out of the imbroglio. But the possibility of revolution in Nigeria will be dependent on the degree of 'social consciousness' among the ethnic nationalities of Nigeria. "However," says M.C. Alli, "whether or not Nigeria is ripe for a revolution is a question bearing on the fact that Nigeria is a collection of nationalities and interest groups that are unable to act in concert without relapsing into divisionism or babel" (Ibid.). But divisionism or Babel does not completely rule out ethnic nationality revolts as exemplified in the Biafran movement which after fifty years of Civil War has once more resurfaced with greater vigour. Besides, the upsurge of ethnic nationality agitations for self-governance will continually be fuelled by historical circumstances because:

> The thaw in the Cold War since World War II has focused the attention of the world populations and nationalities within nation states on their respective ethnic or community patrimonies and created new competitions for central power and resource control. The breakup of the impregnable Soviet Union, India/Pakistan, Ethiopia/Eritrea and the East European nations did not take long to

impact on African nationalities often bound by tenuous incongruous state structure (p. 93).

The issue in contention concerns the structuring of Nigeria to the benefit and comfort of all the ethnic nationalities that constitute the Nigerian polity. Such act of restructuring should substantially and comprehensively ameliorate the pandemonium on ground. Hence, M.C. Alli counsels for caution if not "extreme angst and emotions may warrant outbursts suggesting a break up, but so would the present structure and their rigidities lead eventually to the biafranization of Nigeria" (p. 100). And granted that "equality of nationalities may be far-fetched, but equity is inevitable, or else, all will lose all" (p. 99). He then calls for a truce by way of a Sovereign National Conference of all the ethnic nationalities. He further advocates that "representation at the Sovereign National Conference should therefore be by individual ethnic delegations and not through the medium of one man one vote" (p. 100). Obvious from the foregoing, is the suggestion that Nigeria as a plural society should toe the line of pluralistic democracy which should be the foundation for a pluralistic democracy based on the rule of law and the historico-cultural experiences of the people.

Conclusion

A nation under siege is definitely at war. It is either that the nation crushes its assailants or the assailants crush the nation. Since the time of the amalgamation in 1900 (when Lord Lugard forcibly put Nigeria together) to date, Nigeria has been under siege. At independence, the baton was handed over to the internal colonizers thereby making our self-autonomy a mere token. The irony of it all is that the peoples and cultures boxed into the enclave called Nigeria are several millennia old. If one goes by the documentary run on Nigeria Television Authority (NTA) in 2008, the peoples and cultures that comprise Nigeria today lived around the Rivers Niger and Benue more than forty thousand years ago. Meanwhile, colonization till date is just about 300 years old. Colonization wants to completely wipe out the cumulative memory of 39,700 years and forcibly shorten our memory within a gruesome 300 years. But since the human spirit is stubborn and it propels the human memory, there will continually be an upsurge of ethnic nationality consciousness, thereby necessitating a clash between the past and the present. This is the tragedy and the sham of what it means to be a colonial amalgam or a new state.

To operate within the historical circumstance created by colonialism is to totally accept the myth of the hermetic hypothesis, which states that the existence of the entire black world began from the moment of discovery by the white explorers. This is short of saying that Africans were pre-logical, that reasoning among Africans started from contact with the Europeans. It further implies that Africans lack the mental capacity to run their own affairs. As suggested by Immanuel Kant in his book entitled, *Anthropology from a Pragmatic Point of View*, the best that can be done is to train Africans to ape other people's way of life.

But since evidence abound to show that Africans are the pioneers of history and civilization, it follows that contemporary Africans has no choice in the matter but to demonstrate their capability for self-organization. To do otherwise would amount to forfeiture or self-abandonment. By way of conclusion therefore, the book, *The Federal Military of Nigerian Army: the Siege of a Nation*, besides being timely, challenges Africans at large and Nigerians in particular, to wake up from dogmatic slumber and answer to the call of civilization by embarking on a journey of self-rediscovery which should trigger off the quest for national rebirth.

References

Alli, M.C. (2001). *The Federal Military of Nigerian Army: The Siege of a Nation*. Lagos: Malthouse Press Limited.

Anyanwu, K.C. (1981). *African Philosophy: An Introduction to the Main Philosophical Trends in Contemporary Africa*. Rome: Catholic Book Agency.

Aristotle (1984). "Nichomachean Ethics", in *The Complete Works of Aristotle*, vol. 2, (ed. Jonathan Barnes). Prince Town, N: Prince Town University Press.

Bentham, J. (1975). *The Theory of Legislation*. Bombay: M.M. Tripathi Private Ltd.

Hobbes, T. (2007). *Leviathan*. University of Adelaide – http://ebooks Adelaide.edu.

Kant, I. (1974). *Anthropology from a Pragmatic Point of View*. (Trans. M. J. Gregora). The Hague: Martinus Nijhoff.

Marx, K. (1977), *A Contribution to the Critique of Political Economy.* (with some notes by R. Rojas), Progress Publishers, Moscow (online).
Momoh, C.S. (1994). *Funeral of Democracy.* Auchi: African Philosophy Projects Publications
Montesquieu, B. (1949). *The Spirit of the Laws.* New York: Hafner Pub. Co.
Nkrumah, K. (1978). *Consciencism: Philosophy and Ideology for Decolonization.* London: Panaf Books Ltd.
Nozick, R. (1974). *Anarchy, State, and Utopia.* New York: Basic Books.
Ogundowole, E.K. (2006). *The Amalgam, Kakistocracy and Warfare Society: The Options.* Lagos: Research Correct Counsels Limited.
Ogundowole, E.K. (2011). *Self-Reliancism: Philosophy of a New World Order,* Lagos: Correct Counsels Limited.
Plamenatz, J. (1970). *Ideology.* London: Macmillan.
Plato (1966). *The Republic.* London: Oxford University Press.
Rawls, J. (2001). *Justice as Fairness: A Restatement.* (ed. E. Kelly). Cambridge, MA: Harvard University Press.
Rawls, J. (2005). *Political Liberals.* (Second edition). New York: Columbia University Press.
Stanford Encyclopedia of Philosophy (2005). Online.
Thomson, A. (2007). *An Introduction to African Politics* (Second Edition). London: Routledge.

Chapter 10

The Matter of Justice and Equity in Nigeria: A Reflection on M. Chris Alli

-Dorothy Oluwagbemi-Jacob

Introduction

Giving everyone that which is his or her due is an essential element of justice and wherever there are hues and cries about domination, marginalization, exclusion and other related concepts; one should look closely to find out if the aggrieved are getting their due. In his book titled, *The Federal Republic of Nigerian Army: the Siege of a Nation*, M. Chris Alli raised justice and equity issues with respect to federalism/power sharing, federal character/quota system, the Nigerian factor and revenue allocation. The aim of this chapter is to reflect on the issues thrown up by Chris Alli's contestations. Specifically, this chapter subjects the policies of federalism/power sharing, federal character/quota system and revenue allocation to the litmus test of justice and equity. It is the position of the chapter that given the insights which one's investigation revealed, Chris Alli's contestations are well-founded.

In the opening statement of the 1999 Constitution of the Federal Republic of Nigeria, it is stated that:

> We the people of the Federal Republic of Nigeria firmly and solemnly resolved...to provide for a constitution for the purpose of promoting the good government and welfare of all persons in our country on the principles of Freedom, Equality and Justice, and for the purpose of consolidating the Unity of our people...

One assumes that 'people' in this constitutional arrangement refers to all Nigerians without exception and that the freedom, equality and justice referred to therein apply to everybody regardless of one's ethnic and religious affiliations. Equality, freedom and justice are core universal values that promote unity, harmony and peace. Ignore or disregard them in the policies and practices of the agents of the state or in the treatment of individuals and the result one gets is alienation, antagonism and conflict.

In the recent past in the Nigerian polity, there had been hues and cries regarding domination, marginalization and discrimination. These are pointers to the fact that these hallowed principles of equality, freedom and justice have either been thrown overboard completely or selective in their application. Nigeria would have been a safe and secure haven for all the ethnic groups, whether major or minor if these principles were followed. But the reality of the Nigerian situation is that there had been a huge gulf between ideas and reality, principles and practice, hence, the assorted complaints about domination, marginalization and discrimination. That calls for sovereign national conference, referendum, restructuring, true federalism and devolution of powers are getting louder are indications that some people are feeling short-changed relative to the constitutional provision of "promoting the good government and welfare of all persons in our country on the principles of Freedom, Equality and Justice." Issues of equality and justice arise regarding the distribution of resources and dividends of social cooperation to the component groups in Nigeria, whether major or minor.

The aim of this chapter is to reflect on justice issues as raised by M. Chris Alli, in his book titled, *The Federal Republic of Nigerian Army: the Siege of a Nation*. Alli does not articulate any particular theory of justice. But one can glean from his views that he is miffed by certain policies and practices of the agents of the Nigerian state. It is clear from his submissions that policies pertaining to federalism, federal character, quota system, revenue allocation and what he calls the Nigerian factor stand in clear violations of justice principles.

Subsequently, this chapter highlights the essential elements of justice with a view to appraising Alli's claims of justice breaches on the side of the agents of the Nigerian state relative to some of the ethnic groups in

The Matter of Justice and Equity in Nigeria: A reflection on M. Chris Alli

Nigeria. To accomplish its major objective, this chapter is divided into three sections. Section one gives insight into the essential ingredients of justice. Section two gives a brief insight into the political configuration of post-colonial Nigeria with a view to preparing the ground for the issues that constitute the bones of contention for Alli. In section three, an attempt is made to evaluate Alli's views relative to the core principles of justice and to show whether or not the Nigerian state in its policies and practices has lived up to the expectations of justice in its treatment of some ethnic groups or the populace generally. This section also embodies the conclusion.

The Concept of Justice: a theoretical account

Justice is a concept that has meaning in a social context where people with various interests exist. Relevant issues of justice come to the front burner whenever people begin to reflect on the social, political and economic arrangements within which they live their lives and organize their activities. Etymologically, justice is derived from the Latin word, "*jus*", meaning right or law. The *Oxford English Dictionary* defines the "just" person as someone who always "does what is morally right" and is disposed to "giving everyone his or her due". "Giving everyone his or her due" is central to justice and wherever there are agitations in the society; one should look deep to find out whether the aggrieved are getting their due. The *Oxford Dictionary* offers the word "fair" as a synonym of justice.

As a philosophical chapter, one wishes to go beyond the etymology of the word, as well as the dictionary definitions to consider, for example, the nature of justice as a desirable quality of political society, and how it applies to social and political decision making. As a principle of equity, justice takes into account the inalienable and inborn rights of all human beings and citizens, the undeniable rights of all individuals to equal protection before the law, of their civil rights, without discrimination on the basis of race, gender, national origin, religion, disability, age, ethnicity or other characteristics.

Utilitarianism

The nature of justice is articulated under assorted theories. One of the popular theories of justice is utilitarianism, the view that actions, policies and institutions are to be judged in terms of the extent to which they maximize overall happiness or wellbeing. Utilitarianism assumes a variety of forms; however, each of them embodies consequentialism, impartiality and maximization as essential ingredients.

Utilitarians are consequentialists for the reason that they assess actions and policies solely in terms of consequences such generate. Considerations that are 'backward looking' (such as what people deserve in the light of their past behaviour) are not counted on this view; all that matters is the future effects. In other words, utilitarianism considers law and punishment forward-looking. What has the best consequences for society is just in the sense of its implementation producing most (societal) goods.

Utilitarians are impartialists because they give equal weight to the wellbeing of every person. No preferential treatment is given to the interests of the agent or her close relations, consequences for everyone are to be counted and no one's wellbeing is given more weight than the others.

Finally, utilitarians are maximizers because among all possible options, they single out that which results in the greatest overall wellbeing as the exceptionally acceptable choice. Regarding what good should be maximized, the utilitarians agree that the right action is that which maximizes the good.

A number of objections have been raised to utilitarianism. The most worrisome has to do with the fact that insofar as utilitarianism concerns itself exclusively with consequences, it cannot be squared with justice. Elaborately, critics contend that justice involves giving people their due, and because someone's due depends principally upon her previous actions, an ethical outlook which looks solely to the future fails to offer an adequate account of justice.

John Rawls

In his *A Theory of Justice*, Rawls comes up with a theory of justice as fairness that tries to remedy the shortcomings of utilitarianism. He ends up with the recommendation that the costs and benefits of social cooperation are to be arranged in such a way that the worst off persons have the best possible share.

Rawls makes the point that his account of justice involves two principles, but his second principle is two pronged. Following this, his account may be understood in terms of three distinct principles namely: the principle of *greatest equal liberty*, the principle of *fair equality of opportunity* and the *difference principle*.

The principle of Greatest Equal liberty, which enjoys priority over the other two, specifies that "each person is to have equal right to the most extensive basic liberty for others" (Rawls, 1971, p.60). The principle proposes that each person is to have equal right to such liberties as freedom of conscience, freedom of speech, freedom of political participation, the right to private property, etc., as is compatible with everyone else equally enjoying these freedoms.

The principle of Fair Equality of opportunity requires that offices and positions be genuinely open to all under conditions of fair equality of opportunity. The idea here is simply that each person should be able to compete on an even playing field, so that those with the same talents and motivation enjoy equal opportunities to assume positions of power and prestige.

Finally, the Difference principle asserts that social inequalities are to be arranged so that they are of the greatest benefit to the least advantaged. In other words, deviating from equality is permissible only when it is to the maximal advantage of the worst-off.

For Rawls, unequal distribution of social and economic benefits could be legitimate in so far as the less privileged members of the society gained. Consequently, Rawls somewhat rationalizes inequality as a form of justice in so far as it benefits those who are not well off. Clearly, it is this kind of idea that perhaps undergirds the policy and practice of quota system in Nigeria. That is using a little injustice to achieve justice (Ucheaga 2009: 115.)

Libertarians
The libertarians' stance on justice stems from the inviolability of moral rights. Such libertarians offer an account of justice different from those of Utilitarianism or Rawls. Rights-based libertarians such as John Locke and Robert Nozick frown at the attempt to redistribute goods so as to maximize overall happiness or improve the condition of the worst-off, insisting that such redistribution is typically unjust. They contend that

goods are not merely largess that fall from the skies; they have to be produced and normally are the property of their producer.

The point the libertarians are making is that no matter what good consequences we may wish to achieve, it would be unjust to take the tiniest of the good produced by the individual without the permission of the owner of the good or producer. As the rightful owner of the property, the individual stands a privileged position or moral dominion over it. Efficiency, charity and maximization of happiness are worthwhile goals, but libertarian justice insists that none takes priority over moral rights.

Like the rest of the theories, libertarians have their own critics. Here one examines one of the objections. If one were to follow the libertarians' perspective of moral rights, especially, property rights, then it means that all forced welfare distribution would be unjust. But the critic contends that there is no ample reason to believe in rights in the way libertarians describe it. Though we believe in moral rights, but our own understanding of moral rights is different from the way libertarians understand them. For the libertarians, there can be no "positive" rights to assistance because such rights are ruled out by "negative" rights to be free from interference as long as we do not harm others. (Roughly speaking, negative rights protect one from being harmed, and positive rights entitle one to be benefited).

The question that emerges is: why must we agree that our negative rights exclude positive rights and allow no space for such? The critic asserts that the only scenario that would support this is where our moral rights are unfailingly absolute and they are not. In the absence of a theoretical explanation of why rights must be general and absolute, he says that we cannot conclude that our negative rights rule out the possibility of positive rights. Given our considered belief in positive rights, it seems wrong to insist that all forced redistribution of wealth must be unjust (Wellman 2002).

Distributive Justice

Distributive justice is focused on the proper allocation of things - wealth, power, reward, respect- among different people. It is basically concerned with giving all members what is their due reward. However, it is important to note that while everyone might agree that wealth should be distributed fairly, there is no such agreement regarding what counts as "fair share". The criteria of distribution are usually equity, equality and need. Equity implies that one's rewards should be equal to one's contributions to society, while "equality" means that everyone gets the same amount, regardless of their input.

Equity Principles

Equity is founded on the principle that people should be treated as equals. It is driven by the idea that despite individual differences, all people share a common humanity or human dignity and as such all should count in the moral calculus.

In a society that treats all its members as equals, the varied realms of social, economic, political and cultural will work in synergy for the good of all. Distributive justice and equity are closely linked and more often than not the latter is explored through the lens of the former. Distributive justice involves specifying principles or rules according to which the different goods, services, rewards, punishment, etc., should be distributed among members of a society.

The essential ingredients of social equity include "fairness" in distribution, equality of opportunity, treating people with equal concern and respect and the notion that alike cases should be treated alike, meaning that people with similar characteristics should be treated in the same way in terms of the benefits enjoyed or the burdens suffered.

In interrogating the principles of equity at a general level, one need to: (1) examine the various things that are distributed within society such as power, honour, knowledge, wealth, work and leisure, as well as more tangible things such as food, shelter, transportation and medical care; (2) highlight the sorts of goods and services that people are said to need. These include shelter, physical security and environment, health care, water and sanitation and nutrition, a basic education and so on. People need these things in order to have a full life and all these feature when the issues of justice are mentioned in Nigeria.

Meritocracy

Equity requires that positions in society and rewards should be distributed based on people's merits. This means that someone is required to have acted in a way that elicited some sort of treatment as a response. Under the merit principle of justice, a person may receive a favourable or unfavourable treatment depending on what the person has done. What the person deserves therefore, is a function of the actions or performances for which the individual is responsible. Practically, people applying for positions should be judged fairly according to their qualifications for the position. This principle is violated where factors such as family background, race or place of origin give people access to different types of job. Or where males and females are treated differently in consideration for a job or paid differently for performing similar tasks. Or where a person's social standing or political power is more operative in the sorts of opportunity available than their qualifications for the post (Gerber 2014: 8)

The issue under consideration does not only belong to lawmakers. It is an issue in the public administration and other segments of the society that deal with service delivery. In the area of public administration, the emphasis is on issues of race, ethnicity and gender in employment, democratic participation, and service delivery.

Equality
The core concept of justice is equality. From the perspective of equality, justice demands that the same amount of whatever we are sharing should be given to everyone if there is nothing relevant that distinguishes the possible recipients. There is an intimate relationship between equality and fairness. One's concern about equality has to do with comparative fairness that focuses on how the three major ethnic groups fair relative to minority ethnic groups. Here unfairness consists in the minority ethnic groups being worse-off than the three major ethnic groups in political representation.

A little detail will give us insight into what equality means in concrete terms. When the concept of equality is examined in the social sphere, one is concerned with the extent to which its ideals are translated into practice in the laws and institutions of society. Equality has a variety of forms in the social sphere: civil equality, political equality and economic equality. Here one elaborates upon political equality. This is measured in terms of citizen's participation in their government, the extent to which decisions and policies reflect the popular will. It manifests concretely in the conferment on all adult citizens the right to vote, the right to stand as a candidate for election. It also means that individuals who legitimately win in elections should not be denied the right to execute their legislative or executive functions on the grounds of ethnic or regional alignment or sex. But the enjoyment of political equality may not make real sense in an atmosphere of socio-economic disabilities.

This chapter has not emphasized any one account of justice as fully adequate or uniquely correct. The traditional approaches to justice highlighted here have their own attractions and capture important insights but each by itself does not tell the whole story. The best way to understand why one cares about justice and inequality is to leave theory aside and listen carefully to what actual victims of injustice are saying. Clearly, theories of justice make sense only if one remains sensitive to the actual frustrations of those who long for justice.

There is a need to integrate these traditional approaches to justice in our social policy formulations and instead of selecting one and ignoring others, there is a need to appreciate the real insights, which attract people to each of these standard theories and then remain open to combining these various insights into an integrated whole. It is from this perspective that this chapter examines the issues raised by Alli.

The Nigerian Polity: Chris Alli's Case Study

Nigeria is made up of a variety of tribes, related ethnic or ideological groups and nations linked economically and politically under a common government, a colonially imposed territorial unit. The British colonial government created a unified Nigeria in 1914. Hitherto the British arrival, there was nothing one could call shared national consciousness, culture or language in Nigeria, or was there any sentiment to come together to form one political entity. Clearly, what is known today as Nigeria was created by fiat, thanks to colonial invasion.

At independence in 1960, Nigeria was politically composed of western, Eastern and Northern regions. The Mid west was carved out of the former Western region. It was these regions that reinforced Nigeria's major geographical, cultural and ethnic groupings with the Hausa Fulani concentrated in the north, Yoruba in the southwest and Igbo in the southeast. Other ethnic groups categorized as minorities can be found scattered across the length and breadth of Nigeria. These include the Tiv in the Middle Belt, the Edo in the Mid-West and the Efik, Ibibio and the

Ijaws in the East. This composition subsisted until 1966 when the regions were abolished.

It is important to note that distributional issues were handled at the regional centres which were controlled by the major ethnic groups. Being in control of the power centres, it was alleged that the three major ethnic groups benefited enormously and got the lion's share of everything within their areas of authority, while the ethnic minorities complained bitterly of domination and marginalization (Igbo: 1997). Though the regions were abolished in 1966 and replaced with 12 states structure and subsequently 36 states, hues and cries of domination and marginalization have not ceased. In what follows, attempts are made to highlight some of the issues raised by Alli.

Justice issues from Alli's Perspective: a reflection

It is important to note from the onset that Alli did not articulate any consistent or systematic theory of justice. His approach is rather critical of the existing Nigerian socio-political structure given the essential ingredients that define justice. He proceeds to show that the implementation of certain policies in Nigeria is more in breach of justice principles, fairness and merit than in conformity with such. One may not be wrong in asserting that Alli is a defender and champion of the ethnic minority interests and the ordinary Nigerian citizen as he brings to the fore some of the teething challenges of marginalization and exclusion facing them in the Nigerian polity. Worthy of particular note are issues of federalism/power sharing, federal character/quota system, revenue allocation/formula, and what he calls the Nigerian factor. One's reflection on Alli in this chapter is along these lines.

Federalism/Power sharing

The federal system is decentralized form of governance in which power is shared between the central government and the federating units, which could be regions or states. In true federalism, the federating units are supposed to enjoy some autonomy in political and fiscal terms. The guiding justice principle is political equality. Political equality as already mentioned, is measured in terms of citizens' or composite group's participation in their government, the extent to which decisions and policies reflect the popular will. It manifests concretely in the conferment on all adult citizens the right to vote, the right to stand as a candidate for election. It also means that individuals who legitimately win in elections should not be denied the right to execute their legislative or executive functions on the grounds of ethnic or regional alignment or sex.

What Alli observes regarding the practice of federalism in Nigeria is a far cry from its principles as well as those of political equality. Specifically for him, there had been an overconcentration of power at the centre, leaving the states virtually at the mercy of the federal government. Beyond this, the federal arrangement seems to favour the major ethnic groups, while relegating the minorities. In chapter 7 of his book, Alli makes the point that the constitutional landmarks from 1922 to 1954 that formed the building blocks for the component parts and nationalities constituting the Nigerian union "structurally contained seeds of instability and inequality...that place the portals of power at the steps of the three main tribes (Hausa/Fulani, Igbo, Yoruba triumvirate) within the geographical north, east and west" (Alli, 2001:89).

In practice, for him then, the existing structures do not carry the minorities along or give them a sense of belonging. Political equality in this respect, requires that both the majority and minority ethnic groups, weak and small should be given say at all national representative forums (Alli 2001: 89-90).

Further, according to him, the politics of Nigeria since Independence has been that of number, which denies representation to the minorities excluding and marginalizing them. For him, "scores of component nationalities are discounted while the major hegemonies and large ethnic groups hide behind the game of numbers to stifle minority voices and interests (Alli 2001: 91) Even the annulment of June 12 election (Chief M.K.O. Abiola saga) is particularly used by him to demonstrate that Nigeria has existed in the breach of justice principles than observance as this pertains to political equality.

What are the contradictions of Nigerian federalism as it is? For Alli (2001: 105) these include the land use act and the revenue formula and the fact that the union has been too suffocating for many nationalities that have no access to national power and resources in equitable measure. Further, the federal government has become the monthly paymaster; many otherwise vibrant and enterprising nationalities have been reduced to beggarly, unproductive natives living off the central government…a skewed federal revenue allocation formula that emphasizes land mass, need, population…rather than derivation for sharing the national cake. This reflects the greatest injustice in the national system (Alli 2001:106-107). The assorted calls for restructuring seem to bear Alli out in this regard.

Alli finds the remedy to this state of affairs in the practice of true federalism and this involves an acceptable power and revenue allocation sharing formula. Odu (2008: 26) concurs with him in his view that the revenue allocation formula should be calculated in such a way that each unit of the federation should receive grants in strict proportion to the financial contribution that it makes to the central revenue pool. This is justice in line with proportion.

Federal Character/Quota system
On federal character, the 1999 Nigerian constitution states:

> The composition of the Federal government or any of its agencies and the conduct of their affairs shall be carried out in such manner as to recognize the federal character of Nigeria and the need to promote national unity and command national loyalty. Accordingly, the predominance in that government or its agencies of persons from a few ethnic or other sectional groups shall be avoided.

In principle, the idea of Federal character emphasizes the need to ensure equal and fair representation of all states of the federation. The original intention of the government is to ensure that the affairs of the government at any level are not dominated by a few people from a particular ethnic group or a section of the country (Akinyele: 2012: 14). Akpanabia (2012) sees the federal character as a practice where every nationality is represented in all government owned institutions. Specifically, it was "designed to ensure equity, fair play and order among different ethnic nationalities that make up Nigeria in the distribution of resources, so as to promote national harmony and loyalty for economic development in the polity."

The offices that are subject to federal character application include those of permanent secretaries, director general, director, senior military officers, senior diplomatic posts, managerial cadres in federal and state parastatals, bodies, agencies and institutions. Alli points to marginalization as unequal appointments into federal jobs are the rule rather than the exception; ministerial appointments, commissions and judiciary, various committees of the senate and House of Representatives fall short of the constitutional provisions. These contradictions fly in the face of justice, equity and fairness. Clearly, the whole federal character is unfair as it has only succeeded in achieving the opposite of what it set out to achieve in practice.

Oyeweso (2017: 125) provides further insight into this contradiction in his view that using states as foundation for allocation of offices does not guarantee ethnic balances. According to him, the states in Nigeria are not created along ethnic lines or borders. This has been responsible for a situation where only the majority ethnic groups, the Hausa/Fulani; the Igbo and the Yoruba have benefitted most from the federal character arrangement. States in the Northern region have also benefited more than other regions owing to the large number of states in the region. This seems to underscore the point being made by Alli.

Quota system
The policy of quota system predates that of the federal character as it was already being implemented before 1960. The policy of federal character was officially recognized in 1979 Constitution. The quota system policy was aimed at facilitating equal representation of the various ethnic groups in Nigeria's civil service (Tonwe and Oghator, 2014). It was aimed at creating opportunities for disadvantaged states and requires that "special consideration should be given to candidates from the Northern provinces and other areas where educational facilities were more backward than elsewhere (Gboyega 1989).

These twin policies were aimed at addressing the issues of ethnic representation in the public sector, including issues of admission, recruitment, promotion and appointment. Following these, neither merit nor competence weighs much as far as advancement in the country's public institutions is concerned. Where this has played out evidently is in the admission system into Federal unity schools.

The essential ingredients of social equity include "fairness" in distribution, equality of opportunity, treating people with equal concern and respect and the notion that alike cases should be treated alike, meaning that people with similar characteristics should be treated in the same way in terms of the benefits enjoyed or the burdens suffered.

The 2013 National common Entrance Examinations cut-off marks by states give us a clear insight into the policy and practice of quota system in Nigeria and the violations of the above social equity principles thereof.

State --------------------------------- **Cut-off Mark**

North-central
Nasarawa --------------------------------- 75
Niger --------------------------------- 93
Plateau --------------------------------- 90

North East
Bauchi --------------------------------- 35
Borno --------------------------------- 45
Taraba --------------------------------- 3
Yobe --------------------------------- 2

Northwest
Sokoto --------------------------------- 9
Zamfara --------------------------------- 4
Kebbi, --------------------------------- 9

South East-
Anambra --------------------------------- 134
Imo --------------------------------- 138
Abia --------------------------------- 130

South West-
Lagos --------------------------------- 133
Ogun --------------------------------- 131
Ondo --------------------------------- 127

South-south
Edo --------------------------------- 127
Delta --------------------------------- 131
Rivers --------------------------------- 118
Cross River --------------------------------- 97
Akwa Ibom --------------------------------- 123
Bayelsa --------------------------------- 72

(Orakpo: 2013 Online)

In that national entrance, a pupil from Anambra State was expected to score at least 139 points to gain admission into the unity schools, while his counterpart from Yobe and Zamfara states were required to score only 2 marks out of a possible 200. The implication of that was that while candidates who scored 138 points in Anambra failed to gain admission, candidates from Zamfara with just two points were offered same. One of the consequences of this policy is that in the course of bridging the educational gap between the so-called educationally disadvantaged states and educationally advantaged states, the interest of the educationally advantaged states so - called is undermined. At the same time, meritocracy is thrown overboard giving rise to a situation where less qualified people are admitted.

Alli condemns this state of affairs in his view that "the philosophy of federal character, unity schools, secularity and similar pretensions have instead of institutionalizing fairness, polarized us, enthroned mediocrity and subverted the principles of nationhood." (Alli 2001:122) The whole scenario smacks of inequality and discrimination. If the purpose of quota system is to achieve national unity, it appears from Alli's position that this very purpose is defeated by its outcome. He is not alone in this regard.

Segun Joshua *et al.* (2014) similarly observe that the inclusion of the quota system and federal character principle in the educational sector creates a scenario of discrimination against Nigerians in their own country by virtue of ethnic identification, which is contrary to the provision of the constitution. What principle of justice would justify denying admission to candidates who scored 138 points in an examination while offering the same admission to candidates who scored 2 points? Such a policy distorts our common sense understanding of the principles of equity, fairness, and equality of opportunity. Such a policy exists in contradiction of its very end, which is national unity. Those denied opportunity through this means will feel aggrieved towards the system. The remedy to this is that the component nationalities, regions and states of the federation should have relative opportunities and placements in public sector institutions and governments. This is what Segun Joshua *et al.* (2014: 9) tried to affirm when they said that the policies of federal character and quota system be reviewed in such a way that will bring about the improvement in educational status of the educationally disadvantaged states, while not being injurious to those in vantage position. This appears to be more in tandem with justice principles of equity and fairness. In its present form the policies are punitive and injurious to the so-called educationally advantaged states. At the same time, such makes nonsense of the meritarian principle of justice.

The Nigerian Factor
As already noted, equity requires that positions in society and rewards should be distributed based on people's merits. This means that someone is required to have acted in a way that elicited some sort of treatment as a response. Under the merit principle of justice, a person may receive a favourable or unfavourable treatment depending on what the person has done. What the person deserves therefore, is a function of the actions or performances for which the individual is responsible. Practically, people applying for positions should be judged fairly according to their qualifications for the position. This principle is violated where factors such as family background, race or place of origin give people access to different types of job. Or where males and females are treated differently in consideration for a job or paid differently for performing similar tasks. Or where a person's social standing or political power is more operative in the sorts of opportunity available than their qualifications for the post (Gerber 2014: 8).

The Nigerian factor as perceived by Alli is one area in the sociopolity where the meritocracy as a principle of justice is jettisoned. According to him, the Nigerian Factor is the euphemism for operating outside the laws or rules, or seeking to moderate them (Alli 2001: 135). It is a twister of norms and laws guiding officials and non-officials in the conduct of affairs. Alli asserts that all aspects of Nigeria's national life is affected by this phenomenon namely, constitution, laws, culture, religions, ethnicity and status provide its operational environments and parameters. Within the operational framework of the Nigerian factor, anything goes; merit, intelligence and competence are compromised. The picture he paints is quite depressing: "the constraint to our creativity is referred to as the Nigerian factor - in other words, merit is not a critical factor in national development. What counts is quota system and federal character even if an imbecile or someone, whose medulla is as thick as plank of *iroko* wood, must represent the nation" (Alli 2001: 140). Further, he says:

> office, political or otherwise, symbolizes authority and power in government…What is on ground today is a government by patronage in which merit, capacity and capability are of little use to governance and management of resources. Privileges and rights are dispersed only when a seeker can present a note from a man of power, what you get from government agencies depend on whom you know (Alli 2001: 144).

Could Alli be exaggerating? The fact remains that the phenomenon Alli alludes to celebrates mediocrity and puts square pegs in round holes. One is not surprised at the level of inefficiency pervading the atmosphere in Nigeria. It ensures that competent and qualified people are schemed out besides further marginalizing the ordinary citizens who have no one to speak for them.

Revenue Allocation
The issue at stake in this respect concerns the percentage share which the Federal Government of Nigeria is to give the oil producing states and regions for the resources which it obtains from their location. The derivation percentage controversy in Nigeria goes back to the Riesman – led commission of 1958. Prior to this, the resource producing communities were entitled to full ownership of whatever came out of their land (Elaigwu 2003: 154). With the Riesman-led commission a three party sharing formula was devised regarding what percentage of resource revenue was to go to the centre, state and resource communities. It set aside 50% derivation for the region, 30% for the state and only 20% for the resource communities. After the Riesmann-led commission came the Bin-led Commission, which gave 50% to the regions, 35% to the communities, and 15% to the state. The bone of contention, which raises justice issues, is that the sharing formula is not equitable; it tilts in favour of the centre and thus, works to the detriment of the resource producing communities (Elaigwu 2003: 247).

The Riesman-led and Bin-led committees' agenda was jettisoned with the "Land use act" of 1978 and the 1979 constitution. By virtue of the Land Use Act, all lands and resources beneath were vested in the chief executive of respective states. This was followed by the Petroleum Act. From then on, the federal government has been receiving the lion's share at the detriment of the regions, states and especially the resource communities in the country, where the disadvantaged group who suffer most from resource exploitation resides. Enunciating this further, Alli goes historical: Gowon-led administration gave only 30% to the states and 5% to the resource communities. Obasanjo's Administration (1976-1979) reduced Gowon's 30% to 25%. Shagari's government further reduced Obasanjo's 25% to 3% in 1981. Buhari's Administration in 1984 reduced Shagari's 3% to 1.5% in 1984. The government of Sani Abacha took Babangida's figure to 4.5% then to a further 7% for the resource communities. In the wake of democracy 1999, Obasanjo/Atiku –led administration took Abacha's 7% to 13% derivation for the resource producing communities. That has remained the status since then (Alli 2001: 113)

From the libertarian perspective, the foregoing scenario appears unjust. The libertarians' stance on justice stems from the inviolability of moral rights. Rights-based libertarians such as John Locke and Robert Nozick frown at the attempt to redistribute goods so as to maximize overall happiness or improve the condition of the worst-off, insisting that such redistribution is typically unjust. They contend that goods are not merely largess that fall from the skies; they have to be produced and normally are the property of their producer.

The criteria of distributive justice are usually equity, equality and need. Equity implies that one's rewards should be equal to one's contributions to society, while "equality" means that everyone gets the same amount, regardless of their input. In this connection, Alli raises the issue of fair sharing as this pertains to revenue allocation. The point he seems to be making is that the oil producing communities deserve much more than has been apportioned to them in view of the fact that the oil is harvested from their territory. No matter what good consequences the successive governments in Nigeria may wish to achieve, it is unjust to take the resource of the Niger Delta to develop other regions while neglecting the region. As the rightful owner of the mineral (oil) they stand a privileged position or moral dominion over it.

From the utilitarian perspective, justice demands that the wellbeing of every person matters equally and consequences for everyone are to be counted and no one's being is given more weight than the others. Regarding what good should be maximized, the utilitarians agree that the right action is that which maximizes the good. Alluding to the Niger Delta conundrum on page 89 of his book, Alli points out that the three major ethnic groups (Hausa, Igbo, Yoruba) have been living off the natural resources of (e.g, oil mineral) communities in the Niger Delta while the latter have suffered severe neglect and gross violation of their rights to adequate development and other welfare concerns. According to him, "major nationalities like the Ijaws of the Delta mangroves areas gushing with oil, the mainstay of the nation's economy, have since the fifties continued to wallow in poverty, disease, neglect and environmental degradation while these big three luxuriate in comfort." (2001: 89). What this means is that successive governments in Nigeria have not been adequately taken right actions that translates to maximizing the good of the people in the oil producing communities.

If justice means giving to everyone his due, the impression one gets from Alli's assertion is that the oil mineral producing communities in the Niger Delta have not been getting their due as evident in the debilitating condition of the area. This is an important point. But is the debilitating life condition an experience unique to the Niger Delta region? The answer is in the negative because poverty, disease and neglect are widespread in Nigeria and they touch the ordinary Nigerian regardless of location (North, South East and West). Distributive justice highlights the sorts of goods and services that people are said to need, which include shelter, physical security and environment, health care, water and sanitation and nutrition, a basic education and so on. People need these things in order to have a full life. But one discovers that these basic necessities of life are in short supply across the length and breadth of the Nigerian political and geographical landscape.

Instead of blaming the big three ethnic groups, Alli should rather focus his search light on the ruling elite (the tiny minority) that have presided over the affairs of the Nigerian state since independence. It is this tiny minority and its corrupt practices that deny the larger majority the resources meant for infrastructural development and human welfare. It was in this connection that Jacob Olupona (2017: 16-19) has said that "the Nigerian system creates a closed elite society that provides itself access to the benefits of citizenship, while denying these benefits to others."

Alli (2001: 119) totally and without reservation endorses the derivation principle that compensates each component part of the Nigerian federation in line with what it contributes to the national till from natural endowment, that is, natural resources. Justice demands that the biggest share be given to the oil producing communities who actually own these resources and suffer most from the effects of mineral exploitation. Supporting Alli's position, Odu (2008: 56) says "it stands to reason that areas that generate any form of public revenue should be entitled to a sizeable chunk of revenue receipts there-from."

In other words, the order should be reversed thus: the lion's share ought to go to the communities, followed by the state, then the regions and the least share of derivation be left to the federal government whose role in any "true federalism" is merely that of coordinating the resources of the communities and the state. This is what Alli considers to be equitable and just.

Conclusion

This chapter set out to reflect on equity and justice issues as thrown up by M. Chris Alli in his book titled *The Federal Republic of Nigerian Army: the Siege of a Nation*. To be able to do this, the chapter explored the various accounts of justice, ranging from utilitarians', John Rawls' and libertarians', as well as equity principles. It affirmed following the kernel of truth which each embodies that all need to be integrated in the implementation of social policy objectives.

The chapter also examined the various policies (federalism/power sharing, federal character/quota system, revenue allocation formula and the Nigerian factor), which are bones of contention for Alli. It indeed observed that these policies have justice and equity issues that needed to be addressed. From the perspectives of other authors cited in the work, it was clear that Alli's contestations were substantially founded.

As earlier mentioned in the discourse on the various accounts of justice, the importance of justice does not just lie in the theories but in one's sensitivity to the sufferers or victims of injustice. In this respect, Alli deserves one's approbation for shinning the light through his book. What is left to be done is for the powers that be to hearken to the voice of reason and create an atmosphere of dialogue for the issues raised by him to be debated and appropriate steps taken to address them.

Social equity standards apply to our personal and social relationships with other individuals and/or groups and embody a bundle of rights and duties. Given the position of Alli in his book, social equity is really nothing more than rectifying injustice and doing justice to our fellow human beings who have suffered injuries at present or in the past as a result of their circumstances. So far in the Nigerian context, these have taken the form of discrimination, marginalization and neglect which have caused the victims to suffer a loss of the equal rights and opportunities that enhance their wellbeing. Does one doubt that from Alli's assertions that these have been the experience of many a Nigerian, particularly the ethnic minorities and the ordinary citizen? Alli must be commended for highlighting the contradictions in the Nigerian state. Inequality in ethnic relations, followed by other forms of democratic privation, including highly unequal voice in political affairs and government processes that pander more to the privileged few than to the generality of the citizens cannot make for justice, neither can it promote equity. Equity and justice guided by human rights call for integration of equality of opportunity and its concomitant values, such as non-discrimination, non-marginalization whether of the minority or the majority ethnic groups by any ruler, and recognizing the differential needs of the regions composing the Nigerian polity.

References

Akinyele, R. T. 2012. "Administrative History and Crisis of Governance in Nigeria", *Network of Nigerian Historians Monograph Series No.1*

Akpanabia N.H., 2012. "Federal character as Pitfall for National Development in Nigeria: A Historical Perspective". *Elixir Human Resource Management*, 47A: 9155-9158.

Alli, M.C. 2001. *The Federal Republic of Nigerian Army: the Siege of a Nation.* Surulere, Lagos: Malthouse Press Ltd.

Federal Government Press, Constitution of the Federal Republic of Nigeria, 1999, Apapa-Lagos

Elaigwu, J.A. 2003. *The Politics of Federalism in Nigeria.* Jos: Gravis Press.

Gerber, M. 2014. "Promoting Equality including social Equity, gender Equality and women's Empowerment," 8th session of the open Working Group on sustainable Development Goals, New York, 3-7. 2. 2014, Statement on behalf of France, Germany and Switzerland).

Gboyega, A. 1989. "The Public Service and federal Character," in Ekeh P.P. Osaghae, E.E. eds. *Federal Character and Federalism in Nigeria.* Ibadan, Nigeria: Heinemann Educational books. P. 164-185.

Igbo, E.U.M. 1997. "Towards distributive and social Justice in Nigeria," in F.U. Okafor, *New Strategies for Curbing Ethnic and Religious conflicts in Nigeria.* Enugu: Fourth Dimension Publishing Co., Ltd, 202-222

Joshua, S., Loromke, Ronald E. and Olarenwaju, I. P. 2014, "Quota System, Federal Character principle and Admission to Federal Unity Schools: Barriers to Learning in Nigeria," *Interdisciplinary Journal of Interdisciplinary Studies* (IJIMS), 2014, vol. 2, No. 2. 1-10.

Odu, R.I.E. 2008, *Resource Control: Legal Right of Niger Delta Region of Nigeria?* Lagos: University of Lagos Press.

Olupona, J. K. 2017. "The challenges of Nation building: Ethnicity, Religion and Citizenship in Nigeria," in Festus Adesannoye, ed. *Religion, Ethnicity and Citizenship.* An Occasional Publication of the Nigerian Academy of Letters (NAL) number 15. Ibadan, Nigeria: Nigerian Academy of Letters. 1-27.

Orakpo E. Abayomi A, Adesulu D., Why government should revisit Admission Quota System. *Vanguard* (on line). Available from http.//www.vanguard.com/2013/06/why-govt-should-revisit-admission-quota-system/

Rawls, John. 1999. *A Theory of Justice.* Revised edition, Oxford: oxford University press.

Oyeweso, S. 2017. "Rethinking the Nexus of Religion, Ethnicity and Citizenship in Nigeria: the Imperatives of national Restructuring," in Festus Adesanoye ed. *Religion, Ethnicity and Citizenship.* An occasional Publication of the Nigerian Academy of Letters (NAL), Number 15, 89-158.

Tonwe, D.A. and Oghator E.O. 2009." The Federal Character Principle and Democratic Stability in Nigeria". In: Ola R.F and Tonwe D.A. (eds). *Nigerian Public Adminstration.* Lagos, Nigeria: Amfitop, p.230-256.

Wellman, C. H. 2002. "Justice" in Robert L. Simon ed. *The Blackwell Guide to Social and Political Philosophy*, Massachusetts: Blackwell Publishers Ltd, pp. 60-84.
(http://swww.socialequity.unimelb.edu.au/what-is-social equity/ downloaded 13/6/16

Chapter 11

Neo-Liberalism and M. Chris Alli's Hermeneutics of Federalism

-Maduabuchi Dukor

Introduction

M. Chris Alli, a contemporary Nigerian neo-liberal thinker, can be comprehended from the developmental and transitory paradigm of a post-colonial African nation in dire-stress and pitfalls of nation building *pari pasu* federalism qua 'true federalism'. Between liberalism and neo-liberalism and federalism and true federalism are the socio-political problematic and intellectual ferment, leverages and platforms upon which M. Chris, Alli, as neo-liberal thinker, engaged the actions and inactions, success and failures of the governments of his time in Nigeria. This engagement is on the hermeneutics of federalism qua true federalism and neo liberal political economy in Nigeria. His discourse on federalism is precisely on the problematic and sinews of true federalism in Nigeria in the context of neo-liberal philosophy. Neo liberal thinkers are first and foremost liberal in their thinking but were prevailed upon by the vicissitudes, complexities and demands of contemporary socio political realities and problems to re-engage liberal thought on the new and evolving paradigm dictated by race, people, culture, state, nation and development. Ali, therefore, analysed Nigerian predicament and development as something that should be dictated by people, culture and post-colonial environment.

M. Chris Alli, as a neo-liberal thinker in his book, *The Federal Republic of Nigeria Army*, therefore, engaged federalism from the perspective of Nigerian federalism as both contemporary and neo-liberal concept. His thought is embedded in the fluidity of the concept of neo-liberalism which as an analytical device entails some recent economic, social and political trends to showing that, indeed, we live on a neo-liberal age or a neo-liberal society.

The neo-liberal age or neo-liberal society is however, created by the problems of new associations and societies. Neo-liberal thinking about Nigeria is similarly created by those challenges known to be Nigerian in its multicultural and multi-religious diversity. M. Chris Alli reflected on Nigerian neo-liberal problems thus:

> The origin of Nigeria's federalism is a reverse of the American system in both concept and intent. The American federalism is a coming together by the free choice of small strong units under one umbrella. The Nigerian federation started the other way round, characteristic of all its affairs, first as protectorates with provinces, then as regions and subsequently quasi-states or unified states (Alli, 2001, 104).

The theoretical foil he employs here is not really a critique of federalism as it were in Americana geopolitical stratosphere but a satire of the concept and its imperfections outside its original existential and political ecology. It is rather the imperfections of federalism in Nigeria that are subjected as the token of neo-liberal analysis.

M. Chris Alli as a Neo-Liberal thinker

Neo-liberal political philosophy, as the socio-political mirror and proposition of new age and new challenges, shares a common root with liberalism and, of course, democracy. It refers primarily to the twentieth century resurgence of the nineteenth century ideas associated with laissez-faire economic liberalism. Neo-liberalism in the Nigerian sense, is therefore a case for classical liberalism which is a political doctrine that takes protecting and enhancing the freedom of the individuals to be the central problem of politics and that government is necessary to protect individuals from being harmed by others but recognizes that government itself can pose a threat to liberty.

The vistas and vintages of neo-liberal political philosophy historically is a mirror of Nigerian society which M. Chris Alli addresses in his magnum opus. As an undiluted political thinking it is a remedial and mediation of individual freedom and the threat to liberty poses by government. This neo-liberal attitude is also applicable to economic and social relations among religious and cultural groups in a nation state which in most cases as a phenomenon is undergirded by historical contingency and necessity defined by Historicism. Be that as it may the attitude and latitude of nations and states in adapting liberal approach to their different and various peculiar challenges is the collateral window of neo-liberal political philosophy. In reminiscing on philosophy qua philosophies like African philosophy, Western philosophy, and Indian philosophy as ethno philosophy, neo-liberal philosophy like postmodernism also becomes the philosophy of the new age which studies peoples, and nations with their cultural historical, political and economic differences and experiences.

In his neo-liberal thinking M. Chris Alli would predicate his hermeneutics on federalism on some historical anecdotes which are economic and political issues. He argues that:

> ...before slave trade and colonization became scourge of historical experience Africans had receded from the high pedestal of their great civilizations that sprung from our North African origins and heritage, African traditional societies gathered themselves continuously into new kingdoms as they migrated south wards. Nubia, Abyssinia, Somali, Mali, Songhai, Ghana, Benin, Dahomey and Zulu empire, to name a few. It was against these kingdoms which were beginning to find a niche for our intrinsic black heritage that the slave trade and colonization assaulted with a fury. Their logic was based on the ethnocentric theory of racial superiority. Colonial rule was fully established after the Papal Bull of demarcation or the Berlin West Africa conference of 1885, which indiscriminately shared out Africa, kingdoms and territories to European powers (Alli, 2001: 184).

For good reasons in neo-liberal thought, economic history is a nation's torchlight to unravelling liberal economic contemporary challenge. M. Chris Ali therefore, agrees with Walter Rodney who had stated thus:

> The things which bring Africa into the capitalist market system are trade, colonial domination and investment. Trade had existed for several centuries: colonial rule began in the late nineteenth century

and has almost disappeared. Throughout the period that Africa has participated in the capitalist economy, two factors have brought about underdevelopment. In the first place, the wealth created by African labour and from African resources was grabbed by the capitalist countries of Europe, and in the second place, restrictions were placed upon African capacity to make the maximum use of its potentials which is what development is all about...(Rodney, 1982: 25).

On the other hand, the neo liberal thinking on the economic limitation of liberal economic history of modern African nations is captured by M. Chris Alli's historical analysis of Nigerian socio-economic development, thus:

The ordinary and everyday definition of military intervention in the political affairs of nations will not serve our purpose. Indeed, it is a misnomer to talk about military intervention in Nigeria. What is pertinent is, perhaps, to refer to civil intervention in military governance since independence. The truth is that the nation, since 1960, has been ruled by military and quasi-military personnel with the traditional militancy of pre-colonial authority. Practically, all colonial rulers of pre-Independence Nigeria were soldiers or men who derived their stay from the threat of the use of military power. As far as I can reflect, our empire Days, the district, provincial, regional and central authorities were nearly always in military uniforms, capped in white helmet (Alli, 2001:162).

The historical reality adverted by Alli is not only a litmus test of neo-liberal radical and innovative dehydration of classical liberalism but also diachronic analysis of civil intervention in military governance and vice-versa leading to Nigerian 1999 Constitution widely believed to be a military and undemocratic constitution worthy of neo-liberal afflatus and second order analysis.

Arising from the above is that if a socioeconomic condition leads to economic and political inequalities, the unfortunate persons and nations reserve the right to demand of the state to right the wrongs especially in a plural lopsided society. To address this socio-economic imbalance often created by history, act of missions and commissions of states and even sometimes liberal economic freedom, neo liberalism becomes "a loose set of ideas of how the relationship between the state and its external environment ought to be organized (Blomgren 1997; Maiwes 1998). In trying to tinker with the socio-economic and political challenges of plural and democratic societies neo-liberal political thinking takes a number of open check and blanket assumptions which are often interpreted to mean that policies inspired by neo-liberalism could be implemented under the auspices of autocrats as well as within liberal democracies. The critical and suspicious attitude of neo-liberal thinking to liberal establishment will mean that proponents of neo-liberalism are often, in the critical liberative, portrayed as sceptics of democracy:

> if the democratic process slows down neo-liberal reforms, or threatens individual and commercial liberty, which it sometimes does, democracy ought to be sidestepped and replaced by the rule of experts or legal instruments designed for that purpose. The practical implementation of neo-liberal policies will, therefore, lead to a relocation of power from political to markets and individuals and finally from the legislature and executive authorities to the judiciary (Thorsen and Lie, 2006:15).

This captivates the neo-liberal tinkering in Nigerian predicament with the (new Nigerian age) clamour for devolution of powers and resource control for equity, fairness and justice as well as in Alli's neo-liberal hermeneutics of liberalism in Nigerian contexts

M. Chris Alli has ingeniously displayed neo-liberal tinkering of Nigeria's liberal democratic injustice. With his remedial readjustment of the condition of the weak and the disadvantaged in a lopsided political economy he appropriated John Rawls' liberal political reforms and with his minimal state conception relative to the interest of the naturally endowed and disadvantaged he lends credence to Robert Nozick reduction of states power. It is under this theoretical and empirical presupposition that M. Chris Alli's critique of liberal political philosophy of Nigerian federalism is called neo liberal tinkering of federalism.

M. Chris Alli is an ardent critic of the liberal economy of the twenty-first century Nigeria drawing his theoretical sledgehammer from his personal experience and the experiences of disadvantaged individuals in the Nigerian polity of his time. Even in practice he was on the side of the appraised minority at any time he was given the opportunity to contribute to either national discourse or intelligence debate within the top brass of military circles. He unreservedly not only added his voice to the voices of the oppressed Niger Delta people of Nigeria, no matter whose ox was gored in a military cabinet, as an activist in the military government he argued thus:

> In 1992, as the board discussed the activities of Ken Saro Wiwa and Ogoni movement for self-realization, there were strong accusations that Ogoni movement was insurrectional in character and formation with an implied secessionist objective. It was posited that Ogoni movement ought to be crushed ignoring its political and social imperatives and motivations. This was inadvertently the view of certain elements with the ethnic origins in the Big True. With my intervention attention was further drawn to the genuine governances of the oil producing areas and the compelling need for the federal government to take a visionary and agrarian view of the Ogoni and other similar situations that abound and still do around the nation. It was pointed out that neither the creation of states nation-wide nor the existing federal revenue formula would address the wrongs of a people whose fortunes have turned to misfortune because they belong to a federation within which they must remain, Willy willy or by threat of force. This is a condition only minorities understand well in Nigeria (p.80).

The Big Three alluded above is for M. Chris Alli the exploitative majority groups in Nigeria whose affluence at the expense of the oil or wealth creating areas of Niger Delta and the nascent politics of neglect of these minorities has taken a vicious dimension in Nigeria's political economy. The political economy of Nigerians is however at the rearing end of this vicious game of the Big Three. The minority is mired in neglect, disease, pollution and poverty in the midst of liquid gold, their awareness of the status quo, inequity and unjust exploitation was bond to grow in time. It was bound to grow in rising crescendo, and to reach revolutionary proportions, Alli asserted. Chris Alli interventions and interlocutions are suggestive of the Adam Smith's advice on political economy thus:

a political economy, proposes two distinct things; first, to provide a plentiful revenue or subsistence for the people, or more properly to enable them to provide for themselves and secondly, to supply the state or the common wealth with revenue sufficient for public services. It proposes to enrich both the people and the sovereign" (Adam Smith, 2007 BKV1. The neo-liberal political economy with which M. Chris Alli is analysing the predicament of the oppressed minorities of the Niger Delta communities in Nigeria is a system which should lent voice to the prescription of Adam Smith that the role of the state is to enable the people to provide for themselves and to provide for the subsistence of the state through the maximization of the individual freedom in the liberalized market for the common good of all in the context proper federalism or true federalism.

What scientifically and theoretically casts M. Chris Alli in the mould of a neo-liberal political tactician, theoretician and prophet of the struggle of the exploited minorities is what he wrote and has become the revolution in Nigeria characterized by oil pipeline vandalization, kidnapping of oil workers, crude, oil theft, agitation for resource control, armed struggle against government and multinational interests in oil exploration and agitations for successions and devolution of powers.

Ali's hermeneutics of new liberal political economy could be posited in between the far left and far right political ideologies, to be precise, he is in between Robert Nozik's minimal state and John Rawls' liberal political reforms but more articulately on the side of the later with considerable measure of neo liberal market reforms which identifies with the oppressed and the exploited in a lopsided, unfair capitalist laissez faire economy under the guise of federalism. His neo-liberalism is in an appropriate answer to the defects of liberal political economy and the monstrous political compound called federalism in Nigeria, albeit, which draws him closer to John Rawls than Nozik. He seeks and advocates for human face in politics and in inter personal relations and hence he uses the entrepreneurial adventure and neo-liberal economic and political thought to analyse the predicament of the poor and the oppressed in Nigeria and wherever. The neo-liberal political and economic thought is being employed by M. Chris Alli as a theoretical handle to argue against robbing individuals of discipline, initiative and hobbling private enterprise by the intrusion of the state.

As we observed earlier M. Chris Ali's political and economic thought has a lean connection with the liberal egalitarianism of Robert Nozik, an America philosopher at Harvard whose work, *Anarchy State and Utopia* (1974) was a response to John Rawl's *Theory of Justice*. However, being a centre left libertarian, Alli would be uncomfortable with a theory which prescribes drastically minimal state and near extreme freedom for the individuals, a freedom that would be counterproductive to the officialdom of the state. He would subscribe to the sovereignty of the state punctuated with political, social and economic interventions with neo liberal nuances. This inclination inherently draws him closer to John Rawl's theory of Justice as fairness. Like Rawl's, he critiqued the inequality created by the state in some circumstances, for instance, the Nigeria condition where the state has "destroyed the principle and practice of fiscal federalism and democracy in the country, rendering the state's and local governments' finances anaemic." (Alli p. 115).

He caricatured the Nigerian state and the control of the three big ethnic groups - Hausa/Fulani, Igbo and Yoruba for unduly exploiting the Niger Delta communities from whose land the nation oil wealth is extracted with actions and policies that undermine the development of the areas. "The big three have turned parasitic and lazy, overwhelmed by the largesse of the Niger Delta wealth…they constitute expenditure conduits, a contractocracy' and putting nothing enduring in place, for now or for future generations." (p. 116). For Chris Ali the plight of minorities under the Nigerian state is of universal negative import to humanity. This is a concern that raises the spectre of minimal state, libertarianism, militarism and awesome statehood.

M. Chris Alli's four statements against Unitary Federalism

M. Chris Alli's hermeneutics of federalism consistently views limited state, self-governing entitled, regions, resource control and devolution of powers as antidote to unitarism as federalism and military government which characteristics are as follows: (1) the central government has grown unwieldy and wasteful, there was over-centralization of power, executive, legislature and judicial control in the hands of single individuals (2) there is also a very strong linkage between the military, oil resources and coup d'état as soldiers ravage the nation to assuage personal and group appetite for power and wealth (3) the unitary system under which state and local governments, monthly collect revenue allocations from the centre with no value added, no productively generated, no growth in local productive activity, is a basket case. (4) unlike what we had in the 1963 regional Constitution, existing structural arrangements have prevented local resources to generate development, revenue, employment and economic activity in their areas. The pervasive healthy competition among the four regions in the past contrasts poorly with the resource-wasting propensity of our present unitary system. According to him instead of the above unitarist structures,

> equity and good judgement demand that component nationalities, regions and states of the federation should have relative opportunities and placement in public sector institutions and governments springing from a federation of nationalities, each component part should derive as much as it contributes to the national till commensurate to its inherent energies or natural resources. To create the right national equilibrium for promotion of unity and participation, it is expected that certain disadvantaged communities and regions may be specially provided for, and their relative advancement promoted at no irrational cost or deprivation to others, or at the expense of other areas (pp. 119-120).

The above four statements constitute the moral, political and existential framework upon which M. Chris Alli rejects a unitary government or constitution, advocates for proper federalism and opts for neo-liberalism to quench the fire of the humanitarian crisis in liberal democracy using the relative modulation of liberalism called neo-liberalism.

As a neo liberalist, he would (a) appeal to natural law to answer questions of obligation, right and reason (b) stress individual rights justified by reason (c) assert an equilibrium between government and subject (man) (d) argue that power and authority are to be judged by reference to their purposes as well as the regularities of the natural law that define natural obligations and duties.

John Rawls Principle of Justice and M. Chris Alli's minority question in Nigeria

The stand points of M. Chris Alli is a bold attempt to reconstruct the liberal theory of federalism in Nigeria in order to bridge the gap between the rich and the poor as well among ethnic nationalities in Nigeria. As a neo-liberalist he is reconstructing the Nigerian federalism into a proper federalism where some arbitrary distinction and proper balance are to be interpreted on the basis of John Rawls' theory of justice. And like Socrates, Plato, Aristotle and Rawls M. Chris Alli is concerned with the normative and practical common good of any social contract and like the social contract theorists such as Thomas Hobbes, John Locke and J.J Rousseau he would not question the validity of consent and franchise in the measurement of economic and political privileges. But as a post-modern social contract theorist and a neo liberal political and economic thinker he would judge the social contract theories of Hobbes, Locke and Rousseau on insufficient basis for justice and proper federalism in a Nigeria characterized by inequitable distribution of wealth among individuals and nationalities, wasteful central, or unitary government, military and militarized leadership and corruption.

Ali shares with John Rawl's the view that the social basis of self-respect for any individual or group is predicated on (a) basic civil liberties and political rights (b) economic goods like income, wealth, institutional authority, economic power and social position. This expresses justice as a complex of three ideas, liberty, equality and reward to services contributing to the common goal. This means that what justice and fairness share in common is reciprocity (Dukor, 2004:22). The two principles are what constitute John Rawl's two principles of justice which M. Chris Alli treats justice and fairness in the Nigerian situation but the contrary of which Ali brought out in his critique of the derivation principle. On 3 December, 1998 the summary of statutory revenue allocation with VAT for the month of November 1998 showed that:

> Lagos State had the highest of ₦501,147,955.42, followed by Kano and Katsina with ₦362, 293,120.42 and ₦349,230,612,90. Rivers State and Delta State, both major oil producers are allocated, ₦301, 971,106.69 and ₦309,380,285.19 respectively. What is more baffling

is that Bayelsa is allocated ₦96,498,649.94 a fitting demonstration of Nigerian equity and justice... the truth of the matter is that, the entity called Nigeria was conceived, constructed, cemented and held together by force, deceit and subterfuge to the ultimate benefit of the Hausa/Fulani, the Yoruba and Ndigbo in the arithmetical progression (p.117).

Ali further analysis shows that a state where the Igbo ethnic group has five state, the Yoruba, seven states and the Hausa/Fulani group and its peripheral states has about fourteen states guarantees the hegemony of the three major ethnics groups over the smaller groups comprising of the Rivers, Akwa Ibom, Cross River, Delta and Bayelsa states who are the major sources of the country's revenue in terms of oil resources appropriation. At a particular period, the revenue allocation formula added up to "Igbo, ₦845,902,953.07, the Yoruba, ₦1,600,652,515.22 and Fulani, ₦3,743,652,515.22 and the oil-producing states comprising Edo, Delta, Rivers Bayelsa, Cross-River and Akwa Ibom collected ₦1,323,306,290.15. The three ethnic hegemonies altogether collected revenues in excess of ₦7,503, 802, 969. 37 (P. 117).

M. Chris Alli's analysis of the figures and facts concerning the appropriation of oil revenue is a vivid construction of a systemic injustice sitting on the tripped nature of the hegemony of the big tribes in Nigeria who appropriate unjustly the naturally endowed oil resources in the smaller tribes of Nigeria. To remedy this kind of errant and extant volcanoes injustice, Rawls, in his theory of justice in a capitalist state would argue for the "economic adequacy for worst off man" (Dukor, 2004:22) while M. Chris Alli in his neo-liberal articulation of proper federalism would argue that "certain disadvantaged communities and regions may be specially provided for and their relative advancement promoted at no irrational cost or deprivation of others". Economic adequacy, a future of the special conception of justice, is attained when the search for food, shelter and work has become routine rather than urgent. It must extend to the citizens who are economically the worst off in a society in order for the society to meet the condition for the priority of the basic liberties which is sufficient wealth for basic liberties to be effectively exercised.

M, Chris Alli's theorized a case for the disadvantage which underlying principle coheres with Rawls' first priority of liberty upon which (a) a less extensive liberty must strengthen the total system of liberty shared by all (b) a less than equal liberty must be acceptable to those with the lesser liberty (Rawls,1971:285), it also agrees with Rawl's second priority of justice over efficiency and welfare where upon " (a) an inequality of opportunity must enhance the opportunity of those with the lesser opportunity (b) an excessive rate of saving must on balance mitigate the burden of those bearing the hardship" (Ibid). The first and second priorities of liberty and justice over efficiency and welfare respectively are therefore as much Rawl's antidote to malignant inequality and injustice in a capitalist society of Europe and America as it is M. Chris Alli take in resolving the deprivations and imbalances in the sharing of oil resources and revenues among the Big Three ethnic groups and minority oil producing tribes in Nigeria. For him liberty' an irreducible minimum with redistributive justice in terms of maximizing the sum or aggregate advantages with equal opportunities should be inviolate principle and praxis of proper federalism in Nigeria. His neo-liberal thinking on the political economy of Nigeria is, therefore , "addressing sufficiently the educational imbalance between North and South with a view to promoting healthy and equitable competitive climate" to stopping the "northern leaders milking the Niger Delta region" and the militarized notion that "you do not argue with a man carrying gun" (p.141).

The aesthetics of M. Chris Alli thoughts on the predicament of the Nigerian governance maladies is in its neo-liberal methodology and justifications. At the same time it is neo-Rawlsian in approach even as one could possibly argue that John Rawls anticipated him in the situation of the disadvantaged and the privileged classes where however, justice must be appropriated somewhere.

M. Chris Alli's perception of an equitable federal character and Rawls' principles of Justice would raise the question, who is the progenitor of redistributive concept of justice as fairness?. Alli argues thus:

> equity and good judgment demand that component nationalities, regions and states of the federation should have relative opportunities

and placement in public sector institutions and governments springing from a federation of nationalities, each component part should derive as much as it contributes to the national till commensurate to its interest, energies or national locational endowment, that is natural resources. To create the right national equilibrium for the promotion of unity and participation, it is expected that certain disadvantaged communities and regions may be specially provided for and their relative advancement promoted at no irrational cost or deprivation to others areas. Such rationalization should be for a given period of time until the weak and disadvantages are pulled up by its own shoestring and special effort especially as the federal government controls the commanding heights of the economy, strategic areas of industry, commerce and administration...(p.120).

In Rawls two principles of justice (1) every person has equal right to basic liberties compatible with liberty for all (2) social and economic inequalities should be the greatest, expected benefit of the least advantaged and attached to offices and positions open to all under conditions of fair opportunity, (Rawls, P. 230). In both M. Chris Alli and John Rawls therefore both the equality of right to basic liberties and the economic goals of the disadvantaged at a particular time and over a certain period are indispensible. For Alli the federal character or quota system of rationally managed would be amenable to an indelible social justice system. This would also have taken care of Rawls apprehensions concerning the fate of the disadvantaged in a prebendal political economy.

To corroborate M. Chris Alli's neo-liberal thesis on just Nigerian political economy, Rawls further explicated his two principles of Justice. "The first of these principles is to take priority over the second; and the measure of benefit to the least advantaged is specified in terms of an index of social primary goods. These goods I define roughly as rights, liberties and opportunities, income and wealth. Individuals are assumed to want these goods, whatever else they want, or whatever their final ends. The least advantaged are defined very roughly, as the overlap between those who are least favoured by each of the three main kinds of contingencies. Thus, this group includes persons whose family and class origins are more disadvantaged than others, whose materials endowments have permitted them to fair well, and whose fortune and luck have been relatively less favourable, all within the normal range and with the relevant measures based on social primary goods (p. 230 and 231). Methodologically, Rawls is more technical than M. Chris Alli even as both conceptions of primary social goods are in grave deprivation among the minorities and the Niger Delta region of Nigeria. In both philosophers, neo-liberalism is extant, redressing economic imbalances is an imperative, equality of opportunity is emphasized, basic liberties are inviolable and condition of the worst off group or the utterly disadvantaged must be addressed.

Like Rawls, M. Chris Alli endorses on ontology of peoples in relation to their members and in relation to one another but this is born out of his exquisite moral and theistic humanistic philosophy of African thought which is characterized by symbiosis, communalism, sanctity of life and creativeness. Perhaps, he may be anti-cosmopolitan like John Rawls, even while remaining a vanguard republican and democrat. Comparing with Rawls is not an innuendo but a convicted reconstruction of a fascinating and titillating convergence of Rawls reformism and Alli's egalitarian ethnics whereupon "the ontology of any composite like the people will have to identify the components out of which the composite is build, characterize the relationship or structure among those components that the composite presuppose... (Pettit, 2000: 44). On the other hand, both are not only humanist in the modern sense of pure secularism but are also great proponents, recycling the doctrine into the hermeneutic visages of neo-liberal political and economic philosophy. Albeit, M. Chris Alli has additional fillip of theism to complete his unflinching stances on consciencism and communal African life.

In both philosophers, however, are extant seven meanings of modern humanism namely: (1) life should be experienced deeply with environmental sensitive awareness (2) nature is thoroughly worthy of attention (3) confidence in human kind (4) equality of rights among humans (5) cooperation and mutual aid (6) evolution is worked out by nineteenth century scientist, and (7) scientific thinking on the need to match theory with experience (Lloyd and Mary Morain, 1954:26)

M. Chris Alli and the travesty of the Military in governance

M. Chris Alli is a democrat because he is humanist and humanist because he is republican and so much so that his neo-liberal and federalist disposition pitched him against the military in politics and governance. For him the façade and cascade of military phenomenon in Nigeria's polity is so over stretched that civilian rule has become an intervention in the historical trajectory of military rule in Nigeria. As he put it:

> the ordinary and every day definition of military intervention in the political affairs of nations will not serve our purpose. Indeed, it is a misnomer to talk about military intervention in Nigeria. What is pertinent is perhaps to refer to civil intervention in military governance since independence. The truth is that the nation since 1900 had been ruled by military and quasi-military personnel with the traditional militancy of pre-colonial authority. Practically, all colonial rulers of pre-independence Nigeria were soldiers or men who derived their stay from the threat of the use of military power...(Alli, P. 162).

The military is one of the main subjects of his neo-liberal intervention in Nigerian politics and because the federal and governance structure in Nigeria is of military inheritance, the military procedurally, theoretically and logically becomes the entry point of his hermeneutics of proper or true federalism in Nigeria. Hence a critique of the military is critique of federalism in Nigeria.

The military in conspiratorial resonance, placed the political class on the political parade square of the nation, drilled them left, right and centre, forward and backward, banned them and then, unbanned them. Then banned then again in stupor, disorganizing in the process, a vital class of the national polity, though lacking in cohesion and experience. Every institution has thus become a hostage of either the military or the virus of militarism (Alli, p. 163). He argues that since Nzeogwu led military coup and the first military Head of the state in the person of General Aguiyi-Ironsi coup culture has assumed a tripod conflict in which military coups have the formula of tribal suspicion or the survival of the fittest following which the North becomes the masochist after the defeat of the Igbo tribal group in the Civil War. "Regional, sectional or tribal coups as they have occurred in Nigeria seek to promote or redress the interest of a major tribe one of the three regions or a distinct military interest," (p. 165) while rationalizing their motivations, the conspirators justify their treasonable acts by appealing to nationalist sentiments of promoting national unity and national interest while they were meant and measured to serve ulterior motives.

Antithetical to democracy as it were, coup culture planning and execution was a game used by the domineering ethnic group or groups to perpetuate themselves in power. The coup culture was a strategic phenomenon usually premeditated and preceded by a strategically coded exercise that passes as underground narrative or conspiracy before air born into a full blown military putsch. In Nigeria military intervention, such as Northern led 'operation-no-mercy' that never saw the light of the day and Kaduna Nzeogwu, 'Operation Damisa' were never upon but conspiratorial and anti-people. Critically, speaking the coup and countercoup of 1st January and July 1999 and July respectively substituted unitary military government which evil but growth is today's unitary system of federalism.

Another antinomy to federalism in, and as a phenomenon of the Big three syndrome in Nigerian politics is a vanguard group of coup intoxicated and power motivated political army officers which M. Chris Alli calls a 'militricians', He says that "they were a hotchpotch of scramblers for notice, office and bout lickers with a convoluted understanding of their obligations to the constitution and the state. Loyalty to an individual was their credo end self-interest was their tenet. They were later to overreach themselves by confronting the authority of the Army hierarchy and arrogated to themselves, the privilege of deciding who cannot rule Nigeria, elections or no elections (P. 170). This is an eloquently articulated picture of Nigerian Military feudal lords (militricians) and the serfs, (ordinarily Nigerians) who depend on the crumbs that fall from the former's table. Alli would in addition describe them as "Army stock of professional coup merchants and artisans" who derailed economic growth and development for many decades in Nigeria.

It is pertinent, however, not to divorce the search for proper federalism or republican system of government in any African context from the implications of the then Western and Eastern Cold War, an era that warranted the reliance of African resurgence on the military as saviours for a continent in search of class leadership and direction. It was a milieu that created soldiers' inroad into leadership platform in the continent as West and East scramble for lackeys and allies without minding whether they were of people government or not. The Nigerian version of the military inroad was what led to the truncating of 1963 constitution and its conversion to a unitary constitution in the form of the present federal system controlled by the quasi-military lords and then civilian oligarchy. For Alli the military interventions in African states were direct precedents of slave trade and colonization, hence power shifted from the traditional authentic African rulers to colonial masters, and then at independence, to political class. What followed was a rash of coup d'état that swept through the continent like a plaque of incurable dimension (p.184).

Apart from that military government is in tandem with unitary constitution it has always been predicated on decrees and concurrent suspension of democratic constitution. This, according to M. Chris Alli, is conducive to the prevalent ignorance of the principles and importance of the constitution. Contrary to democratic norms people of Nigerian have been so intimidated to develop incredible reverence for force as a legitimate authority especially in a culture often founded "on a submission to the will of religious faith…and as such authority should be respected once established." (p.180)

The long military interregnum in Nigeria suffocated the growth of responsible autonomous and free moral democratic agents both in the natural communal habitat of aboriginal members of different nationalities that make up the Nigerian state and in the Nigerian geopolitical contracted system. Military political engineering has been so dehumanizing that it narrows "the scope and horizon for rational, opinion and decision formulation. They also degrade the culture of dialogue. This explains why conflicts frequently result in wars and violence because opponents have little room to manoeuvre in the then red line between friend and foe" (p.185). Therefore for M. Chris Alli, neo liberal political and economic structure built upon representation, democratic choice and proper federalism is the only means of restoring balance in the lopsided power equation in Nigeria which is in favour of the Big Three and most often the northern domination.

Again, Alli argues that "the greatest irony and paradox of the years of military rule has been the destruction of the people's confidence in government." (p.189) As an alternatives political power it constitutes a debilitating politicization with severe impact on its traditions, esprit de corps, efficiency and effectiveness, it has induced more insecurity in the polity since colonial times. "Everything of value in the nation had been reduced to the giver and the taker and the briber. Soldiers were responsible for the dispensation of the largesse of office and they ensured that they did not come out of the system worsted otherwise" (p.188). The military value system and culture had been so entrenched that the psych of the people had been moulded into a frame of militancy and respect for the use of force. Hence Nigerians no longer respond to persuasion and the political class has become a victim of mental condition and subservience that perpetuates a climate of distrust of national institutions; militarism was promoted in concomitance with reduction of human values in the name of military executions and public blood-spilling that defied human dignity and sanctity of life. For M. Chris Alli military rule is a scourge inconsistent with democratic norms save its constitutional duty to protect the territorial integrity of the nation.

M. Chris Ali and Neo-Liberal Federalism

Ali's critique of military rule in Nigeria is a prolegomena to redefining federalism in Nigeria. This he has painstakingly set forth as adumbrated above. His guiding principles are conceptions of fair play, justice and equity based on egalitarian conception of who owns what and who contributes what. As stated earlier Ali's neo-liberal conception of a just ordered society is more or less a telecast of John Rawl's in terms of taking care of the worst off man in sudden state of inequality, redistributing national wealth as and when circumstances dictate while maintaining zero tolerance of inequality of opportunities and deprivation of fundamental human rights. He would agree with Rawls that:

> a well ordered society is effectively regulated by public conception of justice. That is, it is a society of all whose members accept, and knew

that the others accept, the same principles (the same conception) of justice. It is also the case that basic social institutions and their arrangement into one scheme (the basic structure) actually satisfy, and are on good grounds believed by everyone to satisfy, these principles (Rawls, 228).

There are in Alli's work seven principles that will collectively and severally satisfy the conditions of a well ordered society.

Justice

John Rawls conception of justice in seminal papers culminating in a theory of Justice as fairness is a critique and reform of western capitalism with American society as a case study. On the one hand M. Chris Alli's neo-liberal take for modern Nigerian society proceeds with a critique of Nigerian bourgeois corrupt society and on the other hand with a couple of theoretical and practical solutions to the Nigerian socio-economic predicament. Arising from military corruption is an improper, lopsided and untrue federalism wherein there is no adequate and substantive conception of justice. For Alli, "the origin of Nigeria's federalism is a reverse of the American system in both concept and intent." The American federalism is a coming together by the free choice of small strong units under one umbrella. The Nigerian federalism started the other way round (Alli, p. 194). He says that Nigerian federal system is a colossal deception of the highest order amounting to shirking the girth and scope of the voices of nationalities in the union. He advocates what the founding fathers of Nigeria conceived at Independence, that is, self-rule or shared rule through the linkage of individuals, groups and polities.

While maintaining the inalienability of national rights and aspirations, Ali subscribes for a lasting but united union that "provides for the energetic pursuit of common goals while maintaining the respective integrity of parties - a kind of strength through unity in diversity" (p.104). This presupposes, as concerned by the founding fathers, a federation in which all nationalities would develop at their respective paces.

Restructuring

The discarding of 1963 Constitution by the military junta was indeed the destruction of the Nigerian federalism. Implicated in this suspension of the republican constitution is the destruction of those basic liberties encapsulated in Rawl's priority rules of justice and which even the colonial masters granted to Nigerians as right to natural resources. These basic liberties and opportunities were denied through the Land Use Act and the revenue formula which were meant to deprive the minorities their naturally endowed resources. M. Chris Alli's neo-liberal thinking is the restructuring of the unitary and fascist form of federalism to devolution of powers to regions with the federalist list, concurrent list and residual list belonging exclusively to the religions which, of course the regions are empowered by the residual list to develop at their own paces. This will reverse the perfidious arrangement with a "skewed federal revenue allocation formula that emphasizes land mass, need, population and other weird factors rather than derivation, for sharing the national cake" (p.106). It will equally reverse the order where the interest of the Big Three remains paramount in the federal structure.

Equity

It is typically of neo-liberal thinking to advocate for a reconstruction of Nigerian polity by replacing command oriented unitary arrangement with a perfectly operational regional federal system. It is a redefinition of equity, a new revenue allocation formula "even the British in their colonizing wisdom and authority understood federation and equity better than the indigenous Nigerian military/political class and their constitution making mechanism" (p.114).

In line with neo-liberal thinking the equity to be redefined is an economic reform of a the political economy which John Rawls would subscribe as material and extractable resources endowed with any group at any point in time. Like the challenge of inequality in John Rawls in his own time in America, the challenge of unequal revenue not based on any equitable yardstick was critical for the survival of Nigerian federation in M. Chris Alli. He argues that:

> when large tribes (the big three) controlled the main sources of revenue, before and immediately after Independence, that is, groundnut and cotton in the North, cocoa in the West, coal and palm

oil in East, derivation was the single rationale and the minorities were kept on the sideline...when oil was discovered offshore on the high sea and beyond the littoral states, the rights became universal to all states of the federation and so the federal government controls 100 per cent (p.114).

Apart from the lopsided structure of state policy, there were no equity and fairness with regard to ecological damage and health hazard imposed on the natives of the oil drilling revenue area and regions. According to M. Chris Alli thinking, it is only fair and just to restructure the polity in tune with true regional federalism. This is called fiscal federalism because it will create a robust states' and local government finances and render otiose "the unitary system under which state and local governments monthly collect revenue allocations from the centre with no value added no productivity generated, no growth in local productive activity" (p.119).

Citizenship
In M. Chris Alli's neo-liberal political thought, the concepts of citizen and non-indigeneship are rival notions and practices in modern democracy and politics as the later engenders the syndrome of them and us" (Alli p. 123). Religion, tribalism and ethnicism, therefore, colour political affiliations and boundaries of trust and group relations thereby exacerbating mutual distrust and non-indigeneship syndrome, "if you are a non-indigene, you might as well be a foreigner in that environment. In some cases, you might be relieved of a service job or privilege only to find a foreigner or non-Nigerian replacing you totally." (Ibid. p. 122-123) For Alli, between the citizen and the state there are asymmetrical rights and obligation from where citizenship is inhered as "rights and privileges to work, own property and settle permanently. These rights conversely impose certain obligations on the citizen to both the federal and immediate governments in the area of abode, a social contract between the state and the citizen that is mutually beneficial" (Ibid p. 122). This is the demand of a true federation which can only be achieved by the restructuring of the federation to install a balanced power among the component nationalities that form the nation-state.

Secularism

An important index of proper federalism as being articulated in M. Chris Alli's neo-liberal political thought is the inclusiveness of all religions and exclusion of all in the state affairs. The overarching pressure of Islam, Christianity and traditional religions is a burden on the state that must be dispensed for other neutral and noble common values in a multicultural society. Beside there have been social and political discordant issues about religions generally. "The use of religion as a political instrument had been introduced into the geographical space known as Nigeria as far back as the assault on indigenous belief systems began long before the colonialists handed over the state to a new set of neo-colonialists in 1960." (Ibid. p. 125). Therefore secularism no matter how it is interpreted must stick to the logic, that is, separating state affairs from religious matters especially where there is no mono religious culture. While Nigeria is far from being a secular state in the classical sense because of its religious or animist culture, it is certainly "not, Christian, Moslem or Amist state" (Ibid, p. 127). True or proper federalism in a nation-state like Nigeria can only be sustained in an atmosphere of liberal religious accommodation without interference in their affairs.

Rule of Law

In M. Chris Alli's postulation, the rule of law is a catalyst of individuals and citizens liberty and mutual obligations in the interest of the development of the society and that of the individual. Also, concern in form of decreeism instead of rule of law is never in tandem with development and individual's liberty. While military decrees retarded development in Nigeria rule of law promoted development in the West, for instance, in America, Germany and Britain. For him the rule of law is part of the logic of true federalism and military decree as an instrument of law making is anti-development and against the process of mutual culture in a multi-religious and multi-ethnic society. It is antagonistic to the noble rules of checks and balances in modern democracy. As a result of the toxic infections of military decrees, Nigeria has witnessed several periodic system collapse and relapse. Alli asserted that,

> of the new custodians of the people's sovereignty, the press and the judiciary, only the press lived true to its noble obligations in the face of the most evil of governments in the history of the nation...the truth

is really that, like all other national institutions, their affiliations and maladies, the judiciary has proved unable to rise to the occasion as custodian of the people's manifest sovereignty, the protectors of the constitution and the enforcers of the rule of law (p. 131).

Democracy

On M. Chris Alli's meaning of democracy in Nigeria's federalism, there is no menu or element of democracy in the behavioural pattern and attitude of a militarized state. First, democracy is participatory and progressive because it admits variety and two, because it permits criticism. Second, democracy is not about elections alone or choice. It is also about representation in the corridors of power at all levels. This is because the central issue in the Nigerian union is the nationalities who are denied their nationhood and are in fear of losing their respective identities to the Big Three (ethnic nationalities). Third, democracy is about civil rights within the law. It is about empowering the population by its own voice and choice; it is not about imposing the will and comfort of the leader or clique on the people. Fourth, democracy is about transparency in all its ramifications barring clear instances of the imperatives of national security. Fifth, democracy is about subjecting the military to civil power, since the people defend the constitution and not the military. Sixth, democracy is about liberating the human mind for thought. It is about peoples' and individuals freedoms to channel constructive energies for the benefit of mankind. It is not about positioning power. It is about galvanizing the peoples' free choice. Seventh, democracy is neither Christian nor Moslem but it's an affirmation that all men are created equal and free. Eighth, democracy must have infrastructure to sustain and enliven its practice and purpose. Ninth, there must be a free judiciary to interpret and uphold the rule of law without fear or favour to anyone. And tenthly, federation is not about structure and groupings alone, more pointedly, for it to be stable, egalitarian and just, it should have no groups left behind amongst its components (Pp. 131-134).

On the Nigerian factor

One of the most eloquent formulations of anti-federalism and development bottleneck in Nigerian nation building is M. Chris Alli's metaphor of an ingrained and inveterate corruption domino called "Nigerian factor". Alli has the singular artistic, theoretical and intellectual knack to capture this and define it as a road map towards understanding neo-liberal political and economic development howbeit, a Nigerian malady and concept in socio-political studies. The fact that its operation in Nigeria has become a matter of state policy and institutional calculation is suggestive that the factor is either psychogenic in Nigerians or it was a consequent virus of military rule in Nigerian governance, extemporally militarily induced corruption. For M. Chris Alli, Nigerian factor is both a weird logic and a metaphor for corruption. "Nigerian factor is a loose term, presumably, a learning that things are not what they appear to be. It is never 4'0 clock, is too exact. It is either something to 4'0 clock or something after 4'0 clock. To do otherwise is to ignore the factor, to your own peril, and often, at great cost in time, money and health. Everything is moderated by something and most things must be influenced by everything ranging from the tribal, religion, human face, pity, compromise, emotion, sentiments and circumventing the law to outright lawlessness. It is a means to avoiding responsibility for actions, a bridge between cause and effect but may lead often to inaction. It is an escape valve and excuse for failures and incompetence, seeking for and hiding under a scapegoat that will bear the burden of guilt..." As metaphorically as this paradoxical factor is phenomenologically captured by Ali, it has unfortunately and tragically perforated into all axes of governance and character formation of Nigerians and to the detriment of true federalism and neo-liberal economic development.

In terms of its consequences on the national body language, character and governance the Nigerian factor assumes the dimension of a cancerous phenomenon. That is why M. Chris Alli characterized it as a short cut to everything imaginable ranging from the art of governance to management. Lacking in principle, successive military government have boldly exploited this lacuna called Nigerian factor to the detriment of the nation. It is absence of principles, discipline, law and order, rules and regulations in governance which reflects "in the incompetence that ignores all time and space but springs in volcanic action at the eleventh hour where all manner of foul practices for waste and thievery are armed" (p. 139). Since Nigerian factor is a constraint to creativity, merit is not a critical factor in national development. M. Chris Alli's solution to the socio-economic problem of the Nigerian factor is, however, not quota system or federal character, as it were. He rather postulates that,

> all development environments must make allowance for disadvantaged regiments of its population. Such segments should also offer their best or must meet minimum standards or allow time for such impositions to mature for placement in public or private enterprise. Anything short of this is an open promotion of mediocrity (p. 140-141).

This is extemporally of M. Chris Alli's neo liberal solution to Nigeria's predicament, his theory of justice as fairness among ethnic nationalities of Nigeria, reminiscent John Rawls' second theory of Justice as fairness in terms of the principle of equality of opportunity for primary goods as the distributive principle that caters for the worst of man in period of relative wealth and scarcity.

Conclusion

M. Chris Alli's The *Federal Republic of Nigeria Army: the Siege of a Nation*, has an ethno-biographic information on the side-line of theories and praxis for the survival of a nation state. These liberal solutions to the socio-economic problems confronting the post-colonial Nigeria as a country cannot be over emphasized. Nigeria as a developing country, mired in dire political crisis and debilitating social-economic woes, is out rightly a logical candidate of neo-liberal analysis. It is a country which threats to her survival as a state since independence have been political power and revenue resource controlled by the central government [P.204]. It is a country where the Big Three is a phenomenon crying out for a phenomenological inquiry and to compound the socio economic dilemma with a self-serving strategy the three big ethnic groups namely Hausa/Fulani, Igbo and Yoruba appropriates the essence of political power using the factors of populations and land mass. Hence, by synchronic and diachronic accident of history, the issue of the Nigerian national question remains fully unaddressed in terms of democracy, federalism, rule of law or constitutional governance, secularism and revenue allocations.

More importantly, M. Chris Alli in his *magnum opus*, uses the theory, paradigm and tools of neo-liberal thought either by inclination or by deliberation to decipher and recommend an escape route or roadmap, from Nigeria political and economic anaemia and military induced and facilitated unitary federalism. Ali's analytical and philosophical skill is beyond question. His dexterity and flexibility are however with good points as he tries to exclude theoretical and eclectic accommodations as and when necessary but his argument for diarchy when needed is most synthetically critical questions that could engineer uncontrollable controversy, cynicism and scepticism.

He is however cautious to argue that "if it is the will of the people that the military should rule, or be parts of the rulers [diarchy] or attain certain profiles in national leadership, then so be it. The constitution must under all circumstances provide the bench mark" [P.199]. It must be stated that Ali should not be misunderstood but be made to key unto the dialectics and conversation started earlier between I and J. Osei of the University of Ghana. Joseph Osei reply to Dukor's position as follows:

> The case of Dr. M. Dukor. Besides his sympathetic remark on Zik's proposals for diarchy Dr. Dukor in other writings show a favourable disposition towards military rule in Nigeria and presumably the rest of Africa for some unspecified period of time. He argues that African revolution which began with the nationalist struggle against colonialism has reached a stage where the vanguards are Marxist or non Marxists. The important frame work needed to guild them is psychological, cultural, political and economic freedom equity and justice. He goes on to say that it is also not important the type of elite or class to lead the revolution and that all that is pertinent is discipline rigour and commitment to humanity [Osei 2003:3002-303].

As a rejoinder I clearly stated that neither military nor civilian rule is fundamental or primary contradiction to the present state of African revolution. The problem of military rule, like civilian rule in African is ineptitude [Osei: 303, Dukor: 303]. However, this statement is one of my premises, not a conclusion. Osei then argues further, that the problem of military rule in Africa is worse than ineptitude. It is a question of logical incompatibility. If people of a society X desire a way of life that includes the value a, b, c and d etc. then people of society S, cannot also desire or tolerate a form of government that undermine the values of a, b, c and d. Since the military rule by decree and are therefore not committed to any human or civil rights and rule of law, military regimes in theory and practice undermine the democratic values of freedom, justice, equality and respect for human dignity. [Osei: 303].

Like M. Chris Alli, I equally carpeted military rule, in spite of its temporality in answer to Dr. Osei in the following: "but it would be retrogressive in attitude and thinking to wish that the current democratic anomaly persists far too long. This will certainly not allow Black nations to be fully integrated in the committee of nations."[Dukor, 2003:211]. It is only with excellent emotional intelligence that Alli theoretically accommodates diarchy in his neo-liberal thinking of Nigerian condition otherwise like Dukor, he is in tandem with Dr. Joseph Osei on the value of democracy, and above all, he is a strong advocate of neo liberal federalism.

References

Alli M. Chris (2001) *The Federal Republic of Nigerian Army: the Siege of A Nation* (Lagos, Malthouse Press).

Dukor M. [2003] 'The Military and African Revolution" in *Philosophy and Politics: Discourse on Values, Politics And Power in Africa* [Lagos, Malthouse Press].

John Rawls (1997) "A Kantian Conception of Equality" in *Ideological Voices: An Anthology of Modern Politics* Eds. Paul Schumacher, Dwight C. Kiel Ed Thomas W. Heike (McGraw Hill, U.S.A).

Lloyd and Mary Morain (1954), *Humanism Humanist Press*, Washington D.C.

Osei Joseph, (2003) A Deadly Virus Against Emerging Democracies. The power and presence of political manipulation in African politics, in *Philosophy in Politics. Discourse On Values, Politics and Power in Africa* [Malthouse Press, Lagos

Philip Pettit, "Rawls's People," in *Rawls's Law of Peoples; a Realistic Utopian* (Eds) Rox Martin And David A. Reidy (USA, Blackwell Publishing.

Rawls John, (1971) *A Theory of Justice* (Massachusetts Howard University Press).

Rodney Walter (1972) *How Europe Underdeveloped Africa* (Howard University Press, Washington, D.C).

Steven Faller (2007) *The Knowledge Book* (Montreal - Ithaca, McGill - Queen's University Press).

Index

Abacha's regime; 16
Abubakar Tafawa Balewa; 115
Achebe .C.; 119
Activism; 5
Adjutants; 4
African Child; 107
African Communalistic Orientation; 99
African ideas of man; 7
African Philosophy; 1
African Philosophy; 2
African Societies; 48
African State; 49
African tradition; 2
Alhaji Maitama Sule; 17
Ali's family; 101
Alli Adakwo Alabura and Rebecca Ojumori; 49
Alli; 25, 112
Alli's humanism; 7
Alli's positivism; 12
Amalgamation; 115
Anambra State; 4
Antipathy; 84
Anti-Semitism; 140
Appadorai; 14
Armed forces; 7, 38
Army; 3, 23
Asaba; 77
Autocratic leadership; 61
Axiology; 162
Ayoob; 32
Ayotolla Murtadha Mutabbawi 137
Balkan State; 159
Balkanization; 150

Bentham; 11, 173
Bentham's Ethical theory; 84
Bentham's utilitarian ethics; 93
Benthamite movement; 72
Bertrand Russell; 83
Biafra/Nigeria Conflict; 69, 78
Biafranization of Nigeria; 173
Big three; 17, 212
Bin-led commission; 199
Boko Haram; 36, 141
Bristish colonial masters; 157
Britain; 158
Bruno Latour; 16
Catholic Christian religion; 134
Centralization; 171
Chief Obafemi Awolowo; 92
Child; 105
Christian beliefs; 101
Christianity; 4
Christmas and Eidel Kabir; 6
Citizens; 40
Citizenship; 227
Civil Society; 169
Civilian leaders; 151
Classical Philosophical tradition; 1
Collective Security; 40
Colonialism; 28
Colonization of Africa; 160
Colonization; 12
Combatants and non-combatants; 71
Commanding officer; 4
Commodity and raw material; 165
Consciencism; 9
Conscious creation; 2
Constitution; 160

Constitutional conference; 158
Contemporary African; 149
Contemporary teachers; 3
Copernican; 139
Corporate Child; 107
Corrective regime; 67
Corruption; 64
Country's revenue 217
Coup culture planning and execution; 222
Coup plotters; 172
Critical reflections; 3
Critical theorist; 16
Crude Capitalism; 13
Defence Industries Corporation of Nigeria (DICON); 47
Defensive strategies; 35
Dehumanization; 9
Delta Igbo; 25
Democracy; 2, 14, 229
Democrat; 221
Dictatorship; 61
Disadvantaged Communities and regions; 217
Disposition Muslims; 138
Distributive; 188
Doctrine of authenticity; 170
Dual theological heritage; 5
Easter Day; 6
Ecclesiocentric exclusivism; 134
Eclectric tradition; 5
Education; 49
Egalitarian society; 156
Eidel Fitr; 6
Enahoro; 89
Enlightenment's liberalism; 9
Environmental determinism; 64
Epicurus; 90
Epistemological boundaries; 5
Epistemological pluralism; 131, 143
Equality; 184, 190,
Equity; 189, 195, 200, 226
Essence; 162
Ethnic groups; 191
Ethnic identification; 197

Ethnic representation; 195
European religious wars; 140
Excellence; 49
Exceptionalism; 26
Existentialism; 2, 8
Existentialists; 102, 170
Fairness; 186, 195
Faith; 28
Falola; 45
False Federalism; 13
Fanaticism; 124
Fate; 6
Favouritism; 124
Federal Character; 194
Federal Republic; 2
Federalism; 14
Fela Anikulapo Kuti; 165
Felisic Calculus; 85
Fredrick Nietzsche; 174
Freedom; 174, 184
Free-will; 6
Functionalization and politicization; 44
Garrisons; 151
General Buhari; 65
General Obasanjo; 151
Genocides; 26
Giant of Africa; 119
Gidado Idris; 114
God; 5, 101, 122
Gwadebe and General Diya's Coup; 67
Hard work and meritocracy; 103
Hard work and self-confidence; 13
Hard work and self-realization; 6
Harts; 13
Hausa/Fulani; 17
Henry Odera Oruka; 2
Hobbesian state; 74, 141
Holy Bible; 101
Honesty; 7
Human being; 102
Human beneficence; 131, 143
Human freedom; 102
Human life; 29

Human nature; 29
Human populations; 37
Human problem; 3
Human relationship; 127
Human right; 2
Human Spirit; 9
Humanist Philosophy; 7
Humanities challenges; 3
Humility; 124
Hypocritical Society; 174
Idea formulation; 88
Idealism; 5, 8
Ideas; 7
Ideology; 162
Igbo man; 100
Immanuel Kant; 154
Inequality and discrimination; 197
Inhabitants; 154
Inordinate Craving; 123
Institution; 26
Inter-force co-operation; 44
Inter-religious dialogue; 136
Interventionist gangs; 172
Istamic exclusivism; 133
Italian and Prussian Unification; 159
John Rawl's political liberalism; 13, 186
Journalists; 92
Jurgen Habermas; 12
Just; 185
Justice and fairness; 216
Justice; 60, 119, 153, 184, 225
Kaduna riots; 46
Kant's Copernican; 139
Kantian Critical Philosophy; 12
Kantian principle; 78
Karl Marx; 162
Karl Rahner; 136
Kleptocracy; 7
Kwame Nkrumah consciencism; 9
Laissez-faire economic liberalism; 202
Law of nature; 85
Leadership; 149

Legal positivism; 13
Liberal theory of Justice; 13
Liberalism; 12
Libertarians; 187
Life of short-cuts; 101
Lobby; 6
Lord Lugard; 115
Lust; 24
Luxurious state; 153
Machiavellian idea; 60
Maitatsine; 45
Major General Chris Alli; 4, 70
Makinda; 30
Man; 29, 102, 174, 178
Martin Heidegger; 5
Marxist idea; 67
Materialism; 120, 151
Media; 88
Meritocracy; 189, 198
Metaphysical Vision; 7
Mid-West Region; 76
Militancy and violent resistant; 18
Militarism; 37
Military cabal; 151
Military command structure; 97
Military complicity; 41
Military dictatorship; 151
Military force; 36
Military governments; 149
Military hegemonic; 62
Military hierarchy; 61
Military Pariah state; 161
Military; 2
Militocracy; 151, 164
Mind; 9
Minority groups; 156
Minority; 212
Modern army; 31
Modern humanism; 220
Mohammed Christopher Alli; 1
Mono-religious nation; 143
Moral Acts; 11
Moral and political philosophy; 10
Moral Decadence; 118
Moral feelings; 84

Moral nihilists; 74
Moral rights; 188
Moral Values; 119\
Moral Virtue; 3, 122
Morality and National development; 125
Morden Military formation; 8
Mr Okafor; 6
Multi-ethnic; 169
Multi-religious Society; 11
Multi-religious; 169
Nasarawa State government; 41
Nation; 15, 179
National entrance; 197
National Security Organization; 45
National Security; 87
Nationalism; 159
Nationhood; 2
Natural law; 12
Negative rubric; 144
Neo-colonialists; 138
Neo-liberal thinker; 207
Neo-liberalism; 13
New State; 158
Nichomachean Ethics; 152
Niger Delta; 212
Nigeria factor; 104, 230
Nigeria national security; 27, 31, 37
Nigeria police; 39
Nigeria Society; 119, 208
Nigeria troops;
Nigeria's Federalism; 14
Nigerian Army; 1, 49, 57
Nigerian child; 103
Nigerian Civil and Military leadership; 12
Nigerian factor; 17, 168
Nigerian Military; 23, 47
Nigerian Navy; 48
Nigerian Politics; 7, 17, 59, 84
Nigerian problem; 41
Nigerian State; 11, 58, 152, 161, 214
Nigerian Unity; 25
Nigerian Waters; 48
Nkrumah; 162

Northern Coups; 63
Northern ethnic groups; 50
Northernization; 161
Nozick; 157, 213
Nurudeen Alao; 101
Obi of Onitsha; 69
Ochoche; 31
Oil producing states; 199
Oil resource of Niger Delta; 161
Old Eastern; 4
Olu Awotesu; 119
Ombatse; 41
One Nigeria; 127
Onitsha town; 4
Organic theory; 80
Over-indulgence; 106
Paiko Police Station; 44
Pakistan; 171
Patronage; 6
Patron-clientelism; 103
Pauline Hountondje; 2
People Merits; 198
People; 155
Person; 102
Peters; 37
Philosophic heritage; 5
Philosophical entrepreneurs; 1
Pluralism; 101
Police; 45
Policy; 163
Political and moral value; 5
Political instability; 123
Political liberalism; 155
Politics; 58, 65, 152
Positive rubric; 144
Post-colonial African nation; 207
Post-colonial; 91
Post-Independence; 91
Post-Modernism; 15
Power and authority; 104
Power Sharing; 192
Pragmatism; 30
Press empire; 92
Principle of discrimination; 166

Principle of Explanation and Understanding; 8
Principle of Fairness; 81
Principle of Greatest Equal liberty; 187
Principle of holistic Pluralism; 160
Principle of Utility; 84
Professionalism; 58
PROFORCE; 47
Protagoras; 9
Public Money; 120
Qu'ran; 137
Quasi-Ideological speculation; 10
Quota System; 195
Reactive attitude; 84
Realism; 36
Reap; 101
Reasoning; 3
Reductionism; 11
Regular; 34
Religion and ethnicity; 65
Religious belief; 140
Religious crisis in Nigeria; 114
Religious diversity; 141
Religious Exclusivism; 131
Religious Extremists; 141
Religious festivities; 99
Religious leaders; 140
Religious matters; 101
Religious pluralism; 139
Religious tolerance; 3, 141
Republican government; 15
Republicanism; 15
Re-restructuring; 16, 226
Resource control; 128
Restructuring of Nigeria; 175
Revenue allocation; 166, 199
Richard Cumberland; 11
Riesman-led commission; 199
River Niger; 77
Russia; 159
Sagacity; 3
Sambisa forest; 39
School teacher; 100
Secularis; 131, 228

Security and freedom; 154, 169
Security and Militarism; 23
Security and peace; 31
Security dilemma; 36
Security; 2, 30, 48
Sematic and Utilitarian Modulation; 2
Shehu Shagari; 91
Siege Philosophy; 18
Slave trade; 12
Social contractarianism; 152
Social equity; 203
Social inequalities; 187
Social injustice; 124
Social irenicism; 131, 145
Social Millieu; 10
Societal resources; 152
Socio-political idea; 3
Soldier; 23, 65
Sovereign National Conference; 179
Sow; 101
State Security Services (SSS); 43
State Security; 33
State; 155
Statism; 36
Statist Militarist Realist; 17
Statist-corporatism; 36
Stratocracy;
Supra-natural; 3
Surveillance; 6
Sympathy; 84
Technocratic spirit; 50
Temperance and justice; 123
Theism; 5
Theistic consciousness; 6
Theistic humanism; 5
Theological exclusivism; 134
Theory of minimal state; 157
Thinkers and students; 3
Thinkers; 3
Thomas Hobbes; 154
Time-consciousness; 105
Traditional African Society; 9, 159
Traditional religion; 10
Triangle of fears; 17

Triangular factors; 161
Tribal difference; 124
Trojan horse; 92
True Federalism; 194
Trust; 40
Truth and goodness; 144
Ukhum; 91
Umar aka Kabiru Sokoto; 42
Unitary Federalism; 160, 232
United System; 171
Unknown Soldier; 77

Utilitarian; 77
Utilitarianism; 2, 11, 83, 185
Utopian estimation; 46   W
Value; 24, 27
Violence and terrorism; 38
Violent conflicts; 45
Virtuous qualities; 153
Vulgar liberalism; 13
War; 4
Wealth and status; 64
Westphalia Cosmology 23, 31

www.ingramcontent.com/pod-product-compliance
Lightning Source LLC
Chambersburg PA
CBHW071407300426
44114CB00016B/2211